West Country Pilot

Published by
Imray Laurie Norie & Wilson Ltd
Wych House The Broadway, St Ives
Cambridgeshire PE27 5BT England
☎ +44 (0)1480 462114
Email ilnw@imray.com
www.imray.com
2025

All rights reserved. No part of this publication may be reproduced, transmitted or used in any form by any means – graphic, electronic or mechanical, including photocopying, recording, taping or information storage and retrieval systems or otherwise – without the prior permission of the publishers.

1st edition 2025
© G. Macintosh 2025

G. Macintosh has asserted his rights to be identified as the author of this work in accordance with the Copyright, Designs and Patents Act 1988.

ISBN 978 178679 065 1

British Library Cataloguing in Publication Data.
A catalogue record for this book is available from the British Library.

PLANS
The plans in this guide are not to be used for navigation. They are designed to support the text and should at all times be used with navigational charts.

This product has been derived in part from material obtained from the UK Hydrographic Office with the permission of the UK Hydrographic Office and His Majesty's Stationery Office.

THIS PRODUCT IS NOT TO BE USED FOR NAVIGATION.

The UK Hydrographic Office (UKHO) and its licensors make no warranties or representations, express or implied, with respect to this product. The UKHO and its licensors have not verified the information within this product or quality assured it.

© British Crown Copyright 2025. All rights reserved.
Licence number GB AA - 005 - Imrays

CAUTION

Whilst the author and the publishers have used reasonable endeavours to ensure the accuracy of the content of this book, it contains selected information and thus is not definitive. It does not contain all known information on the subject in hand and should not be relied on alone for navigational use: it should only be used in conjunction with official hydrographical data. This is particularly relevant to the plans, which should not be used for navigation. The author and the publishers believe that the information which they have included is a useful aid to prudent navigation, but the safety of a vessel depends ultimately on the judgment of the skipper, who should assess all information, published or unpublished. The information provided in this pilot book may become out of date and may be changed or updated without notice. External links and contact details were correct as at 1 January 2025. The inclusion of a facility or service in this pilot book does not constitute a recommendation, nor any representation as to its suitability. The author and the publishers cannot accept any liability for any error, omission or failure to update such information. To the extent permitted by law, the author and the publishers do not accept liability for any loss and/or damage howsoever caused that may arise from reliance on information contained in these pages, or the use thereof.

Positions and waypoints

All positions and waypoints are to datum WGS 84. They are included to help in locating places, features and transits. Do not rely on them alone for safe navigation.

Bearings and lights

Any bearings are given as °T and from seaward unless otherwise stated. The characteristics of lights may be changed during the lifetime of this book. They should be checked against the latest edition of the UKHO *Admiralty List of Lights and Fog Signals*.

CORRECTIONAL SUPPLEMENTS

This pilot book will be amended at intervals by the issue of correctional supplements which will be published on our website www.imray.com and may be downloaded free of charge. Printed copies are also available on request from the publishers at the above address.

NO AI TRAINING

Without in any way limiting the author's (and publisher's) exclusive rights under copyright, any use of this publication to 'train' generative artificial intelligence (AI) technologies to generate text is expressly prohibited. The author reserves all rights to license uses of this work for generative AI training and development of machine learning language models.

Printed in Malta by Gutenberg

WEST COUNTRY PILOT

Lyme Regis to Land's End

G. Macintosh

Imray Laurie Norie & Wilson

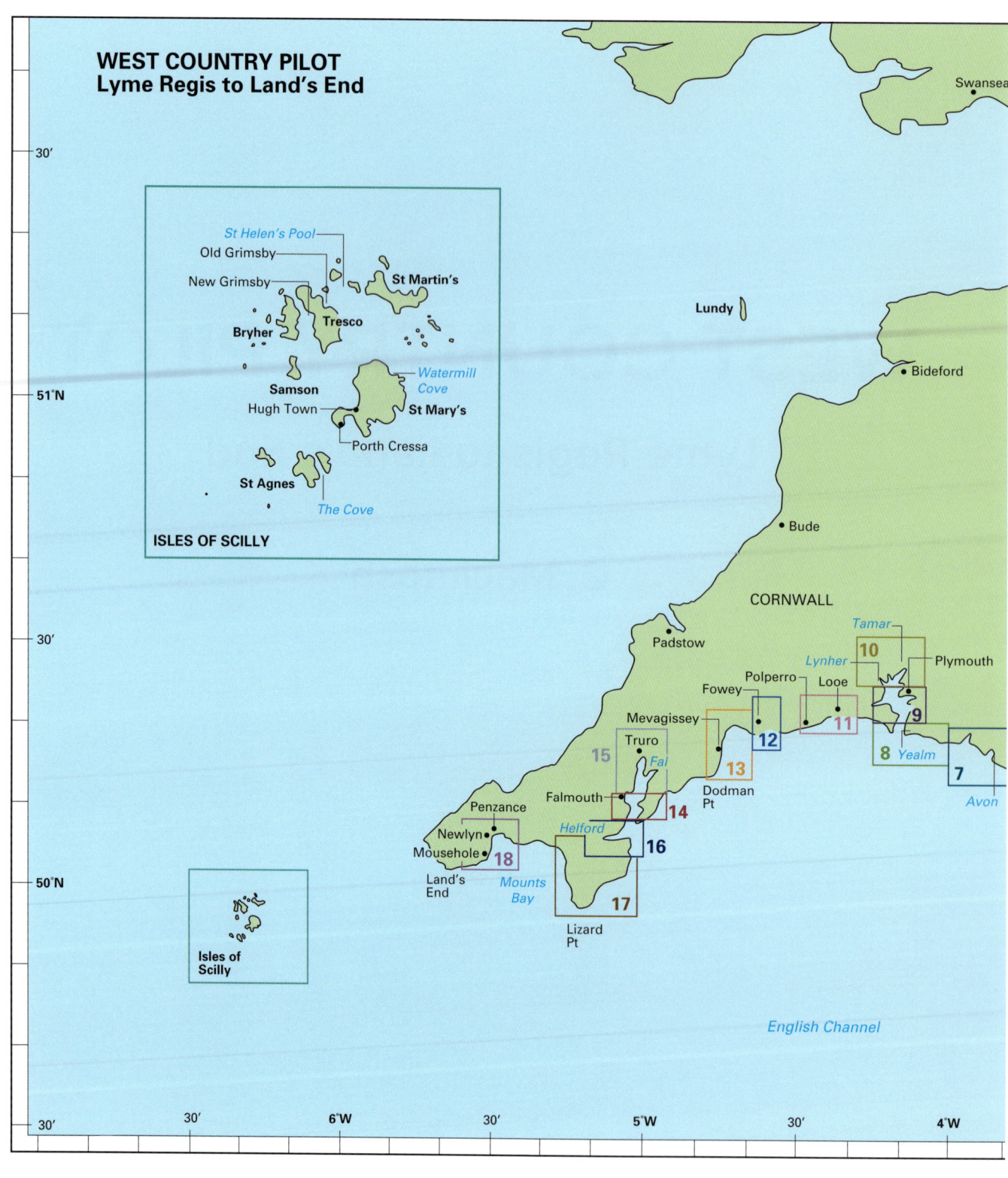

CONTENTS

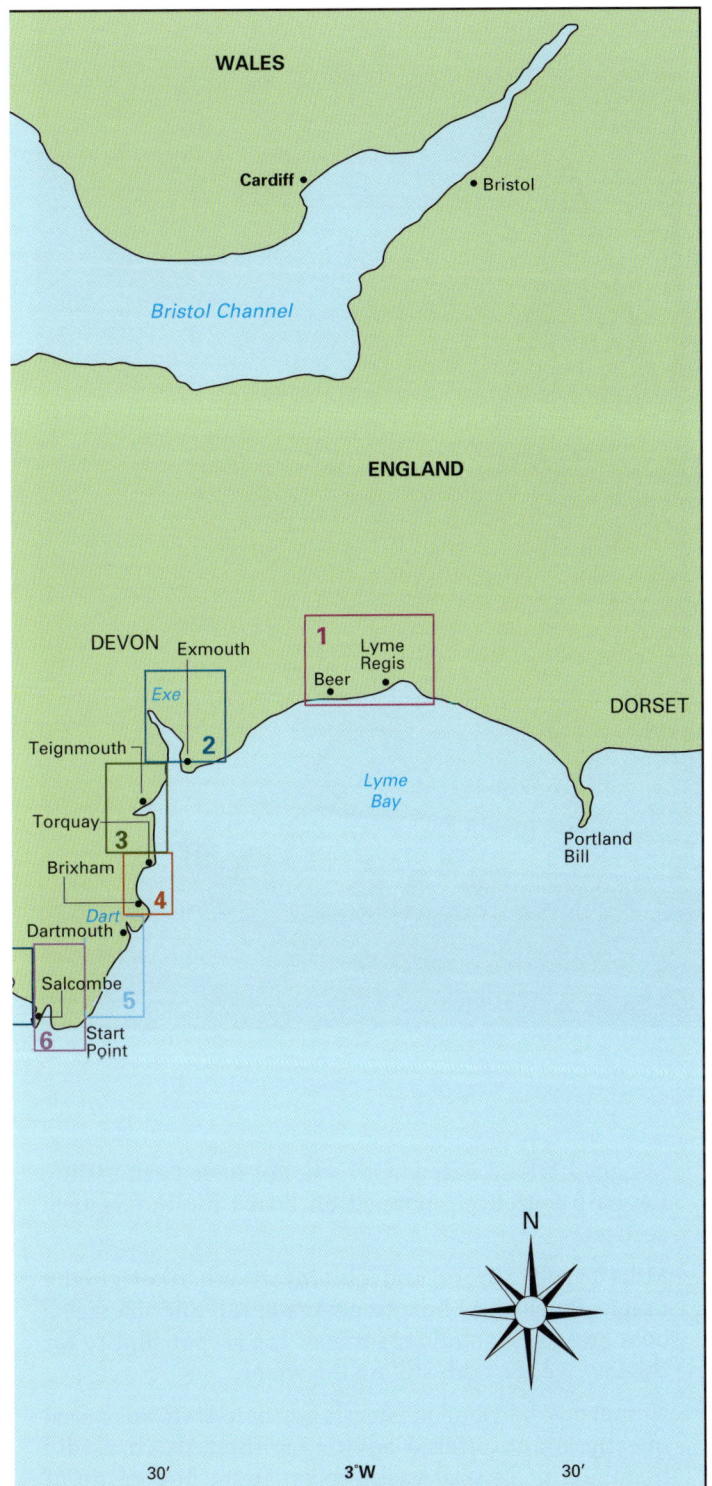

Foreword vi
Introduction 1
Passage Planning 3
Tidal Streams 8
Headlands 12
Abbreviations and symbols 15

1 **LYME REGIS** *18*
    Beer & Axmouth

2 **RIVER EXE** *24*

3 **TEIGNMOUTH** *34*
    Babbacombe Bay

4 **TOR BAY** *40*

5 **DARTMOUTH** *50*
    Totnes & Start Bay

6 **SALCOMBE** *64*
    Kingsbridge

7 **BIGBURY BAY** *72*
    Rivers Avon & Erme

8 **RIVER YEALM** *80*
    Plymouth Sound

9 **PLYMOUTH** *90*
    Cattewater & Hamoaze

10 **RIVER TAMAR** *102*
    River Lynher

11 **LOOE & POLPERRO** *112*
    Talland Bay

12 **FOWEY** *118*

13 **MEVAGISSEY** *126*
    St Austell Bay

14 **FALMOUTH** *132*
    Penryn & St Mawes

15 **TRURO** *142*
    Mylor, Carrick Roads & River Fal

16 **HELFORD RIVER** *150*
    Porthallow & Porthoustock

17 **THE LIZARD PENINSULA** *156*
    Porthleven

18 **PENZANCE & NEWLYN** *164*
    St Michael's Mount & Mousehole

ISLES OF SCILLY passage planning *174*

Index *182*

Steve Lorraine

Foreword

Welcome to the first edition of Imray's *West Country Pilot* for one of the UK's most spectacular cruising grounds. Whatever your craft or experience, I hope it will help you navigate your way around and, whilst I can't claim to have covered every possible spot, there should be enough here to keep the average cruising yacht busy for a few seasons. If everyone who buys this book tries one new port or anchorage as a result, I will be happy.

Like all pilot book authors, I am indebted to a great many people, most of whom have unwittingly contributed in some way (and it's tempting to start by thanking everyone who knows me), but there are some I must mention.

First up is Susan – partner, crew mate, soul mate, first mate (although both our navigator and chief engineer also claim the latter title) – for just about everything.

My good friend Peter, with whom I have been sailing for half a lifetime, hopped on board for the eastern section.

Mike Tyrell (ashore) and John Myatt (afloat) originally taught Peter and I how to navigate, sail and manage a boat and must shoulder some of the responsibility for the fact we are both still on the water.

Numerous harbour masters and their staff answered questions and offered advice for their patch as did members of several yacht clubs, and a fine group of folk I reguarly meet with provided the detailed passage information from Mylor to St Just!

Last, but certainly not least, Lucy Wilson and the team at Imray for keeping the faith.

Fair winds!

G Macintosh
February 2025

INTRODUCTION

The area covered by this book comprises the south coasts of Devon and Cornwall (although technically Lyme Regis is just over the border in Dorset), in the far southwest of the UK. Getting there from the Solent or Northern France involves a passage of a good 100M, more from the south coast of Ireland. The climate is generally warmer than the rest of the UK owing to the proximity of the Gulf Stream, but the weather can be more changeable as Atlantic frontal systems make landfall.

The waters are generally deep and, apart from a handful of well charted/marked examples, hazards are close to shore. Suggesting the best time to visit will inevitably be a commentator's curse, but observational experience suggests the most settled conditions are found between mid-May and the end of June. April might have good conditions one year in ten and the old adage of three good days and a thunderstorm is a reasonable description for the peak period of July and August. There is frequently a bout of wilder weather in September, but its coincidence with the equinox is unproven, and it is often followed by a settled period when the sea is at its warmest in early autumn and the temperature gradient is less. Whatever time is chosen (or dictated by other demands) there is always plenty of sheltered sailing in the big harbours, or bolt holes in the rivers.

The remaining sections before the detailed pilotage chapters are restricted to the basic information required for sailing in these waters, but all mariners should note the following legal requirements:

- Vessels are required to keep a documented log (either written or recorded).
- Skippers/owners are required to comply with SOLAS V (essentially passage planning).

Traditional craft ghosting up the River Fal

INTRODUCTION

- Vessels are required to comply with the International Regulations for Preventing Collision at Sea (also known as the COLREGS).
- Vessels are required to assist another vessel in distress, if practical.

Finally, you may be wondering why this book doesn't cover the Isles of Scilly. Well, Imray already publish a pilot guide for the islands, (*Isles of Scilly*, Royal Cruising Club Pilotage Foundation/David Hackett) which ought to be reason enough, and Scilly is not a destination where any kind of summary is going to provide enough information for a visiting yacht - it is a very different undertaking to destinations on the mainland. By way of example, try taking the narrow, unmarked inshore passage through the Manacles on the east side of the Lizard peninsula, and imagine navigating like that all the time.

Added to this, only a minority of yachts either visiting the West Country, or based there, make it to the islands. For those intending to do so, there is a section on passage planning specifically for the Isles of the Scilly, but please refer to the detailed pilot guide.

Tolcarne Creek on the River Fal

Noss Mayo on the River Yealm

PASSAGE PLANNING
including SOLAS V requirements

If using an electronic device to collate passage planning information, take screenshots so that the information is available offline - merely having the capability to access the information might not comply with SOLAS V regulations.

The sage who was the instructor for my RYA navigation course described passage planning thus:

- Can you get out?
- Can you get in?
- Can you do the bit in the middle?

Simplistic perhaps, but apt nonetheless, and not far off what is now a legal requirement. Most passages between ports in the West Country are of the order of 18-22M meaning they can be made in daylight on a single tide. The following should be considered as essential information required for coastal cruising, annotated for information specific to the area covered.

Distances (miles)

	Scilly	Newlyn	Lizard Pt	Helford R	Falmouth	Mevagissey	Fowey	Looe	Plymouth	Yealm	Salcombe	Start Pt	Dartmouth	Tor Bay	Teignmouth	Exmouth
Newlyn	36															
Lizard Pt	44	16														
Helford R	59	35	15													
Falmouth	60	36	16	4												
Mevagissey	69	46	28	19	17											
Fowey	78	49	34	24	20	7										
Looe	80	57	39	31	29	16	11									
Plymouth	93	66	49	43	41	28	24	13								
Yealm	94	67	50	43	41	28	24	13	4							
Salcombe	104	77	60	52	50	40	36	29	23	19						
Start Pt	108	81	64	56	54	44	40	33	27	23	6					
Dartmouth	116	89	72	64	62	52	48	41	35	31	14	8				
Torbay	118	96	78	72	70	62	55	50	41	36	24	15	11			
Teignmouth	126	104	86	80	78	70	63	58	49	44	32	23	19	8		
Exmouth	131	107	90	84	82	73	67	61	53	48	33	27	24	12	6	
Lyme Regis	144	120	104	98	96	86	81	74	65	60	48	41	35	30	25	20

INTRODUCTION

Moorings at Bantham, River Avon

Weather

Forecasts should be acquired up to three days ahead of an intended passage. Those produced by a meteorologist, such as the Inshore Waters Forecast or Shipping Forecast disseminated by the MCA are more appropriate than a straight depiction of a computer model, commonly available online without human input. They are available at www.metoffice.gov.uk including in text format, which can be read with minimal mobile phone signal, in addition to actual observations from a number of coastal weather stations (e.g. Culdrose). Computer derived internet forecasts should be treated with caution, especially those where the data set cannot be selected. The data set is important as only the 0000GMT and 1200GMT data is a full set at present. 0600GMT and 1800GMT data is not. The main originator of the data is the National Oceanic and Atmospheric Administration (NOAA) in the USA. Its website www.ready.noaa.gov/READYcmet.php has a product which allows the data set and all parameters to be selected.

Falmouth Coastguard covers the area as far east as the River Exe and broadcasts the inshore waters forecasts on VHF every three hours commencing at 0110 local time. Full forecasts including the shipping forecast, gale warnings, naval activity (i.e. Subfacts and Gunfacts) are broadcast at 0710 and 1910 local time. Lyme Regis is in the Solent Coastguard area but the Falmouth transmissions can still be heard and are likely to be more relevant, unless bound further east.

The National Coastwatch Institution (NCI) has lookouts at various points along the coast, and many broadcast local conditions on VHF 65. Details can be found at the start of each chapter and at www.nci.org.uk.

Other sources include Navtex (Station I – Niton) and BBC Radio 4.

Also worth downloading or printing are the Met Office synoptic charts at www.metoffice.gov.uk and there is a useful tutorial for interpreting them at www.rmets.org/metmatters/how-interpret-weather-chart.

Tides

See Tidal Stream diagrams on pages 8-11.
The standard port for this region is Plymouth (Devonport). Dartmouth, Falmouth and Newlyn are also standard ports, but all secondary ports are referenced to Plymouth (Devonport). Official tide tables are published under licence from the UK Hydrographic Office (UKHO). The main source of independent tidal data is the National Oceanography Centre.

For the bulk of the area covered, between Start Point and Lizard Point, the main channel tide sets ENE from half-tide up to half-tide down, and WSW from half-tide down to half-tide up, with reference to HW Falmouth (HWF) or HW Plymouth (HWP) whichever is nearest. HW Falmouth is obligingly 6 hours off HW Dover (HWD) meaning a tidal atlas referenced to Dover can easily be converted to Falmouth. The *Admiralty Tidal*

Passage Planning

Atlas for the English Channel is referenced to both Dover and Plymouth. Tidal streams are generally not strong except near headlands (see separate section) but even a 1kn favourable tide can lop an hour off a nominal 20M passage so it is definitely worth factoring in. Within the bays, the tide largely sets into or out of them with reference to local HW and LW but there is a noticeable onshore set the further west you go, for example at Veryan Bay between Dodman Point and Falmouth.

East of Start Point, the tides tend to follow the coast setting NE from about HWP-0200 and SW from around HWP+0500, and are strongest about 1 hour after the tide has turned (i.e. HWP-0100 & HWP+0600). These times are all about 30 minutes later between Teignmouth and the Exe. At Lyme Regis, the tide rises quickly for the first hour after LW, slackens for about 1.5 hours then increases again for the next 3 hours before appearing to stand for an hour or more around HW. The ebb then runs out for 5 hours. The effect is more noticeable at springs.

In Mount's Bay, the tides are rotatory clockwise affected by both Land's End and Lizard Point, with the E going tide beginning around HWP-0300 turning gradually SE then S becoming SW around HWP+0300 and NW by HWP+0600. Note these are only approximations - the tides in Mount's Bay are notoriously unpredictable, but fortunately the drift/rate rarely exceeds 1kn and is about 0.5kn much of the time.

Vessel

Skippers are responsible for ensuring that their vessel is seaworthy and has the appropriate safety equipment for the intended passage. It is also the sole and inescapable responsibility of the skipper in deciding whether to start or continue a passage. Safety equipment in this context includes charts and navigation equipment (see also System failure on p.6).

Crew

Skippers need to know, or be able to assess, whether crew are fit and well, and any other information which may be relevant. In the vast majority of cases this will never be an issue but even with regular crew, knowledge of a food allergy, or prescription medication could well be relevant for an extended trip.

Dangers

These have been referred to as hazards in this book but the information provided should be used to augment that shown on official charts. Plans should include avoidance strategies such as clearing bearings, transits, minimum tidal heights etc. and the requirements of the COLREGS with reference to deep water channels and traffic separation schemes for example.

Ports of refuge

These will vary according to the vessel and crew but from the perspective of small yachts and motor boats a port of refuge is likely to be somewhere that can be

Newton Creek, River Yealm

INTRODUCTION

Moonrise, Helford River

accessed in any weather, at any state of the tide and where a secure mooring or anchorage can be found within a reasonable time and/or distance from the entrance. Shore access may also be a requirement in some cases and should form part of the decision making process.

Three ports in this area can be considered as meeting these requirements: Falmouth, Plymouth and a combination of Dartmouth and Brixham depending on the wind direction as they are reasonably close together. In anything other than heavy weather from between S and E, Newlyn and Fowey can be added to that list. Unsurprisingly, all these ports have 24 hour VHF coverage, and both all weather and inshore lifeboats.

When arriving in the area from further afield, a prudent plan is to aim for one of these ports.

System failure

Skippers need to consider the means of dealing with system failures. This might include carrying spares (and knowing how to fit them) or portable battery powered equipment, and having the tools and materials to make temporary repairs. But it also refers to the failure of external systems such as GPS which brings us to the thorny topic of electronic navigation. Although very reliable, it is also susceptible to multiple forms of system failure. At the least, you need to be able to find and plot your position, the traditional method being a three point fix. A mobile phone can get a fix from shore based transmitters but they are primarily designed for land use which means coastal coverage is sketchy and there are many so called 'not-spots' in this region due to the topography. Manually plotting your position on a paper chart is quick and straightforward, and many dedicated plotters have the capability to manually enter a position as do some phone apps, which provides an alternative in the event of power failure. However, the official advice remains to carry corrected paper charts and maintain a regular log of your position.

Reporting

It is sensible to let someone else know your plans, preferably a shore based contact. It is also helpful to register your vessel with the RYA SafeTrx scheme (which has succeeded HM Coastguard CG66) as this will greatly speed up any emergency response. SafeTrx can also track your voyage via an app but currently it relies on mobile phone coverage and is map based rather than chart based, so the app should be used with caution.

If help is required, VHF radio is the primary method of communication as it alerts everyone within range (especially if DSC is used), **not mobile phones** which only alert one person. They should only be used as a back-up system.

VHF sets should be checked regularly and before a long passage. In order of preference, this should be done by calling another vessel, a marina, an NCI station or a harbour master. Only call the coastguard if none of these reply. The nearest vessel is the one that will be responding in an emergency and it will be faster if they hear the call first, rather than when alerted by the coastguard.

Passage planning

Lizard Point lighthouse

Anchoring

Entire books are devoted to this subject, so only some basics for this area are covered here. There is some technical aspect to this, but it is not overly complex.

Do not despair if anchoring overnight presents too great a risk. It is perfectly possible to undertake a cruise in the West Country, including the rivers, without the need to do so. Indeed from Falmouth, you can sail to a different destination to anchor for lunch and/or a run ashore, and return to a pontoon or mooring every day for a fortnight, without going to the same place twice.

Ensure ground tackle is sufficient. Chain is a necessity on sand, and heavier is better. For overnight anchoring in this region, 6mm chain is only suitable for very small (day) craft and warp should not be considered at all, apart from as a snubbing line. 8mm is a minimum and 10mm or greater is preferable, with sufficient deployed such that at least one boat length of the chain never lifts off the seabed. Remember that a larger anchor is no substitute for heavier chain; the anchor stops the chain from moving, the chain holds the boat.

Consider both the current and any forecast wind direction. In this area, it is not usually difficult to identify a site that offers protection from the wind. The enemy in the West Country is wave energy and, to a lesser extent, swell. The ambient direction of both is WSW, generated far out in the Atlantic Ocean. In the Western Approaches it is modified by the local conditions and then funnels up the English Channel. Winds with a westerly component tend to accentuate the effect, whereas those with an easterly component initially just increase the sea state, only modifying the waves if prolonged.

The shallower water along the coastline slows down the nearest edge of the wave causing it to 'bend' slightly towards the shore (refraction in technical parlance). Headlands, especially those with an underwater ridge, affect a larger portion of each wave causing more of a change in angle, sufficient that the waves can end up almost parallel to the coast on the lee side. This can sometimes be mitigated by anchoring closer to the headland, for example at Hall Sands near Start Point. The process is repeated as the swell progresses up the Channel. Thus Coverack and Portmellon, for example, both look sheltered from SW but, whilst this is true for the wind direction, the wave energy is refracted by successive headlands and it can often be a rolly experience.

Islands and reefs offer the best protection, the Manacles being a good example where the anchorages just N are usually calmer in SW winds than those just S.

One final point to bear in mind is that the wave direction can change up to 24 hours ahead of a respective change in the wind direction so the forecast is important.

Bearings

Throughout this book, all bearings given are °T (true).

INTRODUCTION

TIDAL STREAMS

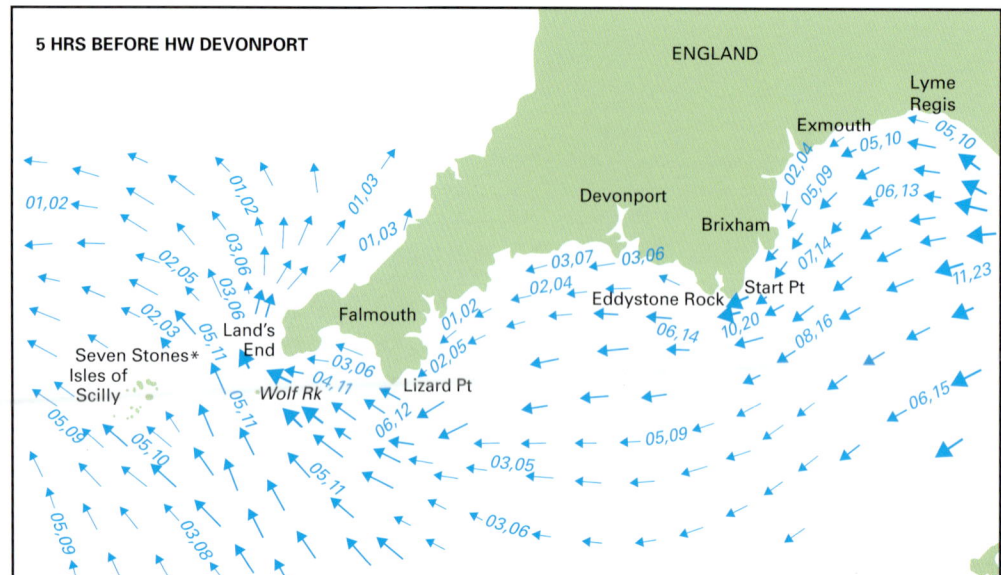

Rates are shown in tenths of a knot for Neap and Spring tides, separated by a comma. Thus '11, 19' is 1·1kn at (mean) Neaps and 1·9kn at (mean) Springs.

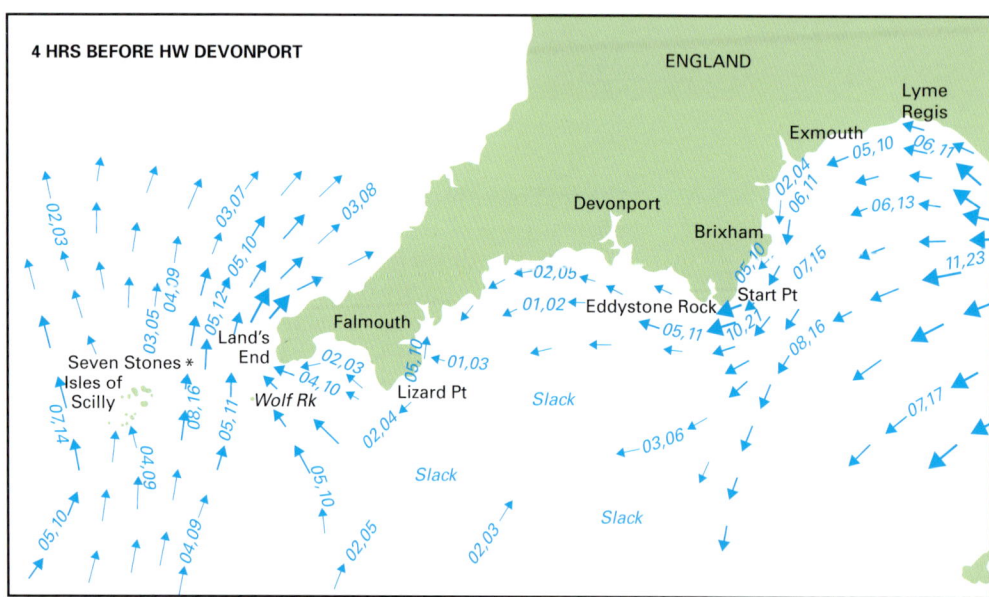

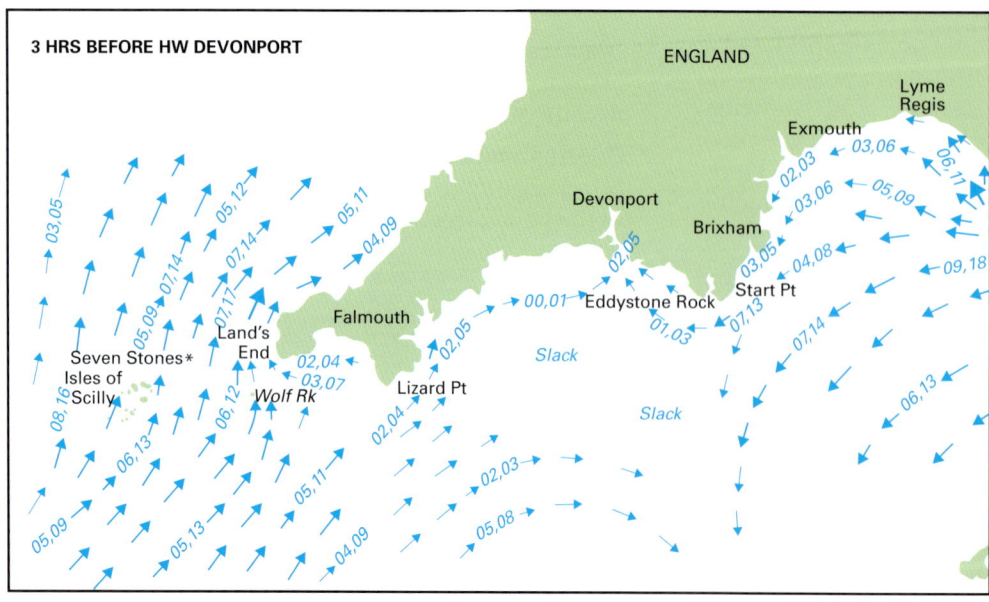

Tidal Streams

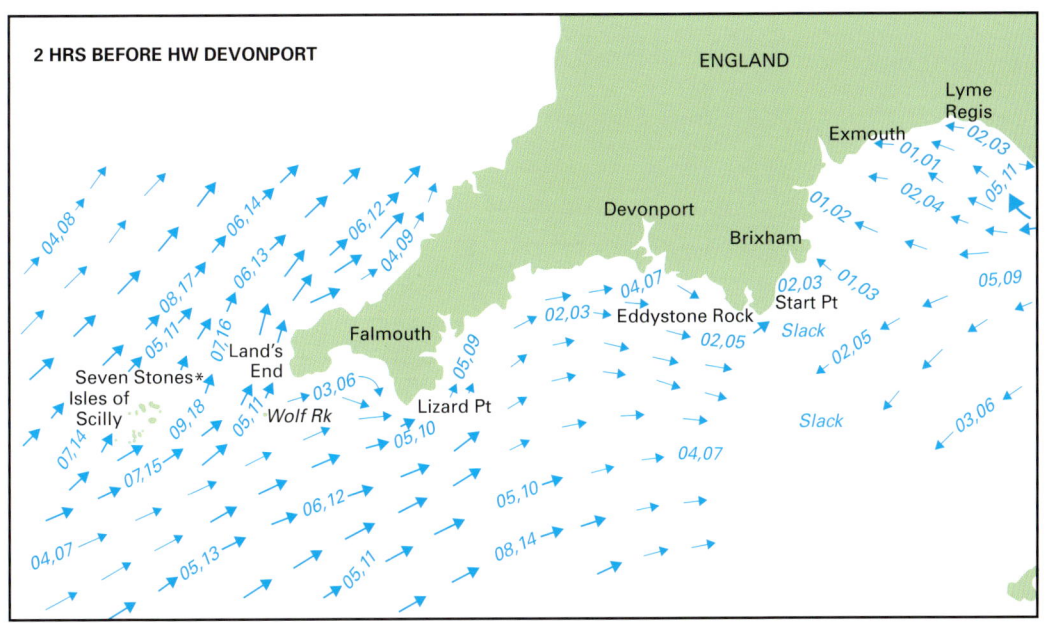

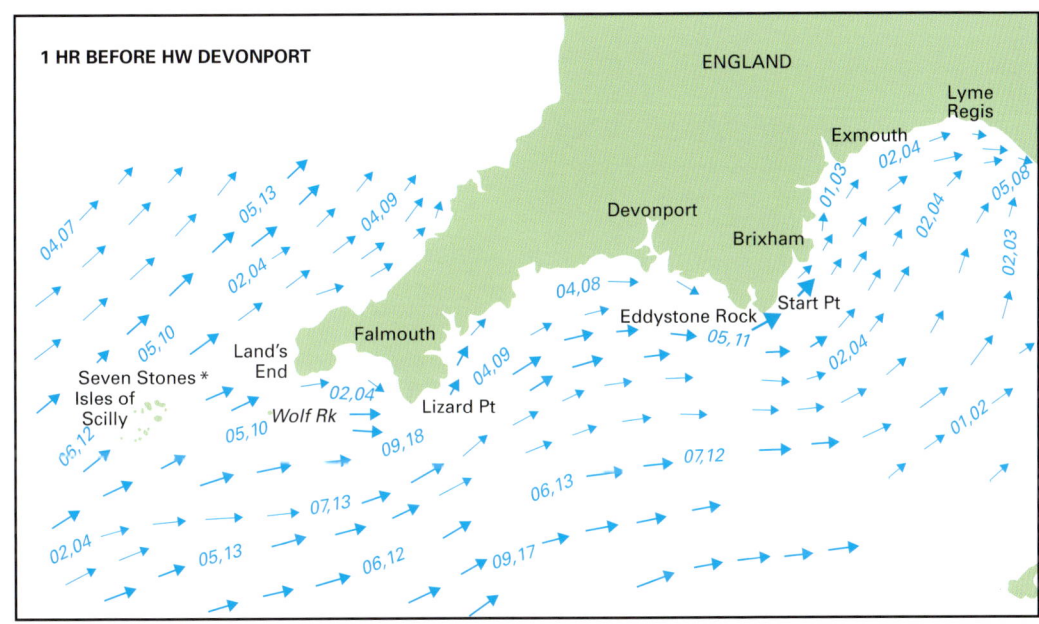

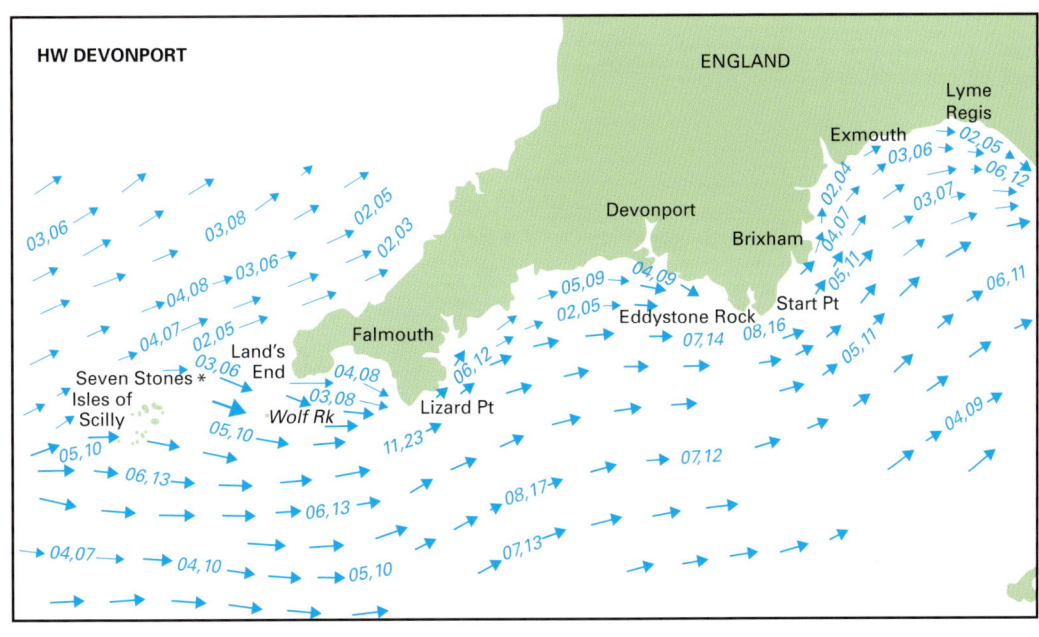

West Country Pilot

INTRODUCTION

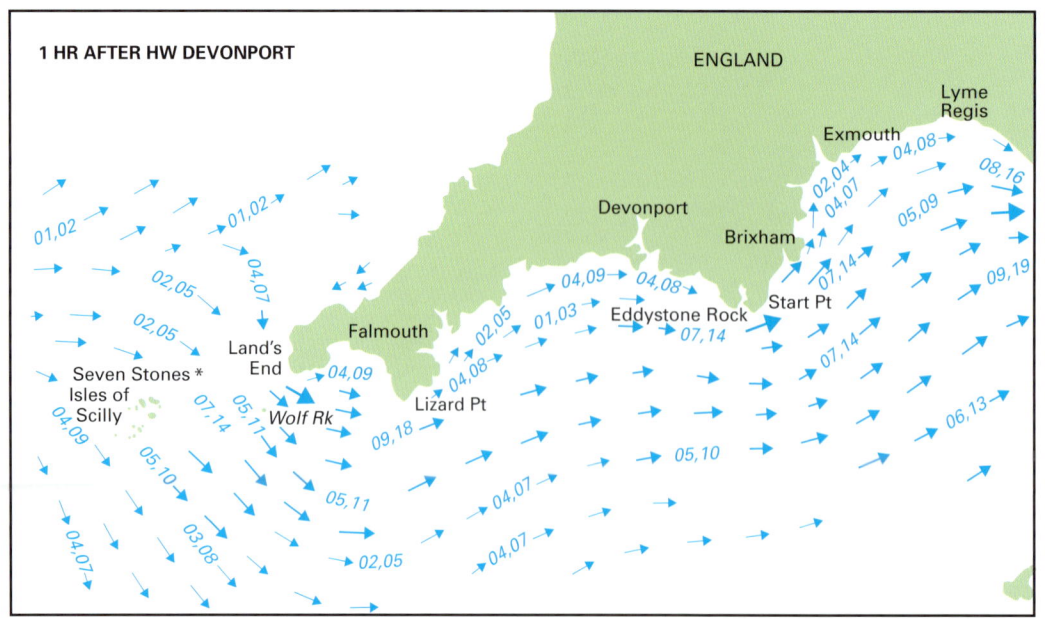

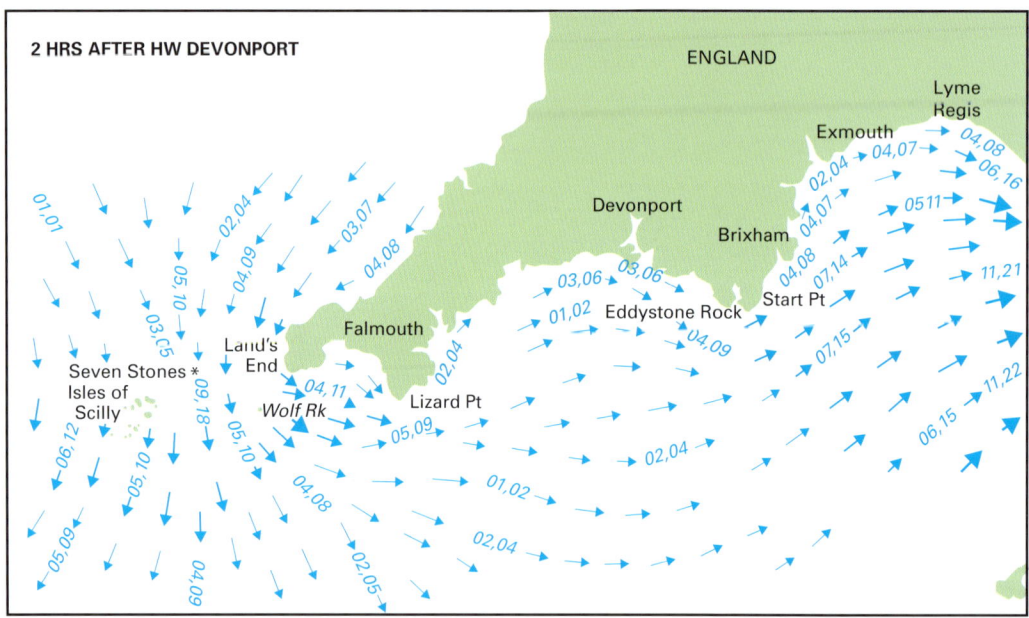

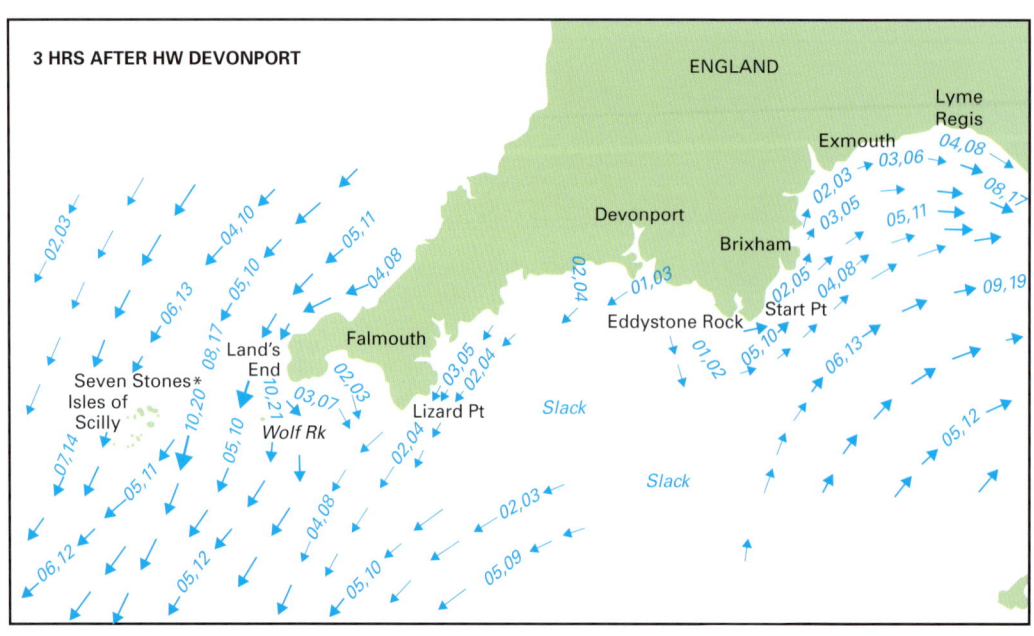

Tidal Streams

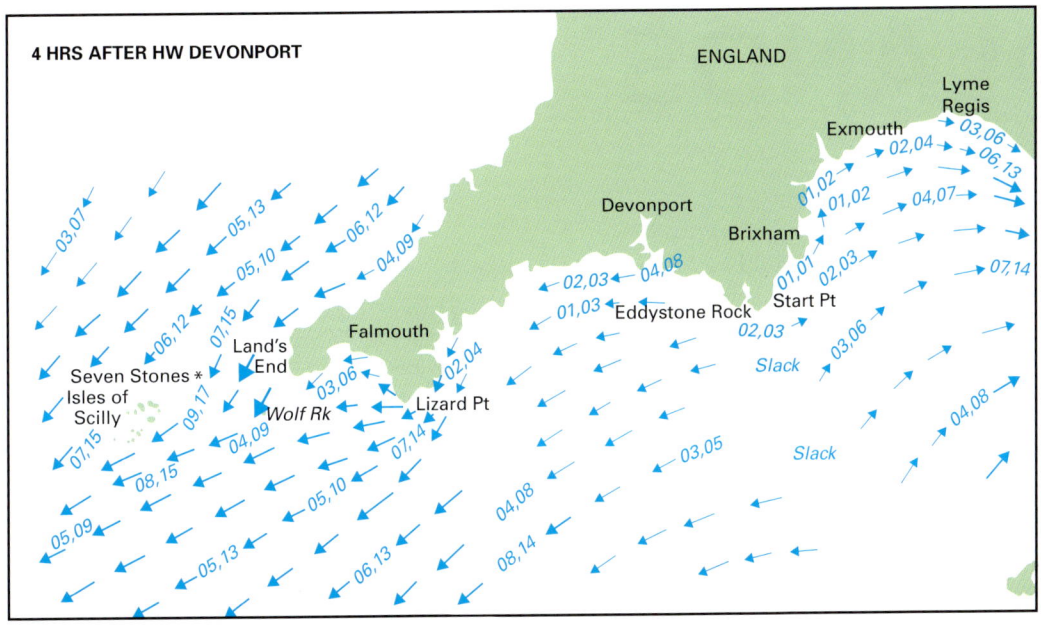

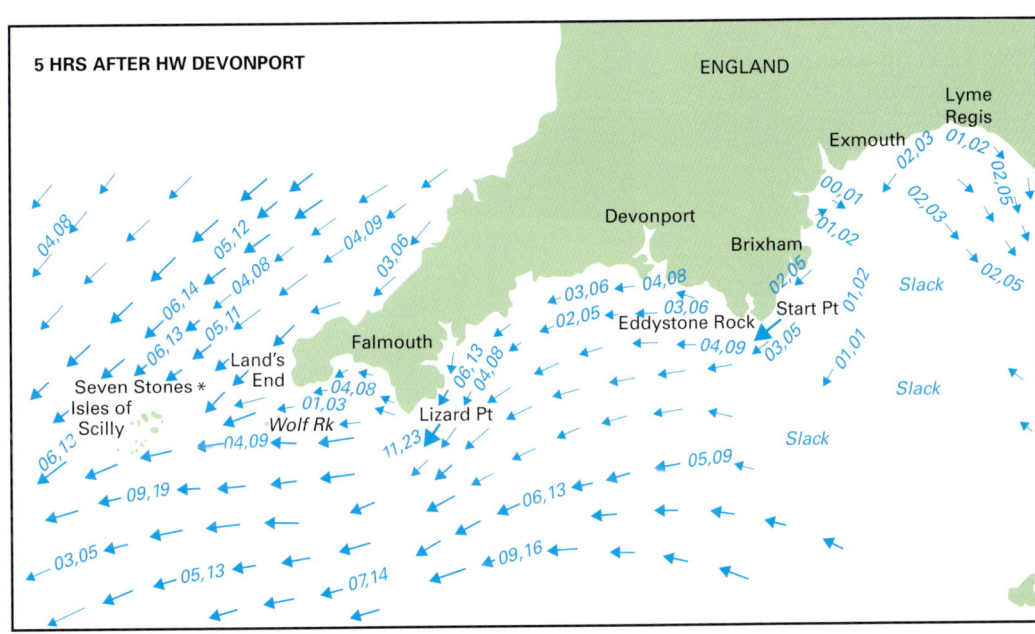

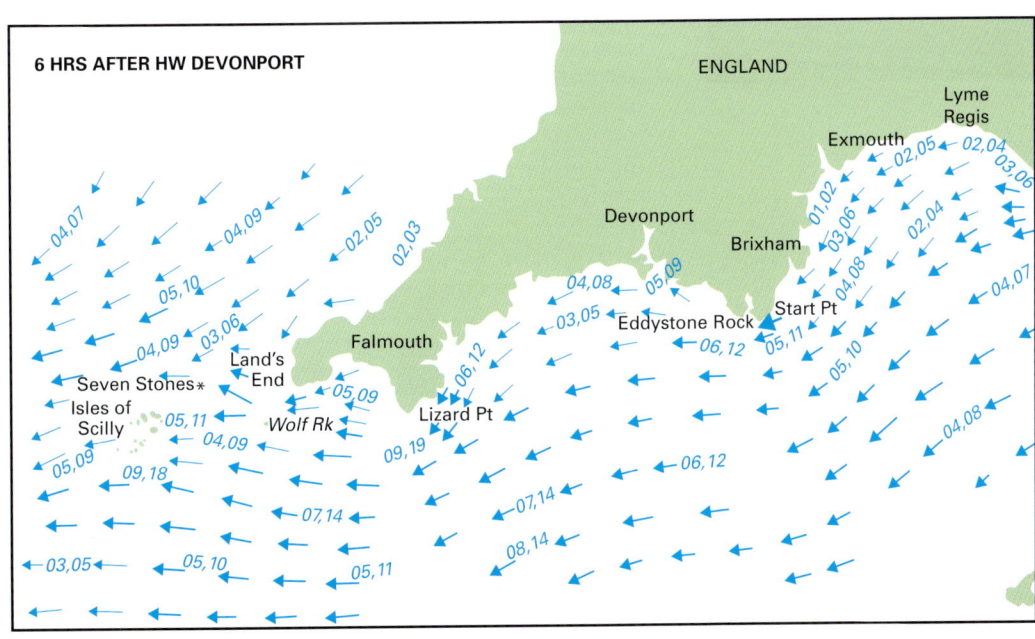

West Country Pilot

INTRODUCTION

HEADLANDS
including tidal strategies

In bad weather, all the headlands listed here should be given a good offing, at least 3M in the case of the two major headlands at Lizard Point and Start Point, and >2M for Dodman Point.

In general terms, it is always better to pass a headland with a fair tide, since the streams are stronger here. Race conditions, or overfalls at the very least, build with the tide and can get quite nasty with a contrary wind, so the distance to aim off will very much depend on the timing. Dodman Point is the only headland with anything resembling an inshore route but even that can get lively in certain conditions. Do not pass close to Start Point or Lizard Point at any time other than in benign conditions, at slack water, just as the tide is turning in your favour. At any other time, stand off a sufficient distance to avoid the races, and proceed with a fair tide.

Beer Head

This is the westernmost chalk cliff on the South Coast 130m high. Streams are weak turning E about HWP-0045 and W around HWP+0540. It presents no particular issues as most vessels will be offshore.

Beer Head

Straight Point

This wedge shaped, red sandstone headland E of the Exe entrance is mentioned for completeness. The presence of a firing range extending SE from it means that it is unlikely to feature in a passage.

Straight Point

Berry Head

This is the first headland requiring proper tidal consideration. It is on the S side of Tor Bay, flat topped with a precipitous drop to sea level from an elevation of 55m. Tides run N from about HWP-0300 and S from around HWP+0300 and reach 3+kn. Overfalls can be encountered as far S as the Mewstones at the entrance to the Dart, and the area immediately N is strewn with fishing floats. In general it is best to stay 1M off, even if heading to/from Brixham.

Berry Head

Start Point

This is the first of the major headlands in this cruising area. It is shaped like a ridge and there are a number of rocks close offshore. The location of Skerries Bank just NE provides an additional planning consideration. Off Start Point the tide runs NE from about HWP-0200 and SW from around HWP+0500 with speeds exceeding 3kn for much of the time. This produces a vigorous race which extends up to 1M S and 1.5M E. Therefore, in anything other than light airs at slack water, plan to give both the headland and Skerries Bank an offing of at least 1M, and stand more like 3-4M off the headland in bad weather.

In settled conditions it is possible to round Start Point close in with careful planning, although if on passage to/from Portland Bill or beyond, there is nothing to be gained. On a passage between Salcombe and Dartmouth or Brixham however, it is worth consideration.

Eastbound, leave Salcombe at HWP-0415 accepting that you will be punching the full flood tide as far as the entrance. Stay close inshore arriving at Prawle Point at HWP-0315 to pick up a favourable 1kn current allowing Start Point to be cleared (avoiding the offlying rocks) around HWP-0230, just as the tide

Start Point

Headlands

Start Point from NE

Bolt Tail

turns N into Start Bay. A fair tide can then be carried NE along the coast to reach Dartmouth or Tor Bay around local HW.

Westbound, leave Dartmouth at HWP+0200 and close the coast at Slapton Sands, once clear of Homestone Ledge and Combe Point. A back eddy runs SW all the way along the beach to Start Point, which should be timed to pass between HWP+0400 and HWP+0430. Arriving later risks being pushed well S, potentially encountering the race. If there is any W in the wind, take the offshore route as the final leg to Salcombe will be choppy, although reasonably short.

Prawle Point

This is a minor headland between Start Point and Salcombe. A small race develops off it but presents no problems to vessels on passage, or if following the directions above for Start Point.

Rame Head

This is another area which is rarely benign and in wind against tide conditions can quickly become rough. Stay 0.5M offshore, preferably with a fair tide.

Rame Head from east

Prawle Point

Rame Head from west

Bolt Head to Bolt Tail

The stretch of water W of Salcombe between Bolt Head and Bolt Tail is always rough and at its worst when there is significant swell. It is best avoided by staying a good 1M offshore.

Dodman Point

Although a minor headland, relatively speaking, it is precipitous and the seabed is uneven. This results in overfalls downstream of it on virtually all tides. Timings follow that of the main channel streams. With a fair tide, unless there is a strong contrary wind, it is possible to pass very close to the shore. It may still be choppy, but for a much shorter time. Note, however, that heading NE with a N wind will result in a wet sail close hauled to Fowey, whilst bound for Falmouth or Helford in a NW wind will be lively, but manageable. There is nothing to be gained by going inshore on a passage between Falmouth and Plymouth or further afield. In wind over tide conditions, or heavy swell stay at least 2-3M offshore.

Bolt Head

Dodman Point

West Country Pilot • 13

INTRODUCTION

Lizard Point

The most southerly point on the UK mainland, the Lizard is a huge granite headland and a true tidal gate, deserving of a menacing reputation. Passing it against the tide should not feature in any passage plan. Tidal streams **average** nearly 3kn and a race extends 2-3M S and SE. There is also Atlantic swell to contend with.

Official tide predictions show slack water 2M S of the Lizard (which occurs only for a short period) at approximately HWP-0400 and HWP+0230. Further out beyond the race, the timing is about 15 to 30 minutes later but 'slack' water is barely perceptible. Close inshore is a different matter entirely with observations varying between 30 minutes and up to an hour earlier. There are no official predictions for inshore.

The most prudent passage plan is to round the headland when sea conditions are slight and winds 15kn or less. Aim to be 2M S of the lighthouse at **HWF+0300** if heading W, or **HWF-0300** if heading E. The latter timing is of more importance if bound for Falmouth because the ebb tide runs strongly S out of Falmouth Bay and down the E side of the Lizard, increasing as soon as the channel tide turns W. This makes for a very long 16M if the timing is late. Westbound, assume that the sea state in Mount's Bay will be a level higher than that E of the Lizard (i.e. slight E of Lizard becomes moderate in Mount's Bay). If late on the tide, or caught out by deteriorating conditions, then stay 4M out to avoid the race (and, eastbound, only turning for Falmouth when St Anthony lighthouse is due N).

When rounding the Lizard for the first few times or on passage, the directions in the previous paragraph should be used. For experienced skippers it is feasible to pass about 0.5M off the headland in benign conditions, making sure to avoid the hazards described in chapter 17, and keeping a sharp lookout for fishing floats which quickly become submerged by the tidal flow. The phrase 'benign conditions' means light airs, slack tide and very low swell, thus proceeding under power. Various waiting anchorages are described in chapter 17 which may help with the timing, especially the closest ones where a subtle change in the sea state is often an indicator of the tidal stream turning.

Lizard Point looking SW

Lizard Point looking NE

Abbreviations and symbols

Abbreviations

Bn	Beacon	Mo	Morse
By	Buoy	N	North, Northwards, Northerly
CC	Cruising Club	NCM	North Cardinal Mark (eg beacon)
CG	Coastguard	NE	Northeast or Northeastwards
Ch	Channel	NEly	Northeasterly
Conspic	Conspicuous	NW	Northwest, Northwestwards
DSC	Digital Selective Calling	NWly	Northwesterly
E	East, Eastwards, Easterly	Oc	Occulting light
ECM	East Cardinal Mark (eg beacon)	ODAS	Ocean Data Acquisition System
F	Fixed light	PAYG	Pay as you go
Fl	Flashing Light	PH	Port Hand
Ft	Foot, feet	PHM	Port Hand Mark (eg beacon)
G	Green	Pt	Point
H	Hour, eg H +15 is 15 minutes past the hour	PWC	Personal Water Craft (jet ski)
hr	Hour, Hours	Q	Quick flashing light
HW	High water	R	Red
HWF	High water Falmouth	S	South, Southwards, Southerly
HWN	High water Neaps	s	second(s)
HWP	High water Plymouth	SC	Sailing Club
HWS	High water Springs	SCM	South Cardinal Mark (eg beacon)
IDM	Isolated Danger Mark	SH	Starboard Hand
IQ	Interrupted Quick flashing light	SHM	Starboard Hand Mark (eg beacon)
Iso	Isophase light	S'ly	Southerly
Kn	Knot, knots	SPM	Special mark
L.Fl	Long Flash	SW	Southwest, Southwestwards
LNG	Liquefied Natural Gas	SWly	Southwesterly
LOA	Length Overall	SWM	Safe Water Mark
LPG	Liquefied Petroleum Gas	TSS	Traffic Separation Scheme
LW	Low Water	UKHO	United Kingdom Hydrographic Office (the Admiralty)
LWN	Low Water Neaps	UTC	Universal Time Corrected (same as GMT - Greenwich MeanTime)
LWS	Low Water Springs	vert	vertical
M	Mile (Nautical mile)	VQ	Very quick flashing light
m	metre	VTS	Vessel Traffic Service
MHWS	Mean High Water Springs	W	West, Westwards, Westerly; White
min	minute	WCM	West Cardinal Mark (eg beacon)
mins	minutes	Y	Yellow
MLWS	Mean Low Water Springs	YC	Yacht club
MMSI	Maritime Mobile Service Identity		
MSI	Maritime Safety Information incl. inshore waters forecast, gale warnings and navigational warnings		

Symbols

	Visitors' mooring		Public telephone
	Visitors' berth		Post office
	Yacht marina		Building
	Public landing		Airport
	Slipway for small craft		Flagpole/flagstaff
	Water tap		Castle/fort
	Fuel		Hospital
	Pump-out facilities		Notice board
	Customs		Wooded
	Public house, inn, bar		Beacon (with various topmarks)
	Restaurant		Mooring Buoy
	Yacht or sailing club		Crane
	Toilets		Chimney
	Public car park		Radio/TV mast
	Hard standing for boats		Water tower
	Launderette		Tower
	Caravan site		Monument
	Camping site		Wind turbine
	Nature reserve		
	Harbour master		
	Travel hoist		

West Country Pilot

INTRODUCTION

Chart symbols

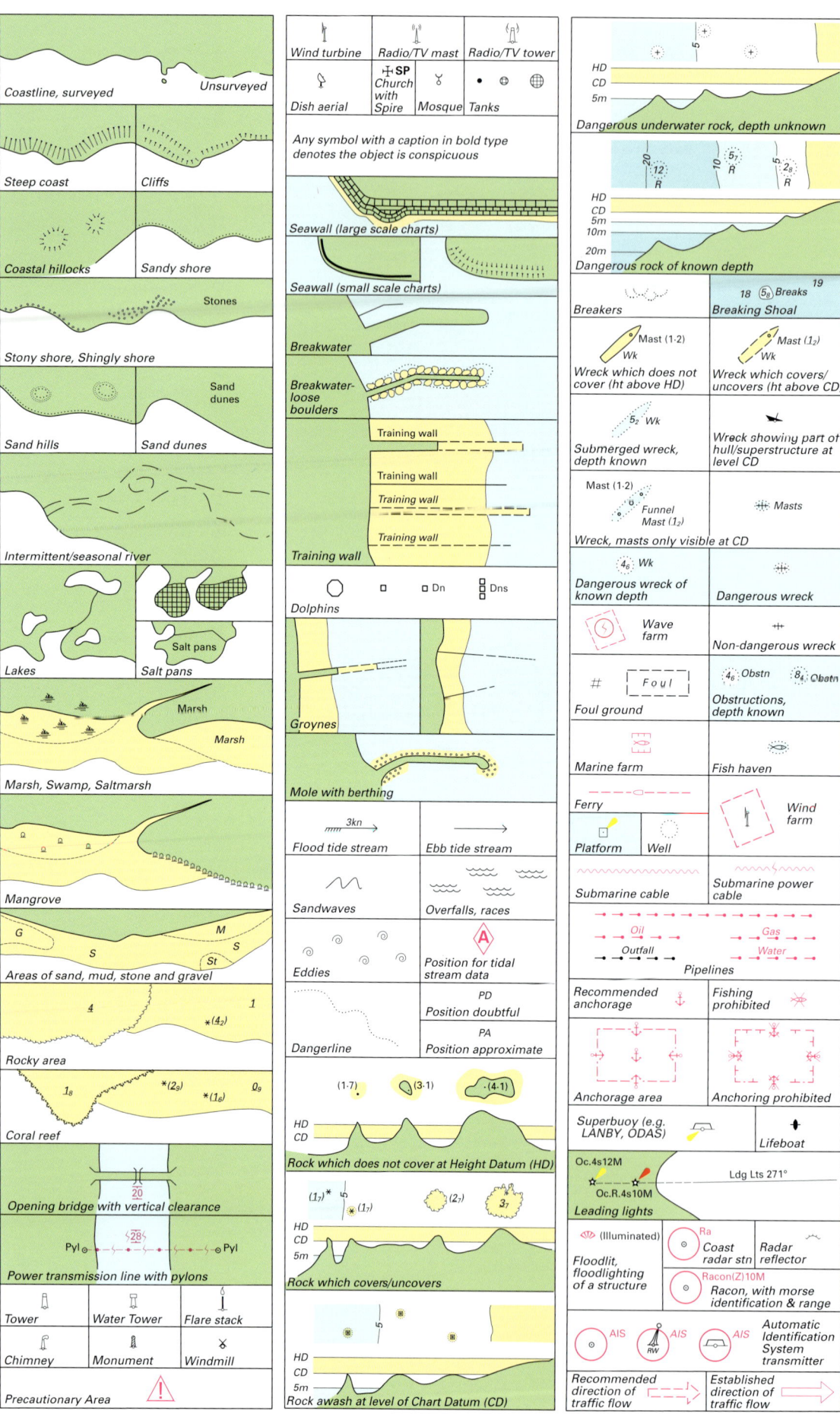

Abbreviations and Symbols

IALA Buoyage System Region A

Lateral marks
Port hand
All red
Topmark (if any): can
Light (if any): red

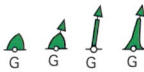

Starboard hand
All green
Topmark (if any): cone
Light (if any): green

Preferred channel to port
Green/red/green
Light (if any): Fl(2+1)G

Preferred channel to starboard
Red/green/red
Light (if any): Fl(2+1)R

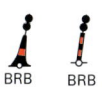

Isolated danger marks
(stationed over a danger with navigable water around)
Black with red band
Topmark: 2 black balls
Light (if any): Fl(2) (white)

Special mark
Body shape optional, yellow
Topmark (if any): Yellow X
Light (if any): Fl.Y etc

Safe water marks
(mid-channel and landfall)
Red and white vertical stripes
Topmark (if any): red ball
Light (if any): Iso, Oc, LFl.10s or Mo(A) (white)

Emergency Wreck Marking buoy
Yellow and blue vertical stripes
Topmark: upright yellow cross
Light (if any): Fl.Bu/Y.3s

Cardinal marks

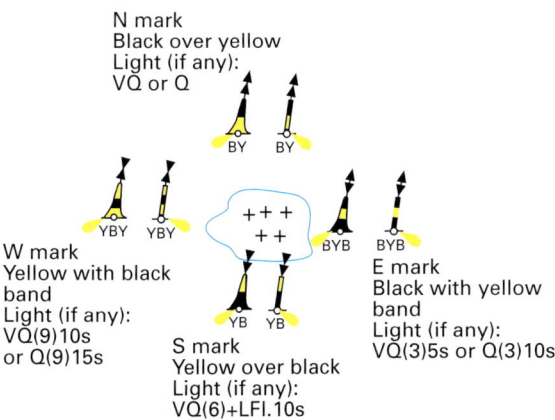

N mark
Black over yellow
Light (if any): VQ or Q

W mark
Yellow with black band
Light (if any): VQ(9)10s or Q(9)15s

S mark
Yellow over black
Light (if any): VQ(6)+LFl.10s or Q(6)+LFl.15s

E mark
Black with yellow band
Light (if any): VQ(3)5s or Q(3)10s

International Port Traffic Signals (IPTS)

			MAIN MESSAGE
1	●●●	Flashing	Serious emergency - all vessels to stop or divert according to instructions
2	●●●		Vessels shall not proceed
3	●●●	Fixed or slow occulting	Vessels may proceed; One-way traffic
4	●●○		Vessels may proceed; Two-way traffic
5	●○●		A vessel may proceed only when it has received specific orders to do so
			EXEMPTION SIGNALS AND MESSAGES
2a	●●● (yellow top)	Fixed or slow occulting	Vessels shall not proceed, except that vessels which navigate outside the main channel need not comply with the main message
5a	●○● (yellow top)		A vessel may proceed only when it has received specific orders to do so, except that vessels which navigate outside the main channel need not comply with the main message

West Country Pilot • 17

1 LYME REGIS
AXMOUTH & BEER

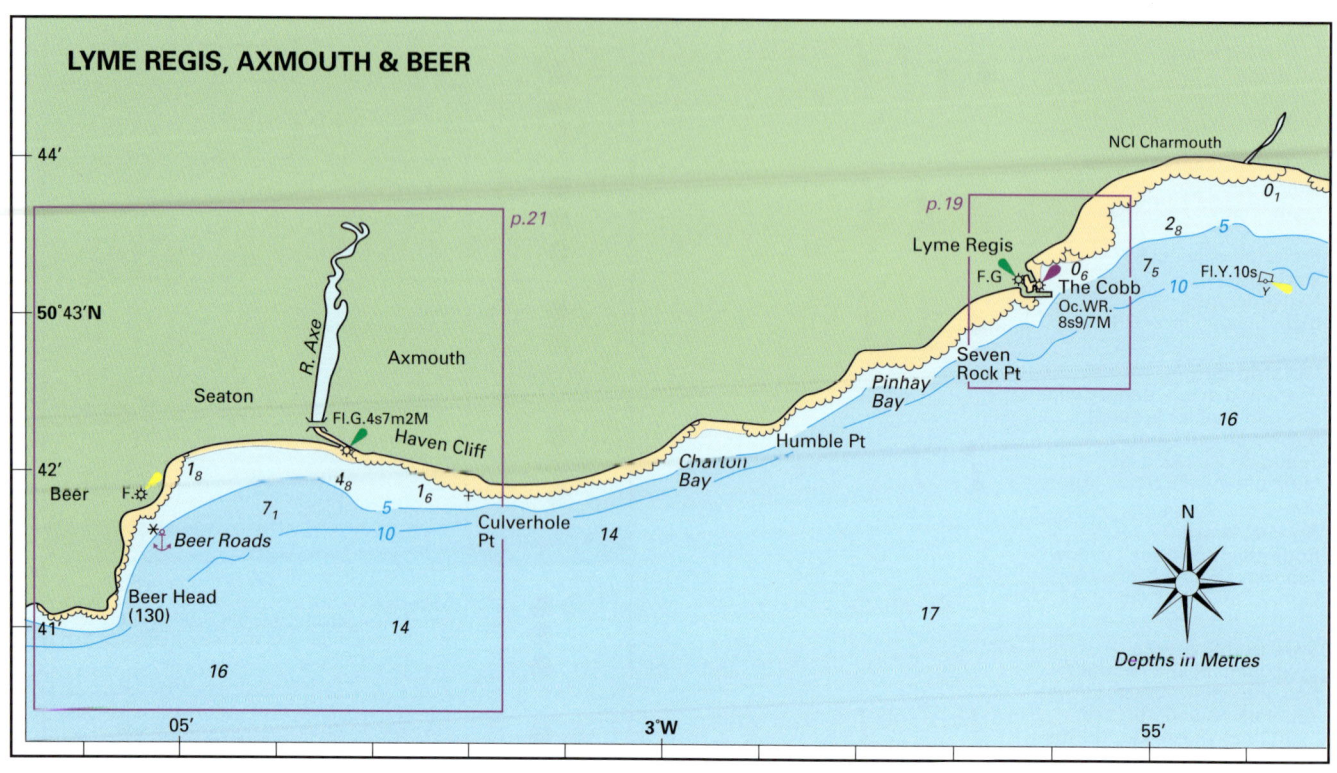

Harbour Master's Office
VHF 14 'Lyme Regis Harbour Radio'
Harbour Office, The Cobb, Lyme Regis DT7 3JJ
☎ 01297 442317 / 07870 240645
NCI Charmouth VHF 65 ☎ 01279 255076

Lyme Regis, on the Dorset/Devon border, lies within the Jurassic Coast World Heritage Site. Although unlikely to be a first port of call, it is useful as a stopping off point for smaller/slower craft heading E up the English Channel, lying only 22M from Portland Bill whereas the Exe is 36M and Tor Bay and Dartmouth 42M.

Landmarks
Golden Cap, the highest point on this stretch of the coast, is approximately 3M E of Lyme Regis. From W, Beer Head is a prominent chalk headland in a mainly sandstone coastline with a conspicuous radio mast inland.

Main hazards
In anything other than offshore winds (i.e. NW to N), this area is unsafe. Even in light winds from other directions, the swell will likely be too uncomfortable for anything more than a short stop.

Beer Head from SE

18 • West Country Pilot

Lyme Regis

Golden Cap just E of Lyme Regis

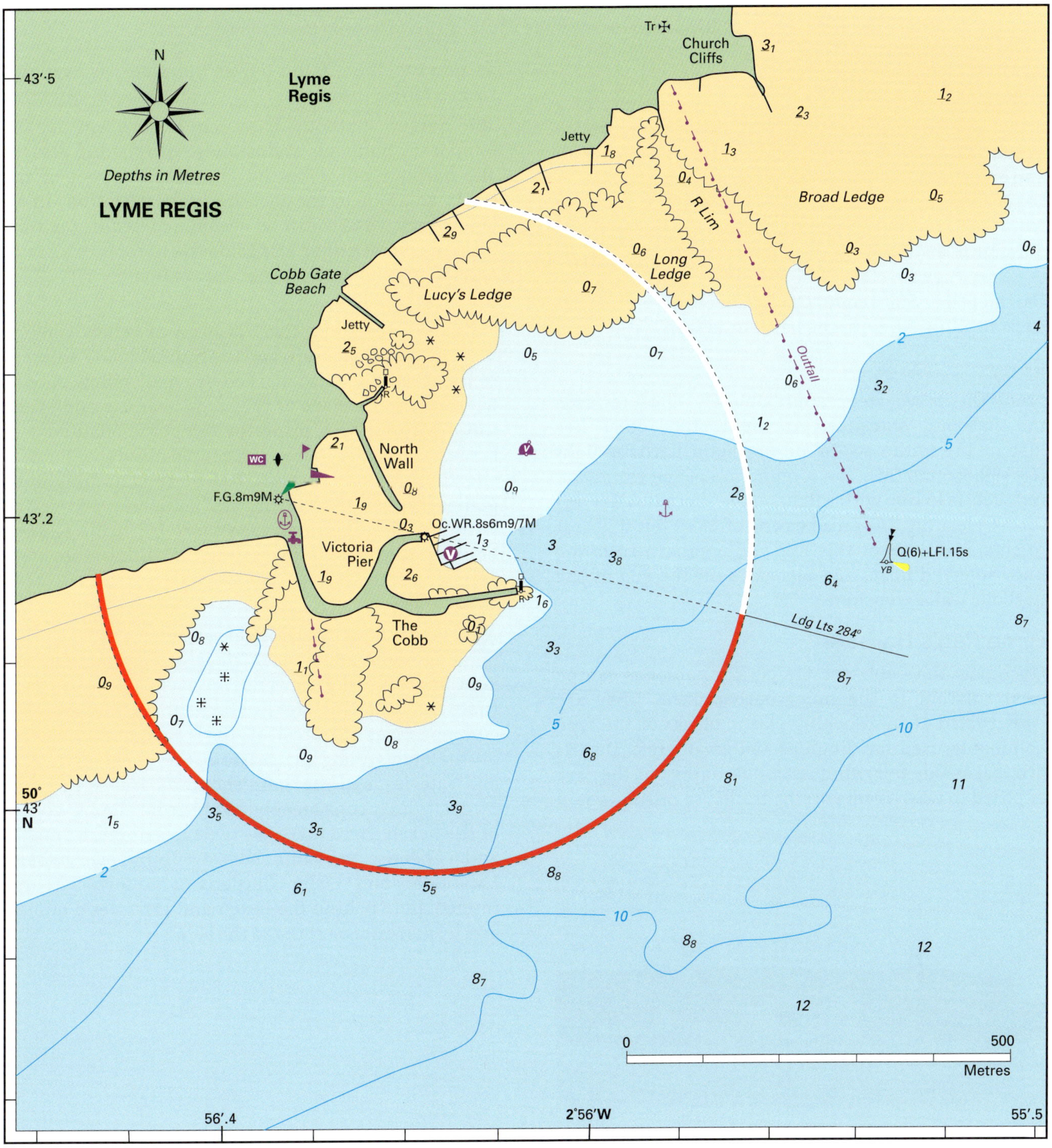

1 LYME REGIS, BEER & AXMOUTH

Lyme Regis Harbour with the summer pontoons centre. The three yachts on the left are on the moorings.

Approaches

From S or E make for a position in the vicinity of a SCM (marking a sewer outfall) 0.25M off the entrance keeping clear of the Cobb, the large stone harbour wall and extension. From here, the temporary pontoons can be seen adjacent to the harbour entrance. Approaching from W, two large marine farms are located off Sidmouth on the direct course to/from Tor Bay or the Exe. They lie close N of the direct course to/from Dartmouth or Start Point. Once clear of these, close the coast heading NE until the harbour is seen.

Entry

From the SCM, steer approximately 280° towards the harbour entrance. At night, this buoy lies just in the white sector of the main harbour light (Oc.WR.8s6m9/7M). The conjunction of the white and red sectors in line with a light on the shore (F.G.8m9M) forms a leading line on a bearing of 284°, but it is best to stay slightly N of this line and approach from the buoy to avoid floats and moorings off the end of the harbour wall extension.

Lyme Regis Harbour

Once past the Cobb, the temporary pontoons can be seen adjacent to the inner harbour arm. They are constructed of interlocking plastic blocks of the type commonly used for dinghies and small craft. Depths are reasonable following recent dredging but they are exposed to wash from passing traffic, so rafting would be unwise. There is no power but water is available from a tap on the quay.

The narrow harbour entrance is adjacent to the temporary pontoons and is busy with fishing vessels. The harbour office can be found at the root of the Cobb, adjacent to the inshore lifeboat station. In an emergency, vessels can be accommodated in the tidal inner harbour, either alongside the harbour wall or at a drying pontoon. Access is approximately HW±2 for moderate draught.

Outside the entrance there is a row of yellow visitors' moorings with pick-ups laid in around 1m LAT adjacent to the swim line (also marked by small yellow buoys). Landing can be made at the steps near the end of the inner harbour arm, or on the temporary pontoons as far in as possible. There are a couple of further landing sites in the inner harbour, but there is nothing to be gained by using them, unless launching/recovering with a trailer, in which case there is a wide slipway between the lifeboat station and the sailing club.

Shoreside

A shower and toilet is available at the HM office during opening hours and a small stock of chandlery is also kept. There is also a shower at the yacht club when open (note the system where the HM kept a key to the yacht club no longer operates). Water is available from a tap on the quay. Along the seafront there are many bars and eateries, and the main shopping area is in Broad Street, which runs steeply uphill from the far corner of the beach. Here there are two food stores, a butcher and a chemist. Souvenir shops are found everywhere. Landmoor and Lister Gardens is a terraced area immediately behind the beach and provides a quieter and less strenuous route to the shops

Summer pontoons inside the Cobb

AXMOUTH & BEER

The small drying harbour at Axmouth and nearby anchorage at Beer Roads lie a couple of miles W of Lyme Regis, and are also only suitable in NW or N winds and an absence of swell. Anchor off the beach at Beer village clear of any local moorings, and an isolated rock in about 2m at the N end. This beach is fairly steep-to and consists of sizeable pebbles which make it difficult under foot, so care needs to be taken when landing or launching. The local boats are hauled up the beach on wooden 'skids' by a winch.

If intending to enter Axmouth, seek local knowledge from the sailing club first and see www.axeyachtclub.co.uk/sailing/pilotage. The drying entrance is extremely narrow and has a dog-leg turn. The tidal stream is believed to reach 6kn at times. Entry should be made at dead slack HW only and in daylight.

Moor as directed by the sailing club and dry out. This harbour is only suitable for small craft (less than 9m) with shoal draught and able to take the ground. Larger

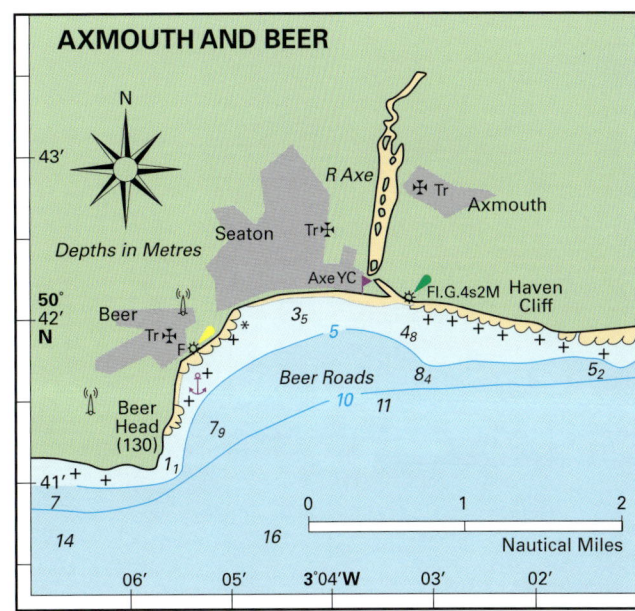

The entrance to Axmouth is well hidden. The small motor boat is just departing

Entrance

1. The shingle bar at the entrance to Axmouth is reminiscent of some East Coast rivers

3. The 'dog leg'. Beware of the shingle building up to port

2. The channel narrows as you enter the harbour

4. Axmouth final approach

1 LYME REGIS, BEER & AXMOUTH

Axe YC pontoons with Seaton beyond

craft can occasionally be accommodated but assistance will likely be required. However, it is preferable to anchor off and visit by dinghy, landing on the beach W of the entrance, or at the sailing club for a short time if the tide allows. Do not attempt to enter or leave in the dark.

Axe Yacht Club has a very good slipway which can be used with permission

Local attractions

Lyme Regis is well known for fossils and many examples can be seen at both Lyme Regis and the Dinosaurland museums, together with organised fossil hunting expeditions along the beaches. The famous Cobb at the harbour has featured in many film and TV productions. The boat building academy at Lyme Regis is renowned and often holds open days for visitors.

Beer is one of the most attractive villages in Devon. There is a village store, a couple of pubs and a restaurant, plus the local fish merchant by the beach sells to the public. Beer also has a chandlery and rigging store. There is a large supermarket at Seaton, very close to Axmouth harbour, and a historic tramway connects the coastal town to the villages of Colyford and Colyton inland. Beer Quarry Stone Caves are some 2000 years old, located just outside the village.

The beach at Beer

Axmouth & Beer

The prettiest village in Devon? Beer is definitely a candidate. The radio mast, top right, can be seen from a distance

Lyme Regis, Axmouth & Beer essential information

Clubs
Lyme Regis Sailing Club
Lyme Regis Powerboat Club ☎01297 443788
Axe Yacht Club ☎01297 20043
Beer Sailing Club ☎07810 754116
Beer Luggers Club

Local Information
Seaton Jurassic, near Tramway

Visitors' berths
Light pontoons, moorings, quay wall via HM Lyme Regis

Additional Berthing
Axe Yacht Club (Club Bosun ☎07842 933610)

Webcams
www.lovelymeregis.co.uk
www.axeyachtclub.co.uk
www.beersailingclub.co.uk

Water
Tap on Cobb at Lyme Regis.
Axe Yacht Club

Fuel
No marine fuel.
Garages at Seaton and Uplyme (1M from Cobb)

Gas
Uplyme Stores

Chandlery
Jimmy Green Marine, Beer.
HM Lyme Regis has small stock

Victuals
Lyme Regis and Seaton.
Small shop and fresh fish at Beer

Nearest Large Supermarket
Seaton, 0.25M W of harbour

Laundry
Pooles Court, Lyme Regis

Repairs
Mears & Son, Axmouth Harbour

Scrubbing posts
None, but possible to dry on slip at Axmouth

Transport links
Bus to Axminster, Seaton.
Trains Axminster to Exeter, Salisbury, London

2 RIVER EXE

Harbour Master's Office
VHF 12 'Port of Exeter'
Trinity Buoy Store, Camperdown Terrace, Exmouth
EX8 1EQ
☎ 01395 223265 / 07864 958658
NCI Exmouth VHF 65 ☎ 01395 222492

The Exe estuary is vast in comparison to other West Country rivers being a good 1M wide for most of its navigable length. A sand bar at the entrance, narrows off Exmouth, turbulent tides and numerous shoals give it the feel of a Thames Estuary haven. The whole area is a Site of Special Scientific Interest. The city of Exeter is reached by canal.

Landmarks

2M E of the river entrance, Straight Point is a red, wedge shaped headland on which sits a very large holiday park and caravan site. There are no other significant landmarks but the estuary can be identified from S as a large, low-lying gap in an otherwise elevated coastline. Within the river, the Brunel Tower at Starcross is visible from all points.

Main hazards

Large parts of the estuary dry, or are shoal, including the entrance which is dangerous in wind over tide conditions. Moorings and anchorages are exposed to winds from every direction, creating uncomfortable conditions in any strength of tide. Waterborne activities of all types take place in the entrance and lower estuary where it can be exceptionally busy at weekends and in the evenings.

Approaches

Approaching from E, it is necessary to avoid the marine farms mentioned in the previous chapter. There is also a live firing range which projects E from Straight Point and extends about 1.5M S, with the E extremities marked by yellow buoys (N edge Fl.Y.3s, S edge Fl.Y.5s). If cruising from Lyme Regis, the best plan is to pass between the two marine farms and continue W until the Exe SWM (Mo(A)10s) is identified. From Portland Bill, or at night, it is best to pass outside both marine farms before shaping a NW course towards the entrance. Note that the lit buoys marking the marine farms have similar characteristics (Fl.Y.5s) to those marking the firing range. From S there are no issues and a waypoint in the vicinity of the SWM will suffice. Interestingly, this is the only SWM in the entire area covered by this book.

Entry

From the SWM the channel over the bar runs approximately NNW and is initially marked with four pairs of lateral buoys at roughly equal spacing, the first pair Fl(2)R.5s/Fl(2)G.5s, then Q.R./Q.G., Fl(3)R.5s/Fl(3)G.5s, Q.R./Q.G. The least charted depth is 0·3m and the buoys are moved as required, although the entrance has been stable for some time now. Keep a good boat's length or more off the buoys, even with adequate depth. From No.7 SHM the channel turns NW and is marked with a directional light at the root of the main slipway (Dir.Iso.WRG.2s6m6M), and an additional PHM, No.10 (Fl.R.3s) marking Checkstone Ledge. Aim for the dock entrance until No.12 PHM (Q.R) is abeam. A sharp lookout is necessary, particularly with the plethora of water sport activities in the evenings and at weekends. Although lit, entry at night is not recommended.

It is essential to identify the SWM from where the first lateral marks can be seen

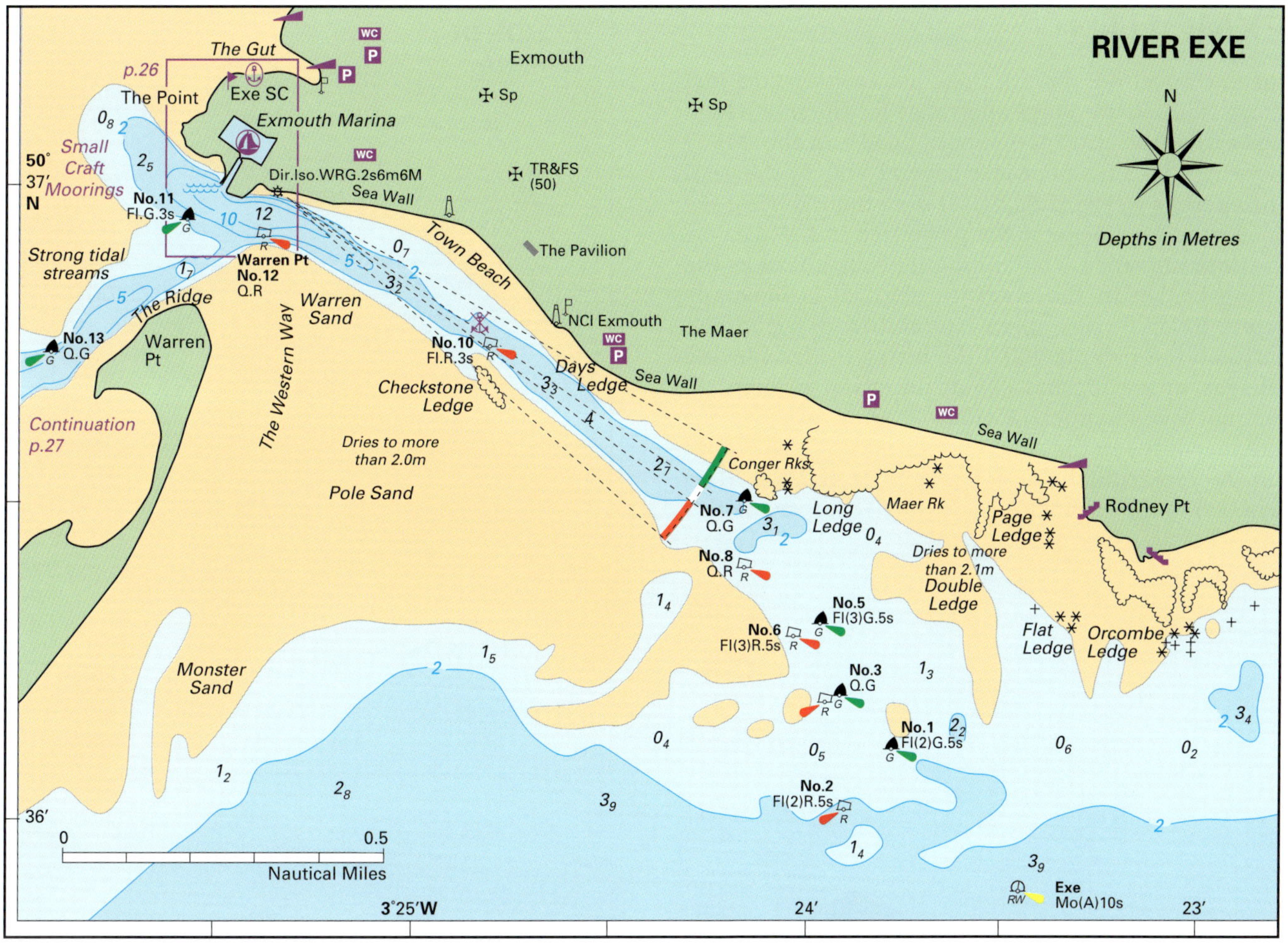

River Exe

The lifeboat station is conspicuous midway along the seafront

The main slip at Exmouth where the tide runs hard

The mainly straight approach channel narrows abeam the lifeboat station

West Country Pilot • 25

2 RIVER EXE

EXMOUTH

The entrance to Exmouth Dock lies to starboard just above No.12 PHM. Make allowance for the tide which rips across the entrance on both flood and ebb. Many moorings lie in a pool just beyond and to the NW, and there is a risk of being set onto them during the flood tide. Anchoring is not permitted in the area off the dock entrance. Visitors should book ahead as the lifting bridge in the entrance channel is normally down. River ferries operate to and from a pontoon between the fish quay and the lifting bridge serving villages upstream and should be given priority in the narrow channel. Visitors' berths are on the hammerheads in the centre of the dock area in about 2m. A creek runs behind The Point N of No.11 SHM (Fl.G.3s) to the yacht club and a small boatyard with a slip accessible near HW.

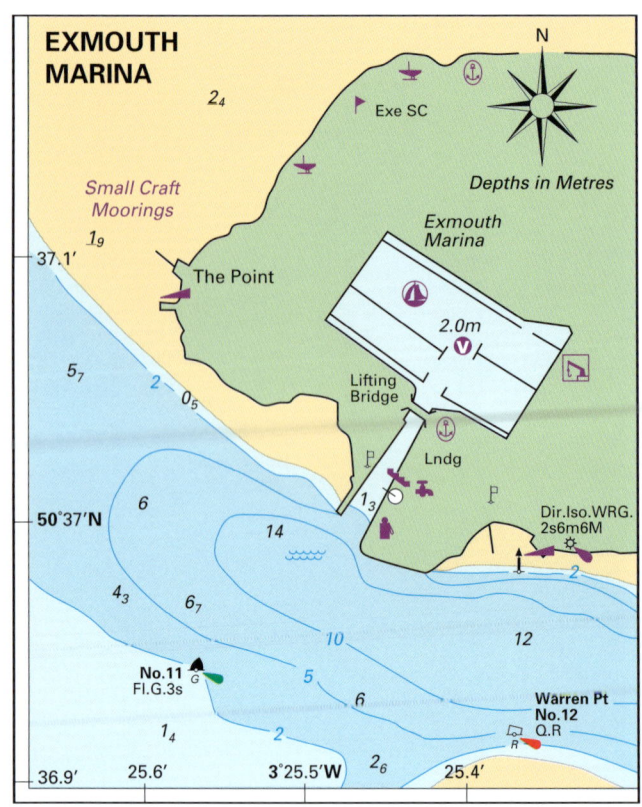

Exmouth Marina entrance with fish quay and ferry berths to starboard below the lifting bridge

Exmouth Marina

Visitors berth on the hammer heads

26 • West Country Pilot

Lower Exe ('The Bight', Starcross, Lympstone)

At No.12 PHM (Q.R.) the channel turns SW and the tidal streams are exceptionally strong. Moorings line both sides of the channel with the fairway between them as far as No.13 SHM (Q.G.) where the channel between the moorings becomes less obvious. Begin a slow turn towards NW, rather than buoy hopping. The sandbank here is growing and the deep water is now further W than charted. Four white moorings (marked EPA) in the vicinity of No.15 SHM (Fl.G.5s) are for visitors, but in any strength of wind they can quickly become uncomfortable, especially if wind rode, and the number of moorings make anchoring a risky prospect. Note the whole of the area of Salthouse Lake S and SW of the visitors' moorings is a nature reserve. A water taxi (or one of the small ferries) operates between Exmouth and Starcross serving the moorings and is the best option for getting ashore, since both destinations are a considerable distance in a tender, even with a favourable tide. There is a possible option for landing at a railway bridge forming the entrance to Cockwood Harbour, although it is very limited by the tide, and the harbour itself is private.

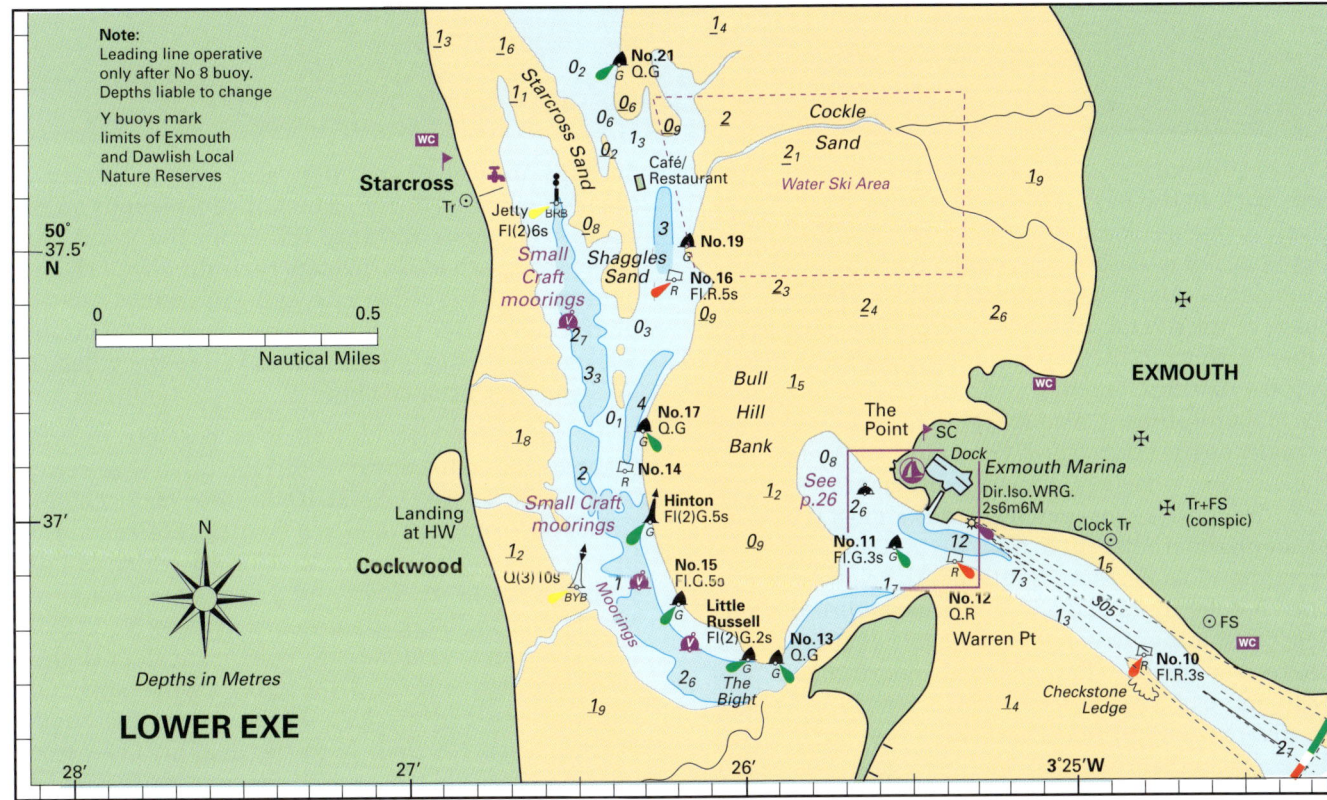

Looking upriver from Exmouth. The visitors' moorings are just right of centre behind the sandbank

2 RIVER EXE

Starcross Fishing and Cruising Club is housed in the iconic Brunel Tower on the waterfront

Proceeding upriver, do not be tempted to transit from one mark to the next. Due to the shoal nature of the river, in some combinations of wind and/or tide, the buoys may lie over the banks and spits they are intended to mark. The best strategy is to follow the curve of the river as it meanders from one bank to the other, favouring the depth sounder over the GPS (if you are visiting from the East Coast, you will recognise normal procedure!). A couple of the lateral marks are actually on the banks/spits. Continue just W of N from the visitors' moorings, allowing sufficient rise of tide as to draught. A shoal patch extends almost the width of the channel adjacent to No.17 SHM (Q.G.) and, apart from the odd hole, there is little depth below half-tide. The channel forks just above the mark with the port arm continuing NNW towards the jetties at Starcross. There is a single yellow visitors' mooring in a pool with 3m, E of a red post PHM, which must be booked in advance with the local yacht club (see facilities) as access from their pontoon requires a gate code or fob. It is feasible to land by tender at the town slip which goes under the railway line, and can be seen from the visitors' mooring, but it appears very muddy except perhaps at local HW±2. The yacht club is housed in the iconic Brunel Tower, which is conspicuous on the shore from some distance off. From the yacht club pontoon, a path leads through their dinghy park and, once through the coded gate, along the railway station platform and over the footbridge. A further 20 minute walk along the main road brings you to the village of Cockwood mentioned above.

With sufficient rise of tide it is possible to cross Starcross Sand to continue upriver, otherwise return to the fork at No.17 SHM (Q.G.). The main channel trends NE from here then N. A floating café/restaurant lies to port near No.16 PHM (Fl.R.5s) which is busy with RIB traffic at times and a designated water ski area is over the bank to starboard as far as No.19 SHM (unlit). From abeam the café/restaurant steer slightly W of N and give No.21 SHM (Q.G.) a wide berth as it is on a bank and marks a wreck. From this buoy a gutway leads NE then N to the quay at Lympstone village. Accessible near HW, it appears feasible to dry out alongside but contact the sailing club first for instructions.

SFCC visitors' mooring downstream of Starcross. Note the strength of the tide

The popular café and restaurant in the main channel off Starcross

Upper Exe (Exeter Canal, Topsham)

Continuing upriver from No.21 SHM, there is a shoal midstream marked by No.18 PHM (Q.R) E of it and some moorings W of it. Yachts can pass either side but above half-tide it should not present a problem. The channel all but dries in places as it continues NNW towards Starcross Yacht Club on the W bank. Note

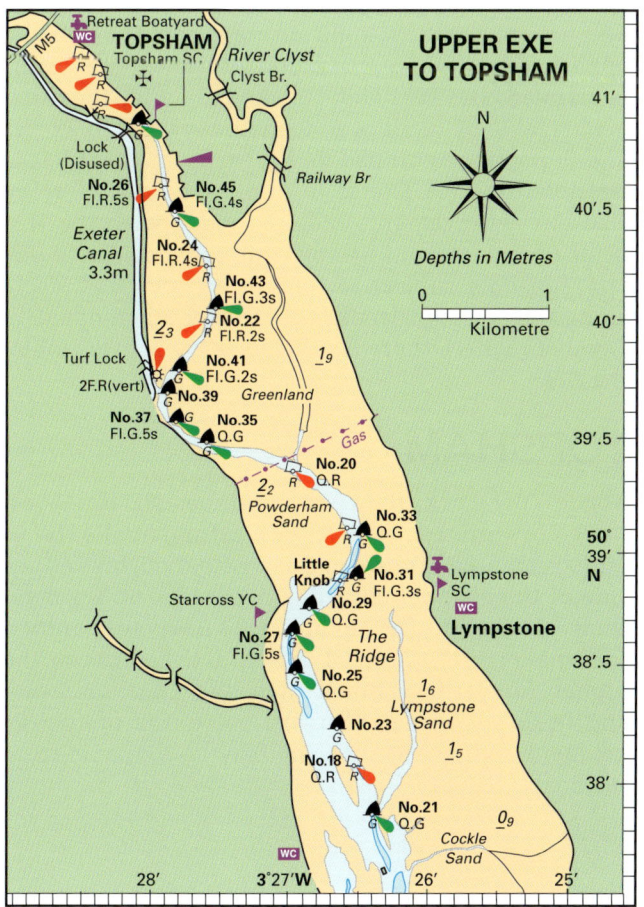

The long quay wall and large slipway at Lympstone

only the starboard side of the channel is marked in this stretch. There is a half-tide slipway at the yacht club, which may be able to provide a temporary mooring. From here, the channel turns NE to a point just over halfway across the river and then arcs round Powderham Sand. Note the three SHMs here may be over the bank. As the channel continues its turn towards W, a group of yellow buoys either side mark a gas pipe, and a gutway branches off N to the River Clyst which is only navigable with local knowledge, and leads to a boatyard beyond the railway viaduct.

The main channel trends further W and runs close to the shore between No.35 SHM (Q.G) and No.37 SHM (Fl.G.5s) before turning towards Turf Lock at the entrance to the Exeter Canal. The lock operates approximately HW-1 to HW for booked transits only. There is no longer a waiting buoy in the vicinity of the

West Country Pilot • 29

2 RIVER EXE

Outnumbered by paddleboards at the Turf visitors' pontoon, next to the pub

lock so it is necessary to anchor off or pick up a spare mooring to await your transit (the HM will normally make contact by telephone). Once cleared to enter, the final approach to the lock is between the pier head and a PHM which dries, so favour the pier head side until you reach the lock gates. If landing by tender and not entering the canal, do not tie up in the approach as it is prohibited. There is a pontoon in the main river just upstream of the lock where tenders can land on the inside at most states of the tide, leaving the outside clear for ferries.

There is a visitors' pontoon just inside the lock to starboard with power available and water from a tap at the corner of the maintenance shed. Four boats (rafted in pairs) can be accommodated here, and a further six to eight on new pontoons on the opposite bank where installation of power and water is planned. The Turf Hotel is close at hand. The canal is navigable by tenders and small/day craft to Exeter and is popular with paddle boarders. In theory, it is possible to reach Exeter in unmasted craft of some size but arrangements must be made with the HM prior to any transit. A ferry runs between Turf Lock and Topsham subject to tide, or a short walk/cycle along the towpath leads to a landing stage opposite Topsham where there is another ferry across run by the HM.

TOPSHAM

Above Turf Lock, the river continues NE for 0.5M, then N towards No.24 PHM (Fl.R.4s) and finally NW in midstream until Topsham Quay with moorings either side of the channel. Berthing is possible at Topsham Quay (contact the HM) or at Trout's Boatyard pontoon for smaller craft, both of which dry. Just above the higher ferry the channel hugs the Topsham bank and leads to Retreat Boatyard below the motorway bridge. A temporary mooring may be available from the boatyard.

Turf Lock approach channel looking downstream at LW. Note the deeper water on the pier side (left)

Topsham

Final approach to Topsham

The Topsham to Turf ferry operates from a small pontoon in the deep channel

Visitors can moor alongside Topsham Quay

Topsham is busy with moorings as far as the motorway bridge

2 RIVER EXE

Trout's Boatyard can accommodate smaller craft which can take the ground

Shoreside

Showers and toilets are located at Exmouth Dock and Turf Lock. The yacht clubs on the Exe all have toilets and showers during opening hours. Exmouth has a good range of small shops concentrated on Rolle Street, a five minute walk from Exmouth Dock, including several food stores, a butcher and a chemist. Topsham has a food store, butcher, baker and chemist and an impressive array of artisan shops and cafés. Both have numerous places to eat within a short walk of the river and Exmouth is becoming something of a foodie destination. There is a convenience store at Starcross. Boatyards at Exmouth and Topsham can cater for most repairs.

Rail lines run down both sides of the Exe from Exeter making it easier to travel further afield when weathered in, or for major shopping expeditions to Exeter.

Local attractions

The flat banks of the Exe make good walking territory and the energetic, or those with cycles, can easily reach the city of Exeter (crossing the river at Topsham if on the east side) which has multiple visitor attractions. Powderham Castle is just north of Starcross and walkable from there or from Turf Lock. On the Exmouth bank, the unusual 16-sided house, 'A La Ronde' (open to the public), is on the outskirts of town heading towards Lympstone.

Topsham upper ferry

Lympstone's alleyways are lined with pretty cottages

Topsham

One of the river cruisers that sail between Exmouth and Exeter

River Exe essential information

Clubs
Exe Sailing Club ☏01395 264607
Exe Power Boat & Ski Club
Starcross Fishing & Cruising Club
☏01626 891996
Starcross Yacht Club
☏07895 504815
Lympstone Sailing Club
Topsham Sailing Club
☏01392 877524
Topsham Small Craft Club

Local information
The Strand, Exmouth
Civic Centre, Exeter

Visitors' berths
Exmouth Marina, moorings, Turf Lock (Exeter Canal) and Topsham Quay, all via HM

Additional berthing
Starcross Fishing & Cruising Club has 1 visitors' mooring
Trouts Boatyard, Retreat Boatyard, both at Topsham

Water taxi VHF 37 'Exmouth Water Taxi'

Webcams
www.exmouthcoastwatch.co.uk
www.starcross-fcc.co.uk
www.starcrossyc.org.uk

Water
Exmouth Marina
Turf Lock

Fuel
Exmouth Marina

Gas
Garners, Exmouth; Boatyards at Topsham

Chandlery
Seawood Chandlery, Pilot Wharf, Exmouth
Boatyards at Topsham

Victuals
Rolle St area, Exmouth
Fore St, Topsham

Nearest large supermarket
Exmouth, 2 miles (bus).
Topsham, nr Retreat Boatyard, 1 mile from quay

Laundry
High St, Exmouth

Repairs
M S Marine Services, Exmouth;
Trout's Boatyard, Retreat Boatyard Topsham

Engineers
JJB Marine Specialists, and at boatyards

Sailmakers
Rowsell Sails, Exmouth
Exe Sails and Covers, nr Topsham

Car Hire
Small firms in Exmouth, mainstream brands in Exeter

Transport
Trains from Exmouth, Lympstone, Topsham to Exeter; Starcross to Exeter/Newton Abbot.
National routes and airport at Exeter.

West Country Pilot • 33

3 TEIGNMOUTH
& BABBACOMBE BAY

Harbour Master's Office
VHF 12 'Teignmouth Harbour'
2nd Floor, ABP Port Office, Old Quay Road, Teignmouth, TQ14 8ES
☎ 01626 773165 / 07796 178456

NCI Teignmouth VHF 65 ☎ 01626 772377

Babbacombe Bay broadly describes the area of coast just N of Tor Bay with Teignmouth, a commercial port frequented by coasters, at its N end. There are several anchorages and the River Teign leads inland to Newton Abbot. The attractive village of Shaldon lies opposite Teignmouth.

Landmarks

Two conspicuous churches adjacent either side of Babbacombe are visible from some distance and are the best guide if approaching from E offshore. Teignmouth lies just N of a high red sandstone cliff topped by pines and has a short pier 0.5M N of the harbour entrance. The Ore Stone, a large granite outcrop just offshore, is visible at the S end of the bay when heading along the coast.

Main hazards

There is a sand bar at the entrance to Teignmouth which, although regularly dredged, is shallow (approximately 1m LAT) and constantly shifts. Tides are turbulent and entry on the ebb should be avoided, especially at springs. Commercial traffic has priority but movements generally take place at the top of the tide. Within the harbour, there is a blind turn and the bank on the Shaldon side ('The Salty') dries 2.5m-3.5m creating eddies at the bends in the river. A large ship anchorage is NE of Babbacombe just outside the 10m contour.

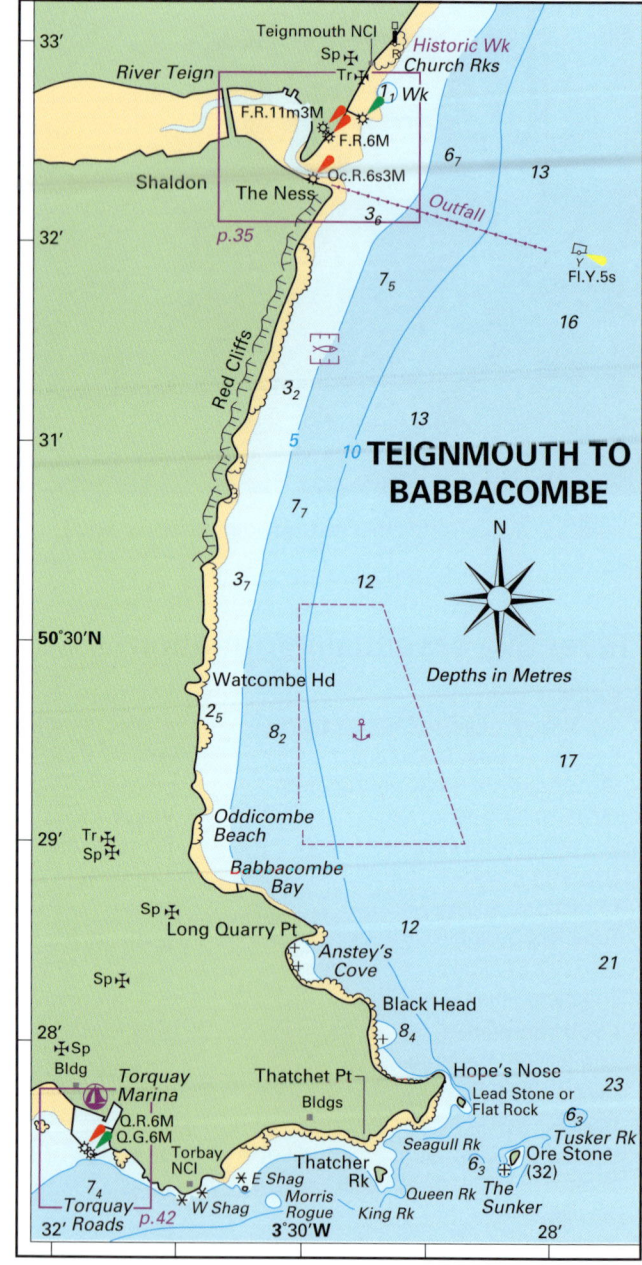

Approaching Babbacombe Bay. Two church spires visible

34 • West Country Pilot

Teignmouth

Approaches

The immediate area is sufficiently deep that it is possible to make directly for Teignmouth from any direction, but remain outside the 2m contour until just N of the entrance, marked by lateral buoys (Fl.G.2s/Fl.R.2s). It is possible to anchor N or S of the entrance to await sufficient tide (or daylight!) but avoid a historic wreck about 0.5M N, adjacent to a fixed red post on the shore. If approaching from S, remain to seaward of the Ore Stone and several other rocks to avoid tide rips and many pot markers. The anchorages at Hope Cove, Anstey's Cove and Babbacombe are accessible at any state of the tide in offshore winds. However, if seeking shelter in bad conditions, head for Tor Bay or Dartmouth.

Entry

Entry to the River Teign requires sufficient rise of tide and daylight. From the first pair of lateral marks steer just S of W keeping a white beacon 'Lucette' (Oc.R.6s4m3M) in transit with the top right corner of a cream structure behind it which is lit (F.R.4m). In practice, binoculars are required to make this out at first, but it is more obvious once abeam the second SHM (Fl.G.2s). At the second PHM (Fl.R.2s) steer W to pass midway between the Lucette beacon and Spratt Sands Inner SHM (Fl.G.2s) then turn slightly WNW

The leading marks of Lucette Beacon and the cream building, shown offset for clarity

parallel with the Shaldon shore to port. The next section is the trickiest as the corner is blind, and a beacon to starboard (Oc.G.6s/F.G.3M from seaward) is on a drying part of the sandbank it marks *and inside it*. If The Salty (the large drying bank in the river off Shaldon) is uncovered, this causes the tide to push you back towards the Teignmouth side and produces an eddy which runs to seaward for a time past the visitors' pontoons and local moorings off the town. When The Salty covers, the flood tide sets strongly over it. Therefore proceed with caution staying in midstream as far as practicable, rounding the SHM beacon several boat lengths off to end up

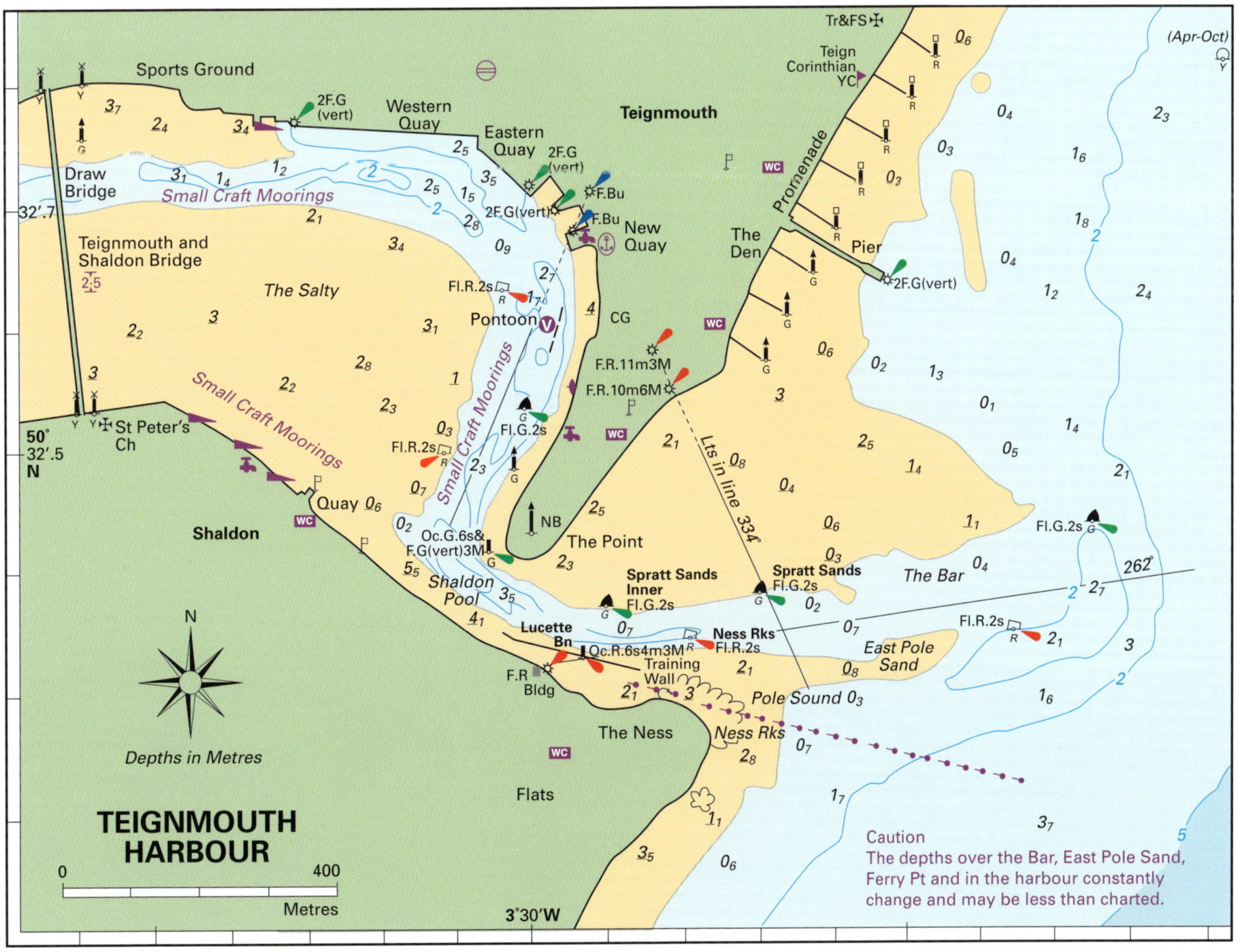

The village of Shaldon (right) and the Ness (left)

heading approximately NNE towards several small quays on the next corner, below the commercial docks. If possible, depart close to HW. Keep an eye out for a small ferry, painted black and white, which plies between Teignmouth and Shaldon. The HM can provide guidance and possibly lead you in if you make contact in advance, which is advisable in any event since there is limited mooring space.

TEIGNMOUTH

The area to starboard inside the spit is known as 'the back beach'. There are many local moorings/trots and the beach is usually covered with dinghies. Approaching the bend in the river there are three detached pontoons, two of which are for visitors. Contact the HM for berth allocation. They are only around 20m long but rafting is possible in settled conditions.

Landing can be made in the corner of the beach near New Quay, or on the hard area in the adjacent dock, but take extra care if returning after nightfall

The SHM marking the end of the beach on the inshore side

(especially under oar) due to the strength of the tide. If the pontoons are full, it may be possible to use a local mooring but check with the HM first. Just upstream of the commercial docks there is a slipway at Polly Steps for launching and recovery. Anchoring is not permitted in the harbour. The Shaldon road bridge is the limit of navigation for masted craft (although it has a lifting section, this is rarely operated except for testing once a year which is a statutory requirement).

Visitors' pontoons at Teignmouth

Babbacombe

Beach landing by New Quay

Short stay landing steps downstream of the docks

Small motorcraft and tenders can reach the town of Newton Abbot subject to tide, and Coombe Cellars is a popular half-tide destination on the S bank.

BABBACOMBE

Located between Teignmouth and Tor Bay, this anchorage is sheltered from winds with a W component. A temporary stop might also be feasible in light southerly weather but swell from that direction is likely to deter most from staying overnight. Anchor clear of the moorings off Oddicombe Beach, taking care to avoid the odd rocky patch, or inside the moorings off Babbacombe Beach if space and draught permit, where it is also more sheltered from any swell. Landing is possible at either location and a

A small harbour arm protects Babbacombe Beach

Babbacombe Beach. It's a long and very steep climb to the town

West Country Pilot • 37

funicular railway connects Oddicombe Beach with the village of Babbacombe at the top of the cliff. Most of the moorings are private, but three are owned by the local inn and are available for visitors. During the day, and evenings in season, all the bays on this stretch of coast get very busy with small fast day boats, RIBs and jet skis and the beaches are understandably packed. Most will return to Tor Bay by dusk, but the area is only really quiet out of season.

Anstey's Cove

This is a very popular anchorage and beach between Babbacombe and Tor Bay, again much used by fast craft and jet skis during daylight hours. Approach from E, and anchor in 3-4m, the only potential hazard being a submerged rock outcrop at the S edge of the entrance. The cove is formed by a fairly deep indentation in the coast and therefore offers slightly better protection than Babbacombe. The holding is mainly good, but deteriorates as the season progresses through near constant use. It should present no problem with heavy chain however.

Hope Cove

The final anchorage in this area is Hope Cove, situated adjacent to Anstey's Cove and in the lee of Hope's Nose which marks the entrance to Tor Bay. It affords better protection from southerly swell than Anstey's Cove or Babbacombe but there is only a small area of beach on which to land, and the same caveat regarding fast craft applies. Favour the S half of the bay when anchoring as the N side is rocky in places.

A funicular railway provides an easier route to Babbacombe

Also, the seabed shelves more steeply than the other anchorages making it more suitable for a temporary stop, but in the right conditions it should be feasible to remain overnight.

The anchorage at Hope Cove

Anstey's Cove / Hope Cove

Teignmouth riverside with visitors' pontoons (centre) and commercial docks (far left)

Shoreside

There is a public shower and toilet at the back beach, Teignmouth; otherwise, showers are available at the yacht club, which is situated at the N end of the main beach, when open. There is a good range of shops at Teignmouth catering for most requirements including a large supermarket a short walk from Polly Steps (see above).

At Babbacombe there are few facilities, although Oddicombe Beach has a public toilet and there is a small food store in the village above the cliff. The hotel at Babbacombe Beach has a restaurant.

Local attractions

The Teignmouth and Shaldon museum, a smart modern building in the town centre, houses exhibits from the local area including a collection from the Morgan Giles shipyard.

Shaldon is a very attractive village with narrow streets and a number of artisan shops and places to eat.

Babbacombe is famous for its model village, best reached via the funicular railway from Oddicombe Beach.

Teignmouth essential information

Clubs
Teign Corinthian Yacht Club ☎01626 798111
Shaldon Sailing Club
Babbacombe Corinthian Sailing Club

Local Information
The Ness, Shaldon TQ14 0HP

Visitors' Berths
Island pontoons and occasional moorings

Additional Berthing
None. HM only

Water taxi
Teignmouth-Shaldon Ferry (cash only) ☎07896 711822

Webcams
www.teignmouth-nci.org.uk

Water
Tap on New Quay

Gas
HS Hire (upstream of bridge)

Chandlery
Seaquest Marine, Quay Road

Victuals
Bank St / Wellington St, Teignmouth; Fore St, Shaldon

Nearest Large Supermarket
On main rd 10min above bridge

Laundry
Brunswick St

Repairs
Riverside Boatyard (NB above bridge)

Engineers
Shaldon Marine, Shaldon

Electronics
At boatyard

Sailmakers
Coastal Canvas, Shaldon

Car hire
Newton Abbot (by train)

Transport
Trains from Teignmouth to Exeter, Newton Abbot. Occasional service to London, Plymouth.

4 TOR BAY

Harbour Master's Office
VHF 14 'Torquay Harbour'/'Brixham Harbour'/ 'Paignton Harbour'
Torquay
Beacon Quay, Torquay TQ1 2BG
Brixham
New Fish Quay, Brixham TQ5 8AW
Paignton
South Quay, Paignton TQ4 6DT
HM Central office ☎01803 208443 / ☎07768 55388 (Security)
NCI Torbay VHF 65 ☎01803 411145

Dubbed 'The English Riviera', this 3M wide bay is sheltered from the prevailing westerly weather and swell. However, large areas inshore are controlled for swimming and other water activities where anchoring is discouraged, so it should no longer be considered a safe anchorage in rough conditions, other than for large vessels. There are good facilities, with large marinas at Torquay and Brixham, and a small harbour at the third main town, Paignton. The area is a popular holiday destination with many beaches and small fast craft, and where motor boats outnumber yachts by a significant margin. Brixham is one of the busiest fishing ports in the UK.

Landmarks

Hope's Nose is a low jagged headland at the N edge of the bay with a granite outcrop, the Ore Stone (32m) just offshore and visible as a small island when approaching from N. At the S end of the bay, Berry Head is a conspicuous flat topped headland with a radio mast and NCI lookout. Visible from a considerable distance, it also gives a decent radar return. A TV mast is inshore of Paignton.

Closer to, there is a large breakwater extending from the S shore at Brixham with a lighthouse at the end, but otherwise the appearance is very much a continuous urban landscape with the exception of the SW corner. There are several white flat/apartment buildings immediately E of Torquay, but none are particularly distinctive.

Main hazards

A deep water anchorage is just E of Tor Bay and a large area of the bay itself, from approximately the 10m contour outwards is also used for anchoring by vessels of considerable size. A yellow special buoy (Fl(5)Y.20s) marks the rough centre of this latter area. S of here, the approach to Brixham is very busy with fishing traffic at all hours.

Numerous offlying rocks are found along the N side of the bay as far as the entrance to Torquay Harbour. Overfalls may be encountered here, and inside Berry Head, building to a short chop in any strength of wind, reminiscent of the Solent or Thames Estuary. Numerous fishing floats are found in these areas.

Approach to Tor Bay from N. Ore Stone left of centre and Berry Head in the distance

Brixham entrance from NE

Tor Bay

A marine farm in Tor Bay. They are very difficult to make out from any distance

Marine farms are also be sited in the bay, S of Thatcher Rock and off Fishcombe/Churston Cove, and are difficult to identify until nearby.

Within the bay from May to September, large areas are given over to swimming and other water sports, marked with unlit small yellow buoys. This includes nearly all the beaches and coves, including some outside the bay. Strictly speaking, yachts and motorboats are not prohibited from entering these areas, or indeed anchoring in them, but it is discouraged, and is a potential hazard due to the proliferation of small craft anchored off the beaches during daylight hours in the season. Water skiers are restricted to an area off Elberry Cove in the SW corner of the bay.

Approaches

From offshore, keep the TV mast behind Paignton on a bearing of approximately 280°, avoiding any large vessels at anchor. This leads to a central position in the bay in the vicinity of 50°26'N 03°30'W (use this waypoint for a first visit). At night, the lighthouse on Berry Head (Fl(2)15s58m18M) is the best initial mark until the TV mast (F.R) can be identified. The smaller lighthouse at the end of the breakwater at Brixham (Oc.R.15s9m6M) is a useful alternative mark, but can be difficult to distinguish within the shore lighting. Keep it bearing WSW to stay in clear water, and closer to SW in rough weather.

Entry

Alongside berthing fills quickly so call ahead, and be prepared to anchor if there is no space. From the above waypoint steer 320° for Torquay, 200° for Brixham or 270° for Paignton (which dries and is only suitable for craft up to about 8m), then follow the detailed notes in the relevant section below. If intending to anchor in the vicinity of Fishcombe Cove it is sensible to head for Brixham in the first instance then skirt the edge of the moorings W of the harbour. This avoids the marine farm.

TORQUAY

The entrance to Torquay Harbour is narrow between large stone piers, Haldon Pier to starboard and Princess Pier to port. It faces approximately W meaning it is essentially blind approaching from S and almost completely blind from the inside. Lateral buoys (Q.G./Q.R.) are laid WSW of the entrance from May to September. Small ferries, tugs and support craft operate from the harbour so it is prudent to call the HM before entering to ascertain if there is any conflicting traffic. Enter the harbour between the pier heads (Q.R.9m6M to port and Q.G.9m6M to starboard) keeping a very sharp lookout, especially for small fast craft which pay little heed to the buoyage. Also, be aware of dinghies and other small craft launching from a large slipway at the root of Haldon Pier. All marks

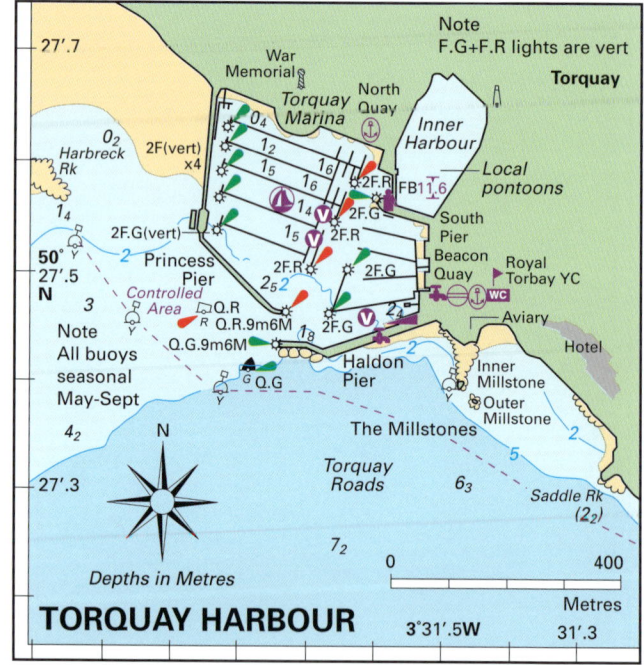

The narrow entrance to Torquay Harbour should be approached with caution

Torquay

The ferry berth looking towards the entrance, with the visitors' berths beyond

are lit. Entry in strong winds between SW and SE, or significant swell from SE or E is not recommended, Brixham being a more sensible option. Even in 20kn of wind from W the entrance can be rough.

Berth as directed once inside. If using the local authority pontoons on the E side of the harbour (Town Dock), this will usually be on the outside of the wavebreak pontoon, directly opposite Haldon Pier, or on the 'Events' pontoon at Haldon Pier itself. The former has power and water. At Torquay Marina (MDL) on the W side of the harbour, some berths are kept for visitors on the port side proceeding up the fairway between the two marinas. A fuel pontoon is to starboard just past Town Dock at South Pier, and the entrance to the inner harbour lies beyond this. The inner harbour is for local vessels but a berth may very occasionally be available via the HM. The entrance is controlled by IPTS signals and consists of a cill with a flapgate and a lifting pedestrian bridge. Access is normally possible at half-tide. Launching and recovery is best done at the large slip by Haldon Pier.

Several beaches lie W and SW of Torquay Harbour, often separated by a lump of rocky cliff. It is feasible to anchor, with due account given to the controlled areas, but bear in mind those nearer the town tend to get very busy with small craft and day boats and beware of a drying rock almost in the centre off the beach adjacent to the harbour entrance.

'Events' pontoon at Haldon Pier

4 TOR BAY

PAIGNTON

The entrance to the drying harbour lies S of Paignton Pier in the lee of a small headland and is very narrow. Overnight berthing for visitors is available, for small craft up to about 8m which can dry out, at a seasonal pontoon alongside East Quay. The harbour entrance is dangerous in E winds above 10kn. Immediately E of the headland, an outfall is marked by an ECM post (Q(3)10s5m3M) and NNW of this is an unlit PHM marking rocks N of the headland, awash at LAT. Give both a wide berth before steering SW towards the entrance, the port side of which is marked and lit. East Quay is to port, with most of the local boats on drying trot moorings. There is a slipway at the sailing club by the root of East Quay. The slip on the opposite side of the harbour is not for public use.

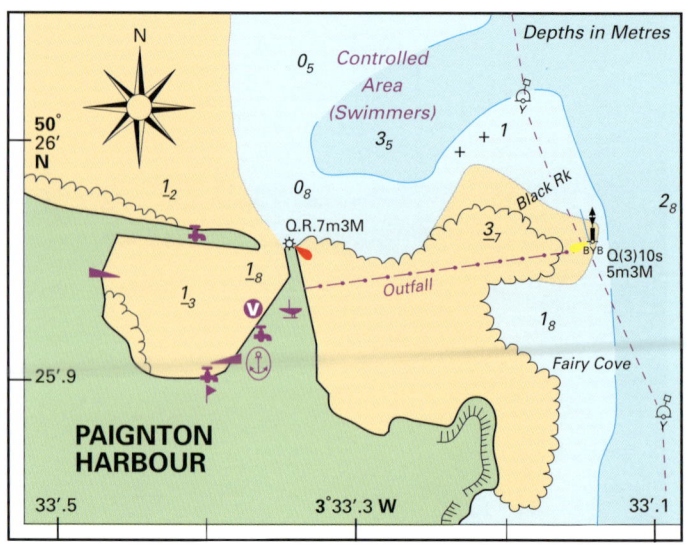

Paignton Harbour entrance with the main slip on South Quay

Pontoons are moored along East Quay (right) during the summer months

Paignton

This ECM outside Paignton Harbour is missing part of its top mark

The Sands

S of Paignton, the wide open beaches for which this area is famous present plenty of anchoring choices with easy approaches. The first of these is Goodrington Sands and a good anchorage can be found outside the controlled zone in 2m-4m LAT. Land on the beach but beware of a rocky patch in the central area by the leisure complex. The heritage rail line from Paignton to Kingswear runs just behind the beach and stops here.

Continuing S, Saltern Cove is a quieter spot, beyond which is a wide beach at Broadsands adjacent to Churston Point. This provides some additional protection from SW winds making it arguably a better option than Goodrington Sands. The buoys marking the controlled zone are in about 2m-3m here so it extends further from the beach than at Goodrington. It is a decent overnight anchorage once the crowds have returned home and there are no obstructions on the beach to hinder landing.

The last of the beaches is at Elberry Cove, a well protected anchorage tucked in the SW corner of Tor Bay. The controlled zone ends just N of this inlet, so it is possible to anchor further in than is perhaps advisable elsewhere. Jet skis and water skiers tend to congregate in this corner, being one of the few areas where water skiing is permitted. This shouldn't present a problem after dark, but during the day the other beaches are likely to provide a more comfortable stay, despite the crowds.

E of Elberry Cove, there is deep water up to the shoreline. Anchoring is possible anywhere along this stretch keeping clear of any marine farms (the position of which may vary from that charted). Bear in mind that there will be at least 6m at LAT, and therefore a minimum of 10m at local HW. A tripping line is advisable as discarded fishing gear seems to be a regular feature here.

At the end of this stretch are the twin Fishcombe and Churston Coves. Once the ultimate bolthole in SW weather, this is sadly no longer the case. Years of near constant use has rendered the holding very poor and several visitors' moorings have now been laid following the discovery of seagrass, so anchoring in the coves is no longer practical, or advisable. It is still possible to

Elberry Cove is inside the water ski area, but is the most sheltered in SW weather

The former bolt hole of Fishcombe Cove. Anchor outside if the moorings are taken

West Country Pilot • 45

anchor off though, but there is less protection and the water is deep. The moorings, however, are very well protected from SW to E, and it is still possible to land at the cove, from where Brixham Harbour is within walking distance.

Visitors' moorings between Churston Cove (far side) and Fishcombe Cove

BRIXHAM

Brixham is a major working fishing port with a large marina and two other berthing options. Anchoring is not permitted anywhere in the harbour, inside a theoretical line from the end of the breakwater to the headland E of Fishcombe Cove (i.e. not Fishcombe Point which is W of the cove).

The approach bearing described earlier (see Entry p.42) clears the breakwater by a sufficient margin, but if approaching from E (having rounded Berry Head for example) then stay 0.5M off the end of the breakwater until the fairway buoys are identified as large fishing vessels may sometimes be encountered. Although it is possible to enter Brixham at all states of the tide under any conditions, caution should be exercised in strong winds from N or NW when the approaches can be quite rough. Dartmouth, or even Torquay, may be safer options in these conditions.

The main fairway is on approximately 155° and is marked by two pairs of lateral buoys. The first pair (Fl.G/Fl.R) is abeam the end of the breakwater and the second pair (LFl.G/LFl.R) about halfway to the

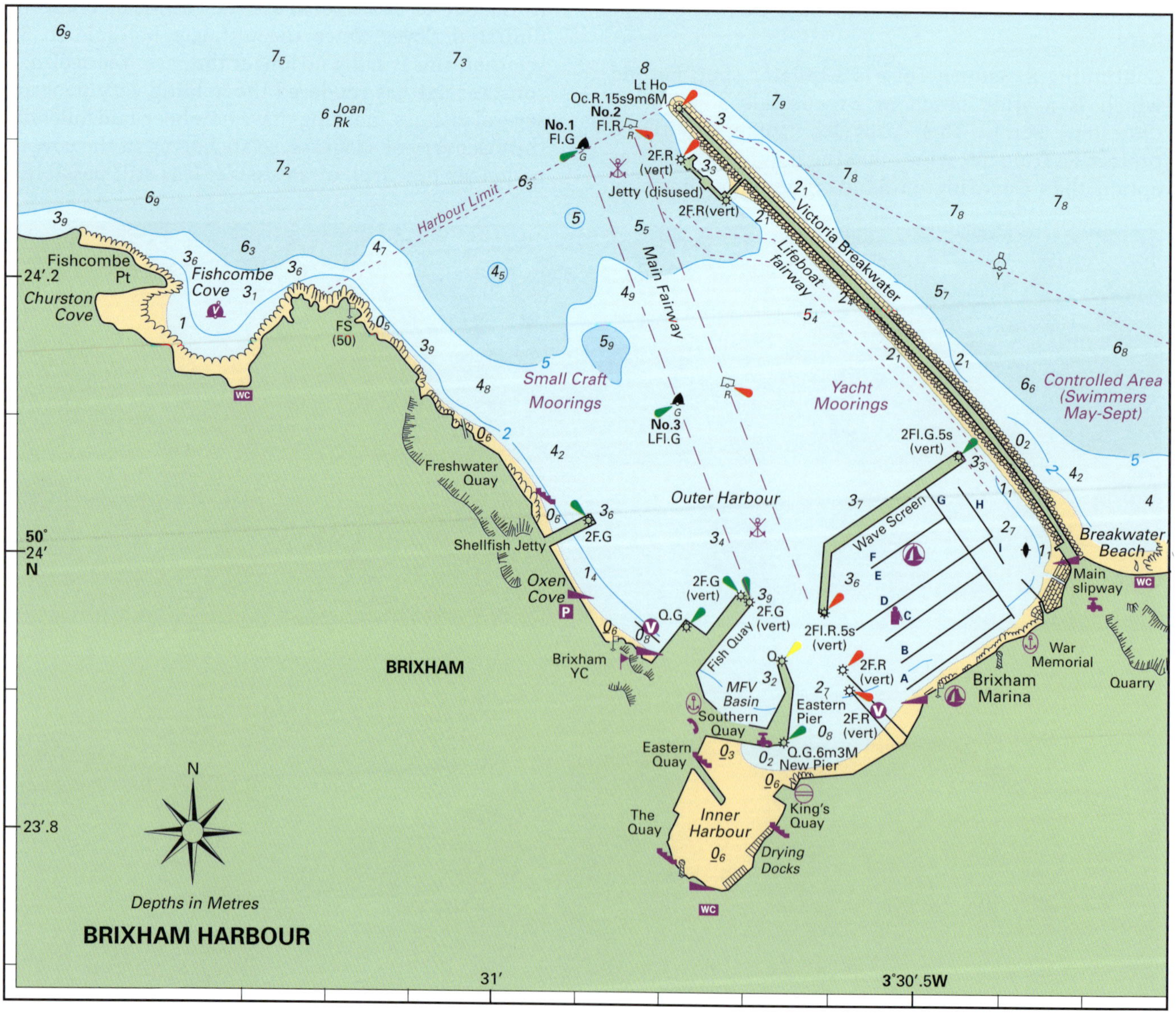

Brixham YC visitors' pontoons are right below the club

pier heads (F.G/F.R) at the entrance. Private moorings line both sides of the fairway but entering at night is straightforward. There is another fairway running past a disused fuel berth along the inside of the breakwater. This is for the lifeboat and access to Town Dock for local craft and should not be used except to access the public slipway.

Approaching the pier heads the main fishing vessel dock is inside to starboard, continuously active and brightly lit at night. Fishing vessels also moor along the outside of the starboard pier. Brixham Marina (MDL) is on the port hand side and straight ahead are two linear pontoons extending from the shore, both lit (F.R) at night. The E one is operated by the marina as an events pontoon and is sometimes used for visitors, but does not have power. The W one is operated by the HM for visitors and there is power and water on the pontoon. The inner harbour W of these pontoons dries and is for local boats, but several repair berths and scrubbing grids are available via the HM.

Brixham Yacht Club has two detached visitors' pontoons just below the club. Turn to starboard where the moorings end outside the pier heads, keeping a very sharp lookout for fishing vessels leaving the pier, and follow the edge of the moorings around the outside of the fish dock. The pontoons are adjacent to the root of the quay and steps by a steep slipway give access to the club. The fish dock operates day and night so this is not the quietest corner but it is well sheltered except when the wind has a N component.

Launching and recovery can be made at a number of sites around the harbour. The main public slipway is at Town Dock at the root of the breakwater by the lifeboat station, but note there is limited space for vehicle use near HW. There are also slipways at the marina and the yacht club.

The town beach and lido are E of the breakwater, where it is feasible to anchor off in deeper water avoiding a seagrass bed. It is not advisable to stay overnight due to the fishing traffic.

The landing slip and steps up to Brixham YC. A shallower slip is just W

4 TOR BAY

Berry Head

The tide runs quite hard off Berry Head, N from about HWP-0300 and S from around HWP+0300. Numerous fishing floats are close inshore. Cod Rock (dries 19m) is 0.5M S and should be passed to seaward. About 1M S, St Mary's Bay is a good anchorage with winds between SW and N. It is out of the tidal stream but any SW swell is likely to find its way in. A rocky patch in the SW corner extends as far as the 2m contour. There is another controlled zone here for swimmers from May to September, almost from headland to headland, so it will likely be necessary to anchor with caution inside the marker buoys.

Shoreside

Shower and toilet facilities can be found at the marinas and at the yacht clubs in Torquay and Brixham. Most beaches have public toilets as does Paignton Harbour but they are generally closed at night. Note there are no public facilities close to the HM pontoon at Brixham.

Both Torquay and Brixham have a number of food shops a short walk from the harbours and, as might be expected, a vast array of places to eat. Both have butchers, but the nearest one at Torquay is about 1M (slightly less from Torquay Marina). Paignton has several convenience stores. There is a chandlery at Torquay.

Torquay and Paignton are served by mainline trains with frequent buses to Brixham. This makes Tor Bay ideal for crew changes, or for leaving a vessel if making a voyage in stages. A seasonal ferry service links Torquay, Brixham and Paignton with occasional sailings to Dartmouth.

Local attractions

Tor Bay is of course all about the seaside and there are many such attractions at Torquay, whereas Brixham is very much a working port, but an attractive town nonetheless.

Kents Cavern prehistoric caves and the medieval Torre Abbey are close to Torquay Harbour and Babbacombe model village is a short bus trip. Torquay Museum houses an Agatha Christie gallery. Brixham is where William of Orange landed in 1688. There is a model replica of the Golden Hind in the inner harbour open as a museum, and a lido at Shoalstone near the root of the breakwater.

A pleasant walk leads to Berry Head National Nature Reserve and NCI station with panoramic views. Keen walkers, or those with cycles on board, can head over the hill to the River Dart at Galmpton, the shortest route being from Elberry Cove. However, there is an easier option on the heritage rail line from Paignton, which runs along the sands before traversing the hill and running down the eastern side of the Dart to Kingswear.

Tor Bay essential information

Clubs
Royal Torbay Yacht Club ☏01803 292006
Paignton Sailing Club ☏01803 525817
Brixham Yacht Club ☏01803 853332

Local Information
English Riviera Information Centre, Vaughan Parade, Torquay

Visitors' Berths
Pontoons at Town Dock, Torquay; Paignton and Brixham

Additional Berthing
Torquay Marina (MDL) VHF 80 ☏01803 200210
Brixham Marina (MDL) VHF 80 ☏01803 882929

Water Taxi
Ferries (seasonal) link harbours

Webcams
www.brixhamyachtclub.com

Water
Marinas and Town Dock

Fuel
South Pier, Torquay and marinas

Chandlery
Seawood Chandlery, Torquay

Victuals
Torquay town centre; Fore St, Brixham

Nearest Large Supermarket
Nr hospital, Torquay (by bus)

Laundry
Tor Laundry, Union St; The Laundry Room, Brixham

Repairs
Most likely at Brixham, contact HM

Engineers
Smith Marine, Paignton
Breakwater Marine Engineers, Brixham

Riggers
Seahorse Yacht Rigging, Torquay & Brixham

Electronics
Tecmarine, Brixham

Sailmakers
Westaway Sails (office nr Town Dock, Torquay)

Scrubbing Posts
Brixham Inner Harbour

Car Hire
Most brands in Torquay (nearest adjacent to railway station)

Transport
Mainline rail stations at Torquay & Paignton (bus from Brixham).

Agatha Christie

The best-selling author of all time was born and brought up in Torquay, working there as a nurse during WWI. Many of her works were penned in Devon, and some are based here. She moved to London but kept a holiday home at Greenway on the River Dart which featured in several plots, and visited Burgh Island several times writing a number of novels there.

Torquay hosts an annual Agatha Christie festival in September and there is a walk in Torquay featuring locations from her life and work. The local museum has an Agatha Christie gallery but a larger collection is now at Greenway, where the house and extensive grounds are open to the public. The Agatha Christie garden at Torre Abbey in central Torquay has many of the plants on which Christie based poisons in her books. Burgh Island is also open to the public although the Art Deco hotel is private.

The locations in Torquay are easily reachable on foot from the harbour. Greenway is opposite Dittisham (Chapter 5) so it is possible to land by tender if moored there, or by taking the ferry from Dartmouth. Finally, the heritage railway which runs between Paignton and Kingswear has a stop at Greenway Halt (which has to be the best option).

Burgh Island (Chapter 7) is best visited by tender from the adjacent anchorage and, if the tide is up, there is the opportunity to travel on the unique sea tractor in the footsteps of Hercule Poirot.

One of two massive ramps at Torquay built for D-Day

Even the jet skis have pontoons at Torquay!

Brixham Battery Military Museum, Fishcombe

5 DARTMOUTH
TOTNES & START BAY

Harbour Master's Office
VHF 11 'DartNav'
6 Oxford Street, Dartmouth TQ6 9AL
☎01803 832337 / 07968 839846 Emergencies ONLY
NCI Froward Point VHF 65 ☎01803 262173

The Dart is the first of the classic West Country rivers. The town of Dartmouth is well sheltered on the W bank inside a zigzag entrance, with the imposing Britannia Royal Naval College on the hill above. Numerous berthing options make it a popular destination and the river is navigable for some 10M inland to the market town of Totnes. The upper reaches are particularly attractive.

Landmarks

An obelisk beacon (24m unlit) is 150m above sea level NE of the entrance and is visible from all directions.

Start Point is a major headland 8M SSW of the entrance beyond the wide sweep of Start Bay, with a lighthouse and radio masts. Closer to, a row of white cottages is conspicuous S of the entrance, as is Dartmouth Castle where the entrance narrows.

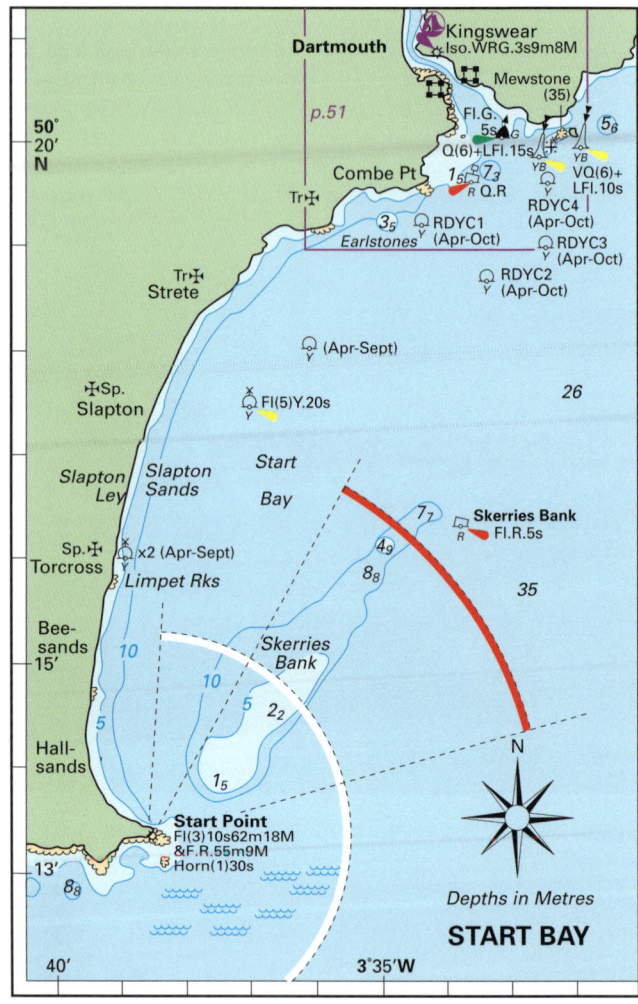

Dartmouth Castle from the river

Main hazards

The entrance, which faces SE, is narrow and funnels. In strong winds or large swell from between SW and SE it becomes rough, worse against the ebb, and may be untenable for small craft in such conditions. Brixham is a safe alternative. Numerous rocks line the approaches, especially on the N side and off Combe Point. Squally winds are often a feature in the final approaches.

Within the harbour, ferries crossing the river below and above the town have priority. There are extensive mud banks above Dittisham, 3.5M from the entrance.

Approaching Dartmouth from SW

50 • West Country Pilot

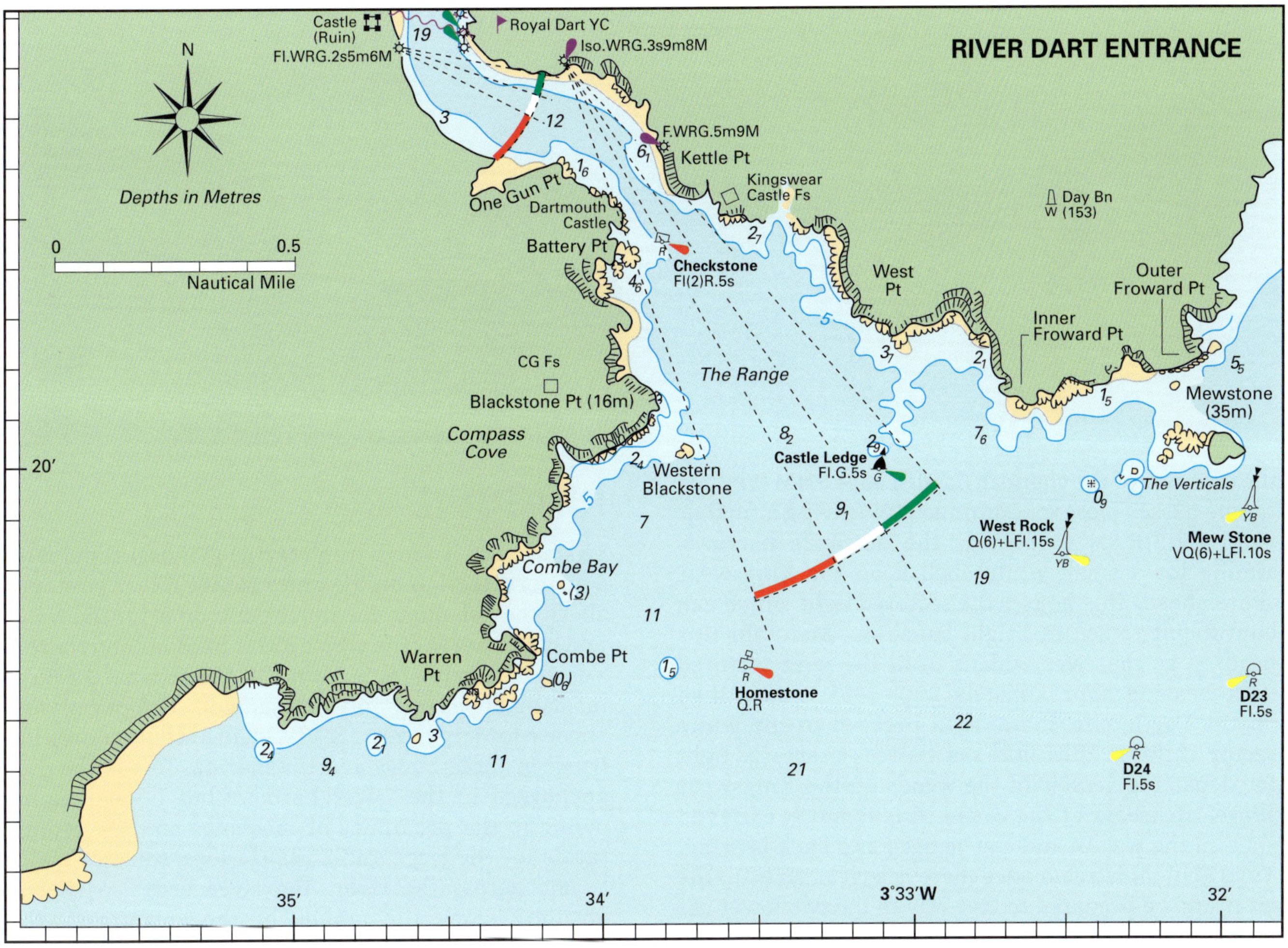

Dartmouth

RIVER DART ENTRANCE

Approaches

From offshore, aim to pass N of Skerries Bank, marked by a PHM (Fl.R.5s), to avoid being swept the wrong side of Start Point.

From N, stay a good 0.5M offshore at Scabbacombe Head in order to clear Nimble Rock (charted depth 1.9m but reported to be less). Start Point open of East Blackstone rock is a clearing transit. A good daytime anchorage is off the beach in the lee of Scabbacombe Head. Approach from E to NE but do not anchor further inshore than the 2m contour. East Blackstone (16m) and Mewstone (35m) should both be passed to seaward. Mewstone is marked by a SCM (Mew Stone VQ(6)+LFl.10s) and a second SCM (Q(6)+LFl.15s) marks West Rock (charted depth 2.1m) at the end of an associated reef. At night, keep Berry Head light (Fl(2)15s58m18M) on a back bearing of 000° until Skerries PHM (Fl.R.5s) bears SW then steer towards it until in the white sector of the first sectored light.

Start Point needs special consideration if approaching from S or W. Follow the strategy in the headlands section at the beginning of this book in the first instance, then stay outside Skerries Bank or hug the coast in Start Bay if conditions permit. From Skerries PHM, head NNE towards the Mewstone. At night, vessels should stay outside Skerries Bank, by remaining in the white sector of Start Point lighthouse until Skerries PHM (Fl.R.5s) bears N.

Entry

From a position or waypoint just SW of West Rock SCM, steer approximately NW for the entrance. The first PHM (Homestone (Q.R)), should be left a good distance to port as there is an unmarked drying rock (Western Blackstone) about halfway to the entrance on

Approaching from N towards the Mewstones

West Country Pilot • 51

Dartmouth entrance

the port side of the channel. Castle Ledge SHM (Fl.G.5s) can be passed close to. Continue NW leaving a further PHM (Fl(2)R.5s) to port as the entrance narrows, aiming for a small white obelisk on the Kingswear shore ahead. This houses the sectored light which can be difficult to see in bright sunshine. Maintain this heading as the river widens until the next sectored light bearing approximately 290°-295° is identified on the Dartmouth shore, then proceed in the white sector. If this is difficult to see, there is a sectored light for departing vessels in the woods on the Kingswear shore, upstream of the castle. This is much easier to spot on the way in and can be used as a back bearing. Turn N in midstream once there is a clear view up the river and be prepared to give way to the two lower car ferries, one of which can appear without warning, and unsighted, from the Kingswear shore just above the Royal Dart Yacht Club. They slow after reversing off the slip to allow their tugs to pivot about the bow, before resuming their course to the other bank. Often one ferry may have to stand off for the other one to leave the slip. A passenger ferry also operates from a jetty adjacent to the Kingswear ferry slipway.

Follow the white sector of the sectored lights at night, initially 325°-331° (Iso.WRG.3s9m8M) until in the white sector of the second light on 289°-297° (Fl.WRG.2s5m6M), following this course until the harbour opens up. Again, the light for vessels leaving (F.WRG.5m9M) may be easier to identify and use as a back bearing on the second leg. The ferries stop running at 2300.

KINGSWEAR

To starboard is Darthaven Marina (Transeurope) with a visitors' section on the outer of two linear pontoons above the fish quay. The inner pontoon is for the water taxi which serves the whole lower harbour and there is a designated area for tenders. Off the marina, the large mooring buoys can only be used with HM permission and are for larger vessels. The main anchorage area lies between these buoys and the marina. This is the only anchorage in the lower harbour but is challenging owing to the proximity of moorings and the ground tackle for the large mid-stream buoys, some of which is laid across the river. The river bed also shelves abruptly along the middle of the anchorage area, which raises the possibility of dragging into the mid-stream moorings. Overall, anchoring here is not for the faint hearted and can only be recommended for a short stay. Harbour rules require sufficient crew to remain on board during the turn of the tide and overnight.

DARTMOUTH

Most vessels opt to use one of the linear pontoons provided for visitors by the HM. Not all have walk-ashore access and some have restricted draught.

A seasonal (May–September) walk-ashore pontoon with all tide access is immediately above the lower car ferry on the W bank, outside the Dartmouth Yacht Club. It is limited to vessels up to 9m on the outside with rafting allowed two deep only, and 7m on the inside at the downstream end. Tenders and dinghies can be left on the inside at the upstream end. Swell can affect this pontoon in SE weather.

The quayside immediately upstream (South Embankment) looks inviting but is known to dry on extreme spring tides, and can only be used with permission from the HM. The next facility is Town Pontoon which is used by ferries during the day. Vessels can berth on the inside at any time where there is between 1.5m and 2.5m LAT charted depth at the pontoon. Rafting two deep is permitted but note that rafted vessels will be in less water and the quayside dries. Vessels can moor on the outside of the jetty

The lower ferries

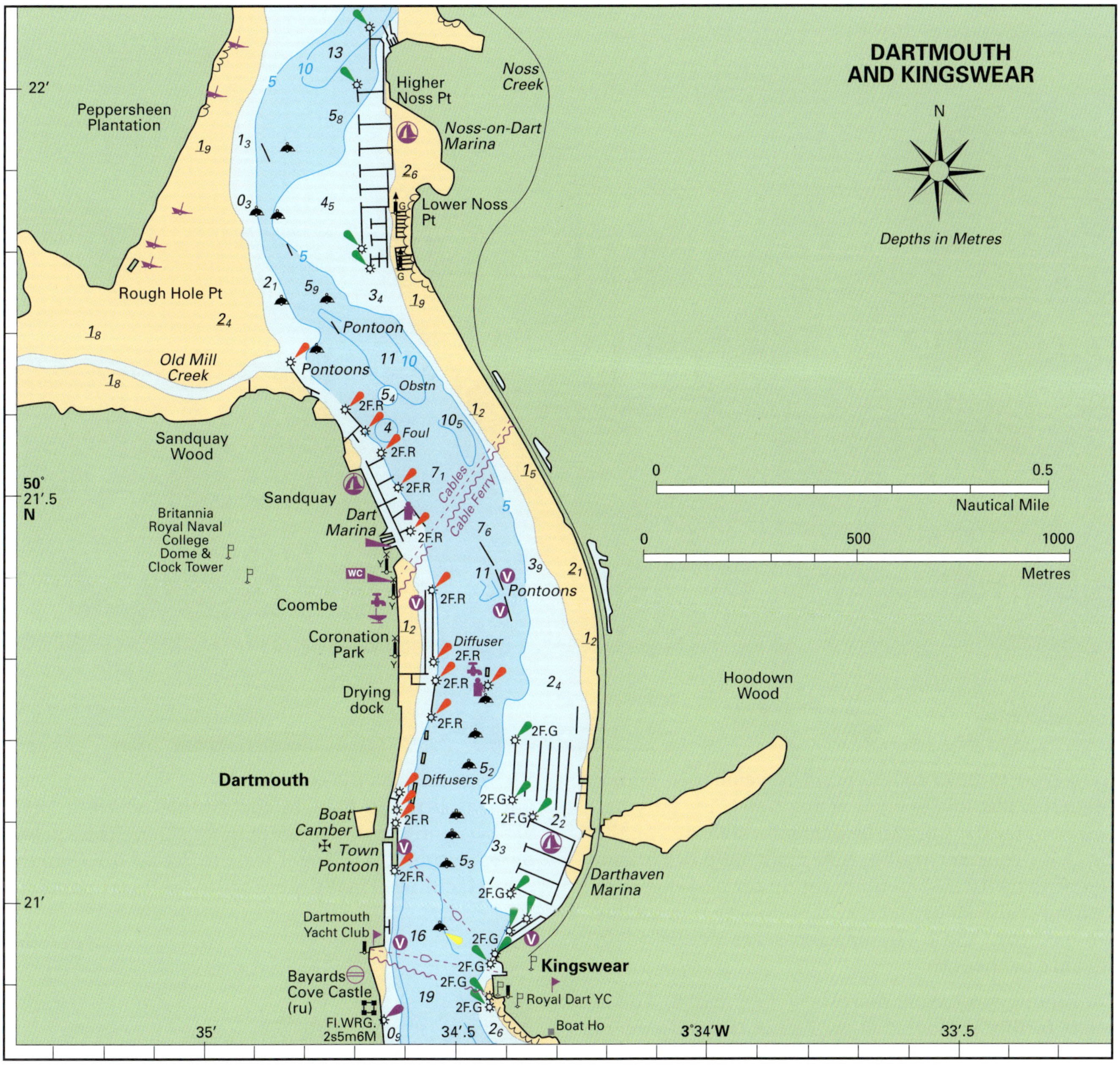

Kingswear

Checkstone PHM and Kingswear sectored light on the corner where the channel turns NW

Britannia Royal Naval College prominent above Dartmouth

from 1700 to 0845 only (except November to March when it is possible to moor at any time). The jetty has power and water but can be uncomfortable during the day with constant traffic. Note that the downstream end of the jetty is sometimes set up for passengers of visiting cruise ships and may therefore be unavailable for mooring. These circumstances are published in advance by the HM.

Continuing upstream there is a fuel barge, and a waste facility is moored at the end of the mid-stream pontoons, which also has a fresh water tap. Allowance should be made for the strong tidal stream when going alongside, and wash if alighting from a tender at the waste raft.

The largest of the walk-ashore pontoons ('DA') is off an area of parkland before the higher car ferry, and is the most popular, often used to accommodate rallies.

Visitors berth on the outside but it is shallow in places, with as little as 1.6m in the middle where a short walkway links to the inner pontoon. There is no power or water and it is a longer walk to get ashore than the other facilities. Finally there are three linear pontoons

Refuse/recycling pontoon and the fuel barge off the town

The deep water visitors' pontoons on the Kingswear side

DA pontoon has shore access

for visitors opposite 'DA' pontoon in mid-stream, but without power or water. Having easy access, this is probably the best option if arriving at night.

There are several landing options if not at a walk-ashore facility, although space is always in short supply. The first of these from seaward are at the yacht club pontoons on either bank. On the Kingswear side, the inside of the marina visitors' pontoon can be used by dinghies and it is also possible to land upstream of the marina at the dinghy rack which is located inshore of the local pontoons. There is also a scrubbing grid at the mouth of Waterhead Creek. On the Dartmouth bank, landing can be made at 'Double Steps' pontoon just upstream of a small craft harbour known locally as the 'boatfloat', or at the adjacent 'Green' pontoon, which dries. It may also be possible to land briefly on 'DA' pontoon if space permits. Launching and recovery is possible at Darthaven Marina or at the harbour slipway upstream of 'DA' pontoon, but extreme caution is needed here because it is immediately adjacent to the slipway for the higher car ferry.

The higher ferry lands close to the main slipway

Dartmouth from the higher ferry

West Country Pilot • 55

5 DARTMOUTH

NOSS & DITTISHAM

The higher car ferry runs on cables and has priority over other vessels. Immediately above on the Dartmouth side is Dart Marina (Indep) which may be able to provide a berth, and then an area of MOD property which is restricted. Old Mill Creek runs W for about a mile with two boatyards where mooring space may be available in a rural setting. The first has half-tide access for moderate draught but the second, at the head of the creek, requires a spring tide as there is less than 1m LAT at neaps. Anchoring off the creek is not permitted. The ground is foul, and it is the turning area for large craft.

Just upstream of Old Mill Creek on the Kingswear side is the redeveloped and expanded Noss on Dart Marina (Premier) on the site of a former shipyard, where visitors' berths may be available.

The river begins to narrow above Noss, with private moorings either side, amidst wooded foreshores typical of the West Country. There is plenty of depth in the channel between the moorings and the river turns NW after 0.5M, narrowing abruptly 0.3M further on at the Anchor Stone, marked by a red beacon (Fl(2)R.5s). Keep at least a boat length off this large drying outcrop where seals might be seen around LW. Below this mark on the same side is an anchorage, historically used by trading vessels heading upstream to Totnes. There is room for a few boats to anchor out of the tidal stream but the bank here is steep-to and, although the holding is reasonable, it would be easy to get pushed on to Parson's Mud which may result in drying at a precarious angle. There is also a risk of dragging into the main channel. Unless intending to dry out, there are better options upstream.

Above the Anchor Stone, the river turns briefly W and the moorings off the village of Dittisham come in to view. The HM provides a number of visitors' moorings

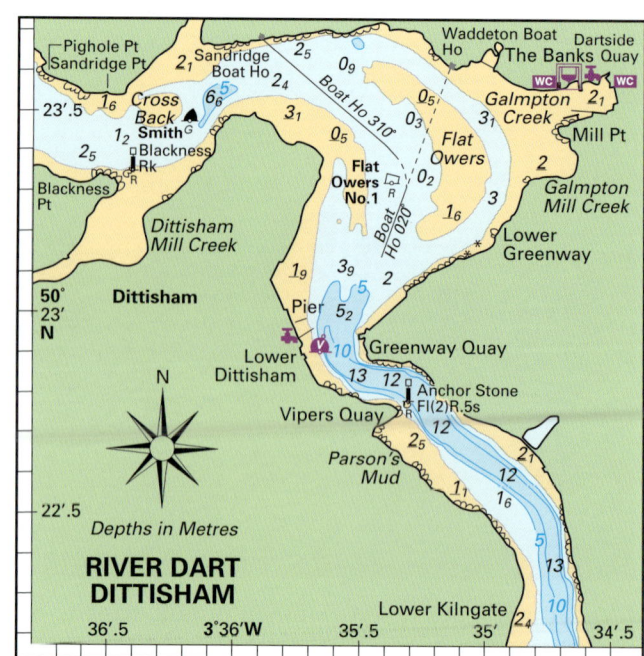

A seal catches the sun at the Anchor Stone

Greenway Quay

Noss & Dittisham

Dittisham village

Refuse and recycling at Dittisham

Upriver to Totnes

The HM harbour guide (print and PDF) is invaluable if heading upstream above Dittisham. A large bank, Flat Owers, extends from the Dittisham shore almost the entire width of the wide open area above the visitors' moorings. A deep water channel runs in a large arc around the outside of the bank, with numerous moorings indicating the deepest part. Halfway round, at the apex of the curve, a drying creek leads towards the village of Galmpton and contains two sizeable repair and laying up yards, one each side of the creek, with access at about half-tide. Continue to follow the line of the moorings heading NW past Waddeton Boathouse and a couple of private slips extending to the LW mark, beyond which the channel turns W until reaching another boathouse, Sandridge. In practice, most vessels will proceed from Dittisham at half-tide in order to visit Totnes over HW and this enables a short cut across the Flat Owers bank. From Dittisham, identify Waddeton Boathouse mentioned above and bring it on a bearing of 020°. Astern, keep a conspicuous house with a large window on 200°. Pass a PHM (Flat Owers No.1) about a couple of boat lengths off and turn NW to bring Sandridge Boathouse

here all marked with a large 'V' with any length or weight restrictions. Nearly all are in deep water and sheltered, except perhaps in strong NE winds. They are very popular and vessels should expect to raft up two per buoy. Moor as directed by the HM and land at the dinghy pontoon as shown on the signs. A ferry crosses the river here and will also act as a water taxi (daytime only).

Waddeton Boathouse. The first bearing for heading upstream

West Country Pilot • 57

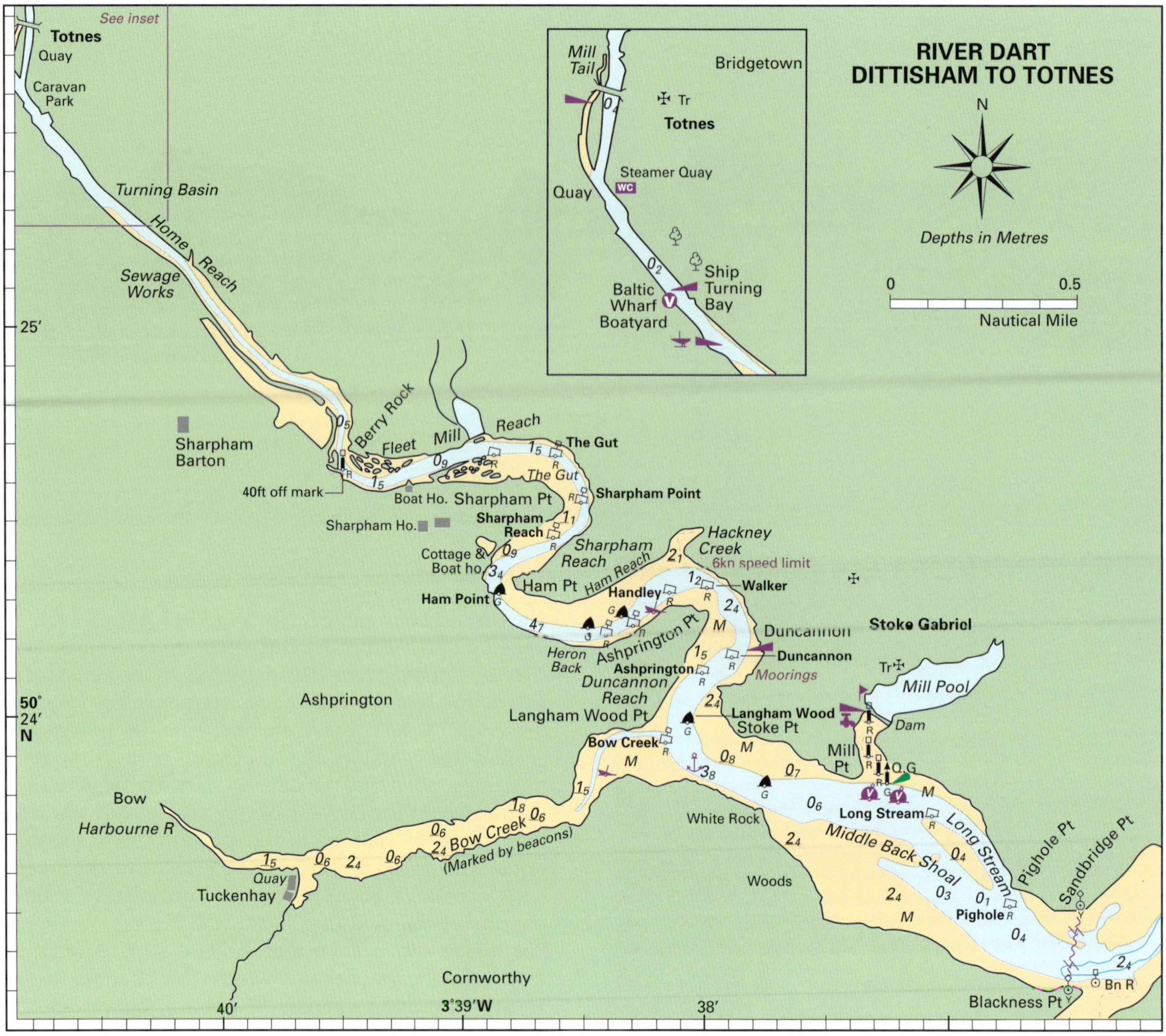

5 DARTMOUTH

onto a bearing of 310°, continuing until the deep water channel is reached at the moorings. The least charted depth on this route is 0.5m and the bottom is mud.

The river is buoyed except for the last mile or so to Totnes and the harbour guide provides more detailed pilotage. From Sandridge Boathouse the channel heads SW past a SHM towards Dittisham Mill Creek, and provides a sheltered anchorage with good holding except in strong W winds. Landing can be made at the hard in the creek where a road leads to the village. A PHM post marks Blackstone Rock at the W edge of the creek where a series of moorings belonging to a small boatyard begins. The yard also has day launching facilities for small craft. Above half-tide the line of moorings can be followed roughly NW but deeper draught vessels may prefer to head further to starboard leaving the next two PHMs (Pighole, Long Stream) to port. There are a couple of visitors' moorings (max 9m) off the drying Stoke Gabriel Creek in about 1m LAT. The creek itself is accessible for very small craft and tenders and is marked by posts. A tide gauge is on the first SHM post and the depth at the landing stage is approximately 0.8m *less* than that shown on the gauge. At other times there is an orange landing stage just upstream of the entrance.

Stoke Gabriel Creek, accessible for small day craft and tenders

Upriver to Totnes

Early morning at Bow Creek

Duncannon Reach heading upstream

From the end of the moorings, steer approximately 260° leaving the next SHM (Stoke Point) well to starboard. A good anchorage is to be found close under the trees on the S shore in an area known as White Rock, and also off the entrance to Bow Creek. The creek is marked by small lateral buoys and is navigable to the village of Tuckenhay for moderate draught vessels or dinghies, where the pub has a couple of alongside drying berths with power which may be available to visitors. The whole area from Stoke Gabriel to Tuckenhay is popular with paddleboarders.

Keep to the buoyed channel above Bow Creek following the instructions in the harbour guide carefully and keeping wash to an absolute minimum. The scenery is among some of the best to be found in this region. Anchoring upstream of Bow Creek is hazardous, even for small craft, and is not recommended. Enough time to return downstream should therefore be factored in, unless intending to dry out at Totnes. Particular care should be exercised in Sharpham Reach where the river narrows, as inevitably this is where large ferries will be encountered. If safe to do so, stem the tide remaining near stationary at the edge of the channel until they have passed. The last mark is a PHM post (40' Off) after which the starboard bank should be favoured as the channel turns briefly N, resuming mid-stream after the next bend. Approaching Totnes, Baltic Wharf repair yard has a drying pontoon on the

5 DARTMOUTH

The final mile

The 40' Off PHM is the last upstream navigation mark

Totnes Steamer Quay where the ferries operate

Drying pontoon at Baltic Wharf

S bank for visitors which must be booked in advance. The HM quay opposite is only recommended for short stays on the tide. The river forks just upstream at the quay where the ferries moor, with private moorings in the starboard fork where occasionally a mooring may be available from the club there. There is a possible berth for visitors at the entrance to the port fork near the pub, but it appears to be permanently occupied.

Steam Packet Inn, Totnes, visitors' mooring right

Start Bay

The 8M wide sweep of Start Bay between the Dart and Start Point is sheltered from the prevailing winds and, at least at the S end, from Atlantic swell. From the Dart, stay to seaward of Homestone PHM (Q.R) in the approaches and remain a good 0.5M offshore until well clear of Combe Point. Between here and the conspicuous church at Stoke Fleming are two temporary anchorages at Warren Cove and Redlap Cove. Both are best approached from WSW with a view to anchoring in 3m LAT. Favour the W side of Warren Cove as it is rocky elsewhere. At Redlap Cove, there is an isolated rock in approximately 2m on the W side. In both locations the seabed should be visible but use a tripping line if in doubt. Landing can be made on the beach at Redlap Cove except at HW.

Blackpool Sands is just SW of Stoke Fleming where it is possible to anchor with care in about 5m, but avoid the central area where there are buried cables. The beach is almost continuous from Strete to Beesands except for a rocky patch at Torcross. The seabed is steep-to but the gradient eases heading S. Although anchoring is feasible almost anywhere, the depth is likely to be close to 10m at the N end, requiring ample scope. The S end is therefore more practical, with the added benefit of more protection behind Start Point from the Atlantic swell. Anchor off the beach at Beesands, or at Hallsands, both of which are useful if waiting for a fair tide westbound.

> ### D-Day Landings
>
> Almost every place described in this book has a connection with the D-Day landings of June 1944, either for the preparation, the massing of troops and equipment or as departure points for the operation itself: huge, well preserved loading ramps at Torquay (Chapter 4), the beach at Trebah on the Helford (Chapter 16), Turnaware and Smuggler's Cottage at Tolverne on the Fal (Chapter 15), used as a base by Eisenhower, to name a few.
>
> The most poignant, however, must be Slapton Sands in Start Bay. In April 1944, amid great secrecy, thousands of US servicemen were taking part in a full scale rehearsal of the beach landings when tragedy struck. A handful of German E-boats encountered the exercise by chance and launched a torpedo attack. In the ensuing confusion nearly a thousand lives were lost, and the episode remained secret for some forty years. The actual Normandy landings took place less than six weeks later in June 1944.
>
> On the shore at Torcross there is a memorial to the fallen, including an American Sherman tank which was salvaged from the sea. There are D-Day memorials at the sites mentioned above and every church and village along this coast has a plaque, memorial or some form of recognition of this historic event.

Yachts at the White Rock anchorage

5 DARTMOUTH

A steam train leaves Kingswear for Paignton

Scabbacombe Sands is a quiet anchorage between Berry Head and the Dart

Shoreside

In addition to the marinas, showers and toilets can be found at the yacht clubs at Dartmouth and Kingswear, both of which are open every day and most evenings in the summer months. Winter times vary. There are also public showers and toilets on the quay at Dartmouth near Double Steps.

Dartmouth has many shops aimed at tourists but there are two food stores and a convenience store, butcher, bakery and a fresh produce market. Kingswear has a convenience store near the railway footbridge to the marina. There is a laundrette opposite the market at Dartmouth. Totnes has all the facilities of a major town and can be reached by bus or ferry from Dartmouth.

The railway never quite reached Dartmouth, so the nearest station is Totnes involving a bus or taxi ride. On the face of it, this does make crew changes a bit of a logistical challenge, but it is not unusual to see yachtsmen in oilskins heading to Paignton on the heritage line (and the author and crew once made the trip home by catching the vintage bus from Greenway early one morning!).

Local attractions

Dartmouth has always been a seafaring port and there are reminders of this in its architecture and monuments. Near the entrance to the river stands the 14th century Dartmouth Castle, a short walk from Town Quay, and Bayards Cove Fort which dates from the Tudor period is adjacent to the lower ferry on the Dartmouth side. Both are open to the public. Britannia Royal Naval College has guided tours, usually on Mondays and Wednesdays with visitors collected from the town.

On the Kingswear side of the river, the main attraction is the heritage railway to Paignton. There is a nice circular walk taking in the daymark and Brownstone Battery, with views across Lyme Bay and towards Start Point.

Upriver is Greenway, a former home of Agatha Christie, where parts of the house and grounds are open. It can be reached by a small ferry from Dartmouth, on the heritage trains from Kingswear, or by vintage bus from Paignton in the summer.

Start Bay is historically significant as the place where practice for the D-Day landings took place.

River Dart essential information

Clubs
Royal Dart Yacht Club ☎01803 752496
Dartmouth Yacht Club ☎01803 832305
Stoke Gabriel Boating Association
Totnes Boating Association

Local Information
Visit Dartmouth, Mayors Avenue
Visit Totnes, Market Square

Visitors' Berths
Pontoons (one shore linked) and moorings

Additional Berthing
Darthaven Marina (Transeurope) VHF 80
☎01803 752242
Noss Marina (Premier) VHF 80 ☎01803 839087
Baltic Wharf (Indep) ☎01803 867922

Water Taxi
VHF 69 'Yacht Taxi' ☎07970 346571

Water
South Quay, DA pontoon, Refuse barge at Dartmouth
Visitors' pontoon at Kingswear, Steamer Quay at Totnes

Fuel
Fuel Barge VHF 06 ☎07801 798861
Darthaven and Noss marinas

Gas
Darthaven, Dart and Noss marinas

Chandlery
Darthaven Marina

Victuals
Fairfax Pl and Victoria Rd, Dartmouth; Kingswear Stores

Nearest Large Supermarket
Nelson Rd (by bus) or Totnes

Laundry
Market St, Dartmouth

Repairs
Baltic Wharf, Totnes
Breeze Boat Maintenance, Dartmouth
Creekside Boatyard, Dartmouth
Dolphin Boatyard, Galmpton
Darthaven Marina
Dartside Quay, Galmpton
Distins Boatyard, Dartmouth

Engineers
Blackness Marine, Cornworthy
Chris Hoyle Marine, Kingswear
Stephenson Marine, Noss Marina
Tonto Marine, Galmpton

Riggers
Rigging Solutions, Galmpton; Lee Rogers, Noss Marina

Electronics
Devon Marine Electronics, Noss Marina
Pulse Marine Electronics, Dartmouth

Sailmakers
Dart Sails and Covers
Edge Sails, Creekside Boatyard

Scrubbing Posts
North Embankment & Hoodown, Kingswear via HM

Car Hire
Totnes (by bus or taxi)

Transport
Bus from Dartmouth to Totnes for trains to Plymouth, Exeter, London
Bus from Kingswear to Brixham, and Paignton for trains.

6 SALCOMBE
& KINGSBRIDGE

Harbour Master's Office
VHF 14 'Salcombe Harbour'
Whitestrand, Salcombe TQ8 8BU
☎ 01548 843791
NCI Prawle Point VHF 65 ☎ 01548 511259

Salcombe is an upmarket holiday town set in rolling hills and is a very popular destination for leisure craft. It is crowded in the season and large dinghy fleets are often hosted for racing. The estuary is a flooded glacial valley (ria) and has several creeks off it for exploring, all forming a Site of Special Scientific Interest (SSSI). The market town of Kingsbridge, 4M inland, can be reached on the tide.

Landmarks
Bolt Head is a distinctive headland with a spiky outline immediately W of the narrow entrance. Conspicuous radio masts are behind and 1M further W towards Bolt Tail at the end of this promontory. Prawle Point is 2M E of the entrance with a NCI lookout. From offshore, Start Point (Fl(3)10s62m18M) is 5M E.

Main hazards
A sandbar extends SW most of the way across the entrance with a least charted depth of 1.1m at the tip. However, this figure should be viewed with a good degree of caution as changes occur frequently. In strong S winds or swell against the ebb, the entrance should be considered untenable, except perhaps for larger craft at HW.

Squally winds are frequently encountered in the vicinity of Bolt Head. It is not uncommon to have ghosted along the coast only to be hit by 20kn gusts at the harbour mouth when attempting to lower the sails.

Numerous rocks line the entrance and the tide runs strongly throughout the harbour. There is much traffic, including swimmers, dinghies and trip boats. The creeks and upper reaches all dry.

Approaches
From offshore make straight for Bolt Head immediately W of the entrance. From E having cleared Start Point (see Headlands), aim to pass Prawle Point 1M off before shaping a WNW course for Bolt Head. A vessel rounding Start Point inshore at the turn of the tide should be able to stay 0.5M off the coast to clear any rocks, and pass Prawle Point close to before any significant overfalls build up. However, stay offshore if the wind is W.

The leading marks are bottom left

The direct approach from NW (Plymouth for example) will close the coast in the vicinity of Bolt Tail. The stretch from here to Bolt Head is always rough, even in seemingly benign weather. To avoid this, remain 1M off between Bolt Tail and Bolt Head, but note the final approach is likely to be rolly.

At night, do not turn for the entrance until in the white sector of the directional leading light (Dir.Fl.WRG.2s27m8M).

Entry
Close the entrance from a waypoint due S of it. Two red/white beacons form the leading marks on 000°. The lower beacon is the leftmost of three on a rock almost at sea level and the upper is on the cliff above. They are difficult to make out but the left hand edge of a conspicuous double-gabled house on the cliff is a good approximation. There is an anchorage on the port side below Bolt Head at Starehole Bay which is subject to SW swell, but is perfectly feasible as a temporary short stay anchorage or to await sufficient rise of tide over the bar. Note the leading line passes over the SW end of the bar. For deeper water, stay W of the transit once past Starehole Bay, approximately 150m from the cliff, and resume the leading line once an isolated house on the cliff to port is abeam. Do not try this trick at night or if there is any significant swell. During peak season (July/August) vessels must proceed under power.

Three PHMs and three SHMs mark a turn in the channel towards NE. Give the first PHM and first SHM

SALCOMBE

East Portlemouth anchorage

a wide berth. Twin beaches, North and South Sands are found to port on this corner. Small day craft may find a temporary anchorage here but both beaches are popular for swimming so caution must be exercised. A seagrass bed lies between two rocky outcrops off South Sands (both covered except at LWS). Larger craft should avoid this corner of the harbour.

Turn NE between the second SHM and PHM. After the third SHM there is an anchorage to starboard at Sunny Cove, more suited to shoal draught although deeper draught vessels will still find room on the 2m contour. The tidal streams run strongly further out towards the buoys. Stay N of the third fairway SHM to avoid the Black Stone, a largish rock/reef visible at most states of the tide. Note the beach is private and whilst landing is permitted at the owner's discretion, fires and barbeques are not allowed.

At night a directional light (Dir.Fl.WRG.2s27m8M) covers the leading line. All three sets of lateral buoys marking the turn NE are lit, but unfortunately with the same characteristics (Fl.R.5s/Fl.G.5s). Roughly abeam of the second SHM, an inner set of leading lights (Front Fl.2s5m8M, Rear Fl.5s45m8M) can be identified, leading 042° up the main fairway past the third PHM/SHM buoys. The lower light can be obscured by anchor lights on occasion but the upper one is always visible.

SALCOMBE TOWN

The first visitors' moorings are found below the yacht club either side of the fairway off Smalls Cove, which is a designated anchorage although the beach is private. This is the case with all the beaches on the East Portlemouth shore but landing is allowed by the owners. Just NE of these moorings, a line of yellow buoys off Salcombe Yacht Club marks a fairway to be used by non-participating craft when dinghy or gig racing is in progress, which is often in the summer! A ferry crosses just upstream of the yacht club and the main area of moorings off the town begins. Visitors' moorings are marked 'V' together with any restrictions (orange buoys are for vessels up to 10m and are in shallower water). The main anchorage is off East Portlemouth between the ferry slip and the fuel barge. However, the holding is poor and the tides run strongly. The edge of the channel is also steep, decreasing rapidly from 7m or 8m to the drying line. In spite of this it remains popular, but should be treated with caution.

On the Salcombe shore upstream of the ferry landing, Batson Creek is marked by beacons and leads to a number of small boatyards and services behind the town. At the entrance there is a refuse and recycling barge opposite the main pontoon landing for tenders (Normandy). Larger craft can moor briefly on the outside for water or crew changes but it is shallow at LWS. Overnight berthing is not permitted. A second pontoon below the harbour office (Whitestrand) has approximately 1.7m at LAT and can be pre-booked for overnight stays. The water taxi also operates from here. The channel then curves gently to port, marked by PHM beacons, past numerous private dinghy pontoons. Shadycombe Creek, to port after the lifeboat station,

Salcombe

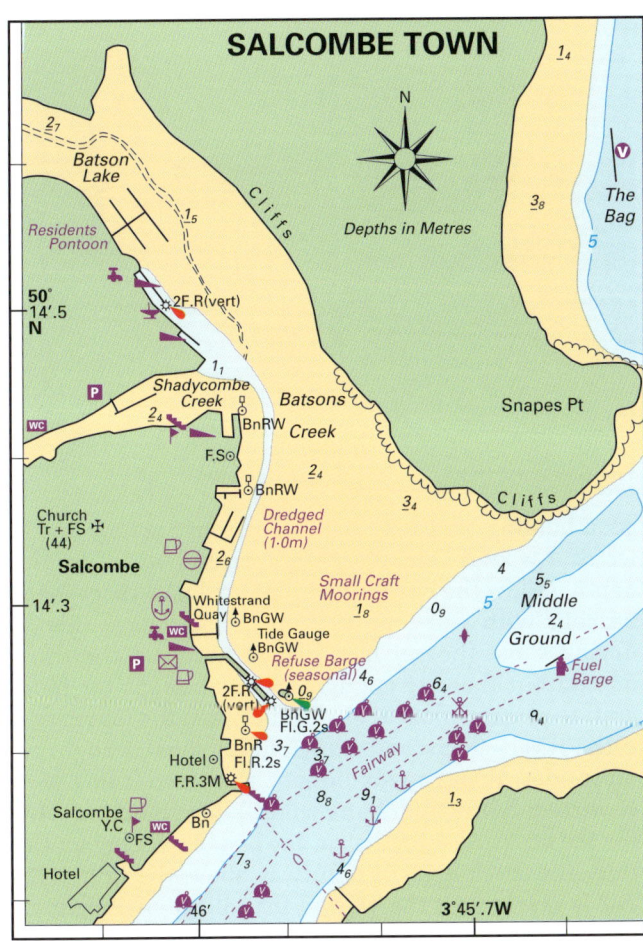

The refuse/recycling facility off the town

is home to a number of small boat builders, repairers and marine services. The creek dries to its mouth so local advice should be sought before entering. Just above this creek is the main slipway and trailer park for launching and recovery, which is possible at most states of the tide. Least charted depth is 0.5m LAT.

A fuel barge is moored above the visitors' moorings, S of a shallow patch known as Middle Ground before a fork in the channel. If following the inner leading lights at night, it will be necessary to pick a route through the moorings after passing Batson Creek. The deepest water is S of the fuel barge, and note the line of the leading lights gets very close to the shore at Snapes Point.

Normandy short stay pontoon

Batson Creek has a large slipway and car park

Shadycombe Creek with many small boatbuilders in the sheds on the right. The forest of masts is Batson Creek car park, used for laying up in the winter

West Country Pilot • 67

SALCOMBE

The Middle Harbour and 'The Bag'

Upstream of the fuel barge, Southpool Creek continues E. The first 0.5M or so is full of local moorings but it should be possible to anchor clear of them and dry out but seek permission from the HM first as it is not a designated anchorage. The creek can be explored on the tide by tender or small craft to a landing stage near the village of Southpool.

Off the entrance to Southpool Creek the main channel turns N and narrows as it passes between two headlands. Moorings are dotted everywhere in the next stretch and some may be available for visitors via the HM in more shelter than those off the town, but with a longer dinghy ride. The first pontoon on the port side is for visitors and is very popular with vessels often rafted. All the other pontoons are private and there is a boatyard accessed by a gutway behind the last pontoon.

Adjacent is an anchorage S of a green/white beacon (Saltstone) off the entrance to Frogmore Creek. The holding here is good and there is less traffic than off the town. The downside is that it is more exposed in moderate or strong winds, and uncomfortable in wind over tide conditions in anything above about F3. A further anchorage is just W of the Saltstone beacon but be aware of a shallow patch between the two spots.

Frogmore Creek leads off to starboard at the Saltstone with a bar at the entrance (least observed depth 0.9m LAT). The narrow channel initially heads ENE towards the first of a series of red/white PHM beacons and there is 1m-1.5m LAT in most of this reach with

The Saltstone mark

good holding, and well sheltered from S winds in the lee of a wooded hill. Keeping a careful watch on the depth, follow the curve of the channel past three PHM beacons with a drying inlet on the starboard side. A drying shoal (horse) has formed just past the third beacon but there is enough water at neaps for most craft to remain afloat at anchor between the fourth and fifth PHM beacons, and sufficient for shoal draught on most tides. This is an idyllic spot, sheltered from SW to N with only the abundant wildlife for company, save for the occasional tender or day boat exploring on the tide. The creek dries to a gutway above the fifth PHM but is marked all the way to the village of Frogmore by PHM beacons. There is a slipway here and vessels which can take the ground should be able to anchor in the final 0.5M reach, although a prior inspection at LW may be beneficial.

Looking downstream from the peaceful anchorage in Frogmore Creek

The slip at the head of Frogmore Creek looking downstream

KINGSBRIDGE

The main channel from the Saltstone continues NNW marked by red/white PHM beacons until it forks at the third one. There is at least 2m LAT throughout this stretch making it suitable for anchoring in light airs only, if somewhat remote. Large expanses of marsh and mud on both sides teem with birds and can only be explored reasonably under oar since they dry up to 4m in places, except for two gutways forming Blanksmill and Collapit creeks on the port side where there is a large area of seagrass. A smaller patch is to starboard opposite the second and third beacons.

At the third beacon, the channel divides and both arms dry. The starboard channel leads to Balcombe Creek and is marked by red *buoys* on the port side (*note* these are numbered consecutively rather than even). There is a swatchway (gap) between No.2 *buoy* and No.5 *beacon* in the Kingsbridge channel, useful if an error was made at the fork.

The port channel from the fork leads to the drying harbour at Kingsbridge and is marked by red/white PHM *beacons*. The channel is easy to follow, except perhaps at HWS in the evening when the sun is low and there may be little of the beacons showing. The W edge of the channel is steep-to in an area of extensive marshland and saltings, so stay a boat length off the beacons. As the channel approaches a headland at Southville, there is a single green/white SHM beacon which must be left a good bit to starboard, and the channel turns W towards a rocky patch on the bank. Remain on this side for a short distance before crossing

The two channels to Kingsbridge are marked either by posts or by buoys

to the opposite bank as the landscape becomes more built up. There is a small (seasonal) yellow buoy here, after which is the final PHM beacon and a further two PHM buoys which should all be left to port. Follow the line of moorings as the channel meanders gently towards a slipway and a row of small craft pontoons on the port side.

Vessels intending to dry out at Kingsbridge are advised to pre-arrange with Salcombe HM before heading upstream. Moderate draught vessels should be able to reach the harbour approximately HW±2. There is space for several vessels up to 9m LOA on the pontoon

Final approach to Kingsbridge

by the access ramp. Larger vessels, up to 11m, moor alongside the quay wall immediately upstream of the pontoons. Bear in mind the quay is public, and it may be necessary to move RIBs and smaller craft from the access ladders before drying out. HM staff will advise on the most suitable berth. Where possible, vessels departing should leave before HW to allow incoming vessels to moor on arrival.

Launching and recovery is possible from the HM slipway at the downstream end of the pontoons but note that access may only be possible near HW when atmospheric pressure is high.

Visitors' pontoon at Kingsbridge

Shoreside

Toilets and showers are available at Whitestrand Quay immediately outside the harbour office, and at the yacht club a short walk from there. There are also showers at the leisure centre in Kingsbridge.

Although most of the shops in Salcombe are squarely aimed at tourists, there is a butcher (where ice is also sold), baker and a small deli, all located in the main street and a short walk from the harbour office. Beyond the lifeboat station in Island Street there is a good sized chandlery and several small boat repairers and shipwrights whose premises have slipways on to the creek. At the end of Island Street is a food store. There is no shortage of places to eat in Salcombe with something for all budgets and tastes. There are two large supermarkets at Kingsbridge within a short walk of the quay.

Local attractions

The estuary has some of the best walking country. A gentle stroll from the town leads to the popular South Sands beach. A ferry runs between here and the town making a perfect circular route for an afternoon, or the more energetic can continue along the coast path to Bolt Head. The eastern side of the estuary is archetypal rural Devon, with peaceful countryside to explore on foot or by cycle including a stunning walk out to Prawle Point, or to the pretty village of Southpool.

Kingsbridge

Salcombe essential information

Clubs
Salcombe Yacht Club ☎01548 842593

Local Information
Market St, Salcombe; The Quay, Kingsbridge

Visitors' Berths
Moorings and Island pontoon
Drying pontoon/quay wall at Kingsbridge
Alongside pontoon (limited hours, prebook only)

Additional Berthing
None

Water Taxi
VHF 12 'Salcombe Harbour Taxi' ☎07807 643879

Webcams
www.salcombeyc.org.uk

Water
Normandy Pontoon & Batson Quay (slipway)
1000-1100 at the pontoon in 'The Bag' Jun/Jul/Aug

Fuel
Fuel Barge VHF 06 ☎07801 798862

Gas
Salcombe DIY, Island Sq
Salcombe Boat Store, Island St

Chandlery
Salcombe Boat Store, Island St

Victuals
Fore St & Island St, Salcombe, or Kingsbridge

Nearest Large Supermarket
Cockworthy Rd, Kingsbridge (by ferry/tender from Salcombe)

Laundry
Church St, Kingsbridge

Repairs
Services in Batson/Shadycombe Creeks
Winters Marine, Lincombe
Stones Boatyard, Yalton
Frogmore Marine Services, Frogmore

Engineers
Batson Creek Marine

Riggers
Salcombe Rigging Services

Electronics
Richard Lewis, Lincombe

Sailmakers
John McKillop, Kingsbridge

Car Hire
Kingsbridge

Sunset, Frogmore Creek

7 BIGBURY BAY
INCLUDING RIVERS AVON AND ERME

Approaching the Avon from SE. Burgh Island left and Bigbury on Sea right

Harbour Master's Office
No VHF
Bantham Estate Office, Bantham, Kingsbridge TQ7 3AN
☎ 01548 560897 / 07890 301238

This 7M wide bay between Plymouth and Salcombe often passes unnoticed by vessels on passage, but contains some good anchorages in offshore winds. For vessels that can take the ground, the River Avon has a spectacular hidden harbour at Bantham.

Landmarks
Bolt Tail is at the E end of the bay with the more recognisable Bolt Head and the Salcombe entrance 3M further E. The Great Mew Stone off Plymouth Sound and the River Yealm lie 3M W of the bay. Burgh Island cannot be distinguished from shoreline, but is about a third of the way across from Bolt Tail and has a conspicuous hotel visible from SE.

Main hazards
There are no dangers up to within 0.5M of the shore except Wells Rock (1.3m) about 1M SE of the River Erme mouth. All the anchorages have rocky areas which require careful pilotage as charts of this area are not detailed. The bay is completely exposed to the ambient WSW swell and only tenable overnight at Burgh Island, in settled weather and winds between NW and NE. Closer to, if people can be seen surfing at Bantham E of Burgh Island, there is likely to be too much swell to contemplate anchoring. The River Avon is immensely popular for wild swimming attracting hundreds of competitors at some events. Due caution should be exercised.

Approaches
Bolt Tail should be given a good offing as there is always rough water but otherwise an approach can be made from anywhere between W and SE.

Entry
It is possible to steer directly for the intended destination once clear of Bolt Tail (westbound) or Stoke Point (eastbound). If taking the scenic route along the coast, remain 0.5M off until in the vicinity of the intended anchorage.

Hope Cove
This small cove is tucked in the lee of Bolt Tail which provides protection from E winds, but the holding is mainly poor so it should only be considered as a temporary anchorage. It has a popular beach and attracts large numbers of day craft. Sound in with the lifeboat shed and slipway bearing about 125°, taking care to avoid the isolated Goody Rock (dries 2.5m), and anchor where the seabed can be seen. Be prepared to move at the first sign of onshore wind or swell. Dinghies can land at the small harbour N of the beach, behind a rocky ledge.

1M N is another potential day anchorage in E or NE winds at Thurlestone. There are large rocky areas, but yachts have been observed at anchor in a deep pool S of Warren Point (identified by the golf course). However, it would be advisable to seek local knowledge first. Approach the N side of the bay on approximately 080°

A small harbour arm at Hope Cove makes landing easier

Bigbury Bay

The daytime anchorage at Hope Cove is best in NE winds

7 BIGBURY BAY

Thurlestone might be a suitable place for small craft

between Warren Point and a drying patch (The Books). Beware of a popular dive site at a wreck SW of this. Very small craft can work their way further SE behind the rocky areas but a sharp lookout is required for isolated rocks, of which one is shown on some charts about midway between a wreck on the shore and The Books, awash at LAT.

Burgh Island

The island, with its famous hotel, is linked to the mainland by a sand bar traversed by a sea tractor when the bar is covered (in reasonable conditions!). Anchoring is possible either side of the bar depending on wind direction but it dries to a minimum of 4.1m so vessels should not cross it.

Most vessels anchor E of the island and this is the better anchorage if intending to enter the River Avon as it affords the opportunity of an inspection at LW. Sound in on a bearing of 030° towards the middle of the beach staying well clear of a red beacon on Murray's Rocks to avoid an unmarked reef extending SE of it. Anchor outside the swim line marked by small yellow buoys. If remaining overnight, anchoring inside the reef just NE of the beacon may provide flatter water, except when the bar is covered near HW, but do not cut the

The infamous sea tractor

corner on entry. It is possible to land on the main beach or the sand bar, the latter being the best option to visit the island, but leave the tender clear of the track used by the sea tractor and other vehicles. An equally good anchorage is found NW of the sand bar with perhaps better shelter when the wind is NE, and without the isolated rocks to worry about. Approach from between SW and NW and beware of a rocky patch at the NW corner of the island. At neaps, it is feasible to anchor in the adjacent Challaborough Cove in a central position away from any rocks.

Burgh Island and the hotel made famous by Agatha Christie

74 • West Country Pilot

River Avon

This is probably the trickiest harbour to enter in the entire region and some pre-planning is essential. If possible, the channel should be checked at or near LW, either by tender or by landing on the beach and walking along the water course. From the anchorage off Murray's Rocks, people can be observed walking across the entrance at LW so assume it dries completely at LAT. The critical parameter is to be in a position to be anchoring or mooring off Bantham at slack water, since the tides run hard and there is little room to take avoiding action if necessary. There is sufficient outflow from the river that slack water off Bantham occurs just before HW *Plymouth* with actual HW being approximately the same time as Salcombe. Therefore, begin the approach from the anchorage at HWP-0030. Initially, keep the last two conspicuous houses on the cliff one above the other on approximately 045° and keep heading towards the cliff until the upper house has 'dipped' halfway below the lower one (i.e. only the top floor of the upper house can be seen). Follow the cliff turning slowly to starboard until the bend tightens and then turn further to starboard to be

Two houses in transit form the initial approach line from the beach (*Note* lower house being rebuilt 2025)

The entrance to the Avon at LWS when it is possible to walk across

The seaward view

7 BIGBURY BAY

The channel then gets close to the cliff

At the corner, the weed was in the deeper part

Aim towards the edge of the high ground – beware swimmers and boards

Keep to the outside of the bend

pointing at the end of the high bank on the main beach (approximately SE). The river bed shallows briefly here and this is the section most likely to vary over time. When last visited, the deepest water was over a weedy line passing to starboard of a small speed limit buoy but there appeared to be at least 2.5m on a direct transit between the lower house and the inner edge of the high bank on exit at HWS. Keep a very sharp lookout for swimmers. A long deep pool begins inside the high bank and the channel follows the outside of the curve, not the inside as depicted on some charts. Although it is feasible to anchor fore and aft in this stretch, the HM would prefer not. Leave other vessels and moorings to port until 200m from the quay, at which point leave one row to starboard. This row usually has HM vessels moored which are olive coloured (military looking) motorised skiffs. Continue past the quay following the centre of the moorings until a small dinghy sailing club on the opposite bank is abeam.

Two reddish orange visitors' moorings are laid at the upstream end of the large sand bank on the edge of the channel, which retains just enough water to float a tender on all but the lowest tides. Alternatively, anchor on the sandbank clear of any moorings. It is largely flat and slopes very gently S which means most vessels will tend to dry out level when facing upstream. The HM recommends setting a kedge to maintain the desired alignment. There are some sand waves on the top but not significant enough to cause a problem and a weedy, slightly boggy area running along the W edge of the sand. This is depicted as the channel on some charts and is fine for anchoring on, but not so pleasant underfoot. Landing is possible at the beach adjacent to the quay and HM office, and is just about accessible at all states of the tide in a tender having launched from the sand bank, but some punting may be required.

River Avon essential information

Clubs
Bantham Sailing Club

Visitors' Berths
Moorings

Additional Berthing
None

Water Taxi
HM provides ferry

Water
Tap at HM office by slipway

Victuals
Bantham Stores
Challaborough Bay Convenience Store

Nearest Large Supermarket
Kingsbridge

Car Hire
Kingsbridge

River Avon

Bantham village. HM Office is left of the yardarm

Anchor anywhere on the sandbank clear of the few moorings. The patch right was softer under foot

The winding river channel can be explored on the tide for some 3M inland to the road bridge at the village of Aveton Gifford, above which tenders might be able to reach a weir 1M further on, or landing can be made at a slipway in the village. It appears feasible for shoal draught craft to anchor with care and dry out in the upper reaches towards the village, and there are a number of vessels on drying trot moorings where the river bed appears reasonably flat. Seek HM advice first.

Launching and recovery on the river is difficult, except perhaps from Aveton Gifford at HW. The roads at Bantham are too steep and twisting for a conventional car and trailer.

There is room to dry out among the trot moorings below Aveton Gifford

The winding channel below Bantham

A perfect day on the Avon. Burgh Island left of centre

River Erme mouth

The Erme is situated approximately 3M NW of Burgh Island and is suitable as a temporary daytime anchorage in winds between NE and NW, protected by low headlands either side. A reef between the headlands formed by the East and West Mary's Rocks provides some additional protection from swell, but makes for challenging pilotage.

Steer towards the headland W of the river from a position 0.5M S or SW. This is Battisborough Island but it is not distinguishable as such from sea level. When approximately 100m off, turn to steer 055° towards a small wooded headland between two beaches (Owen's Point). Sound in to at least the 3m contour before anchoring SSE of Owen's Point. There is a historic wreck off Mothecombe beach (W of Owen's Point) and anchoring is prohibited although tenders can land on the beach. Beware also of an isolated rock on the 4m contour due S of the point (charted). The River Erme itself is private and landing is not allowed, but exploring appears to be tolerated.

Shoreside

There are no washing facilities in Bigbury Bay except for public toilets at Bantham so a degree of self sufficiency is required if staying for long. Victualling is also limited although there is a small store and café at Bantham selling basic supplies (including ice), a convenience store at Challaborough and a small shop at Aveton Gifford.

River Erme

River Erme. Best approach is along the shore in front of Battisborough Island (left)

Mothecombe Beach

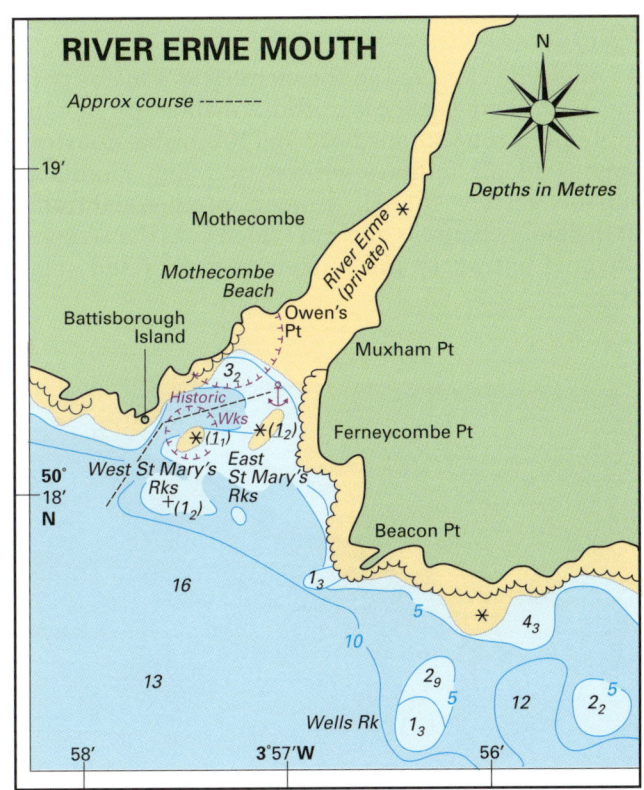

Anchored at the mouth of the River Erme

Local attractions

Most places in Bigbury Bay are daytime anchorages with excellent beaches. Burgh Island has an Art Deco hotel, famous for hosting Agatha Christie on several occasions and the setting for at least one Hercule Poirot mystery (there are potential references in some of her other books). The island makes a pleasant excursion for the day.

8 RIVER YEALM
INCLUDING PLYMOUTH SOUND

Plymouth Sound

Harbour Master's Office
VHF 12 'Yealm Harbour' (occas.)
Yealm Steps, Yealm Road, Newton Ferrers PL8 1BN
☎01752 872533
NCI Rame Head VHF 65 ☎01752 823706

The River Yealm, a classic West Country haven, lies in the outer approaches to Plymouth Sound. At some 3M wide and stretching 2M inland, the Sound is a large natural harbour and true port of refuge, protected by a substantial stone breakwater. Cawsand Bay anchorage lies at the W entrance to the Sound

Landmarks

The Great Mew Stone at Wembury Bay is conspicuous just E of Plymouth Sound and marks the outer approach to the River Yealm. Rame Head is 1M W of Plymouth Sound (4.5M W of Great Mew Stone) and is a conical headland with a chapel at the summit and a NCI lookout. Inshore, the breakwater has a lighthouse at the W end (Fl.WR.10s19m12/9M), a beacon at the E end (LFl.WR.10s9m8/6M) and a fort like structure central, with the urban landscape of the city visible behind.

The main lighthouse on the W end of Plymouth breakwater

Main hazards

As might be expected in the vicinity of a major port, the most likely hazard is traffic. A mandatory moving prohibited zone 250m ahead and 100m abeam/astern applies to all military vessels and any auxiliary/support vessels. There is frequent commercial traffic in the main channels, most of which uses the Western Channel entrance, and numerous yachts and small craft.

Approaching Plymouth Sound and the Yealm from E with Rame Head in the distance

80 • West Country Pilot

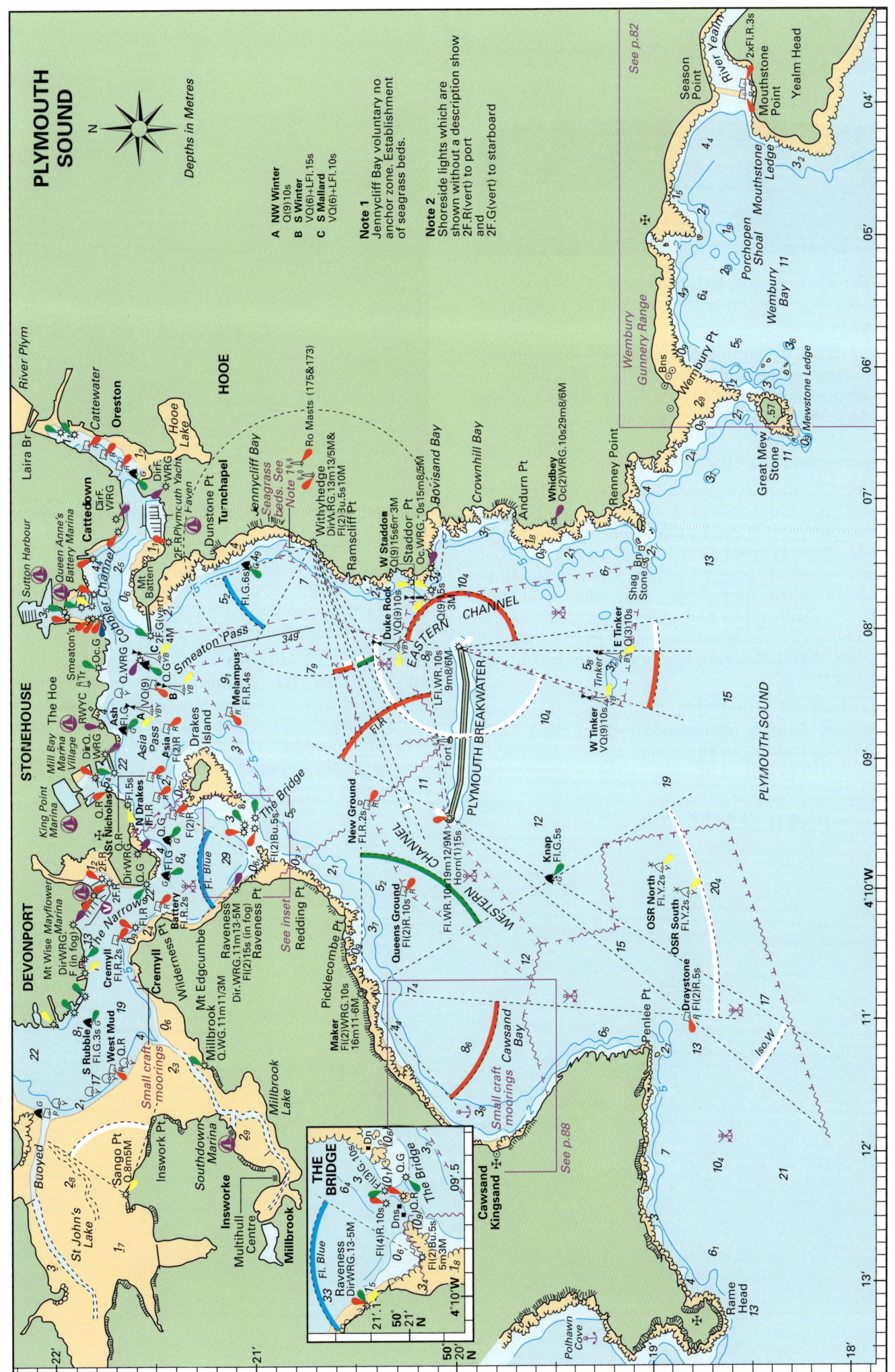

8 PLYMOUTH SOUND

Large cruise ferries operate from Plymouth to France and Spain

In the Eastern Channel, Tinker shoal has a least charted depth of 3m and is marked by ECM/WCM buoys.

Speed trials by large motor boats are occasionally authorised in Cawsand Bay (only observed in daylight) which may cause vessels at anchor to roll heavily and tenders could potentially be swamped.

Approaches & entry

The picturesque River Yealm lies just E of Plymouth Sound. A sand bar and a shallow channel limit access but provide good protection from swell once inside. There is space for up to 70 visiting craft but it gets extremely busy with boats from Plymouth at weekends when, from Friday lunchtime onwards, it may prove difficult to find a berth. Entry and exit is not advised in strong winds or swell from between S and SW. Vessels drawing more than 1.5m should not enter at LW±2.

Stay 0.5M off either side of Wembury Bay until Wembury Church (conspicuous) bears 020°-030°. If arriving from E, an additional clearing bearing of

Wembury Church overlooks the entrance to the Yealm

315° on the radar tower E of Wembury clears the Ebb Rocks at Yealm Head. When due E of the summit of Great Mew Stone, turn NE to avoid a shoal patch with 1.9m least charted depth. Numerous fishing floats and racing marks are found in this area.

The first set of leading marks will then be seen on the hillside in the river entrance, both white triangles with a vertical black stripe. Note that the actual track of this line passes extremely close to a shallow rocky area off Mouthstone Point, and also *does not clear the sand bar at the entrance*. Therefore, stay slightly N of

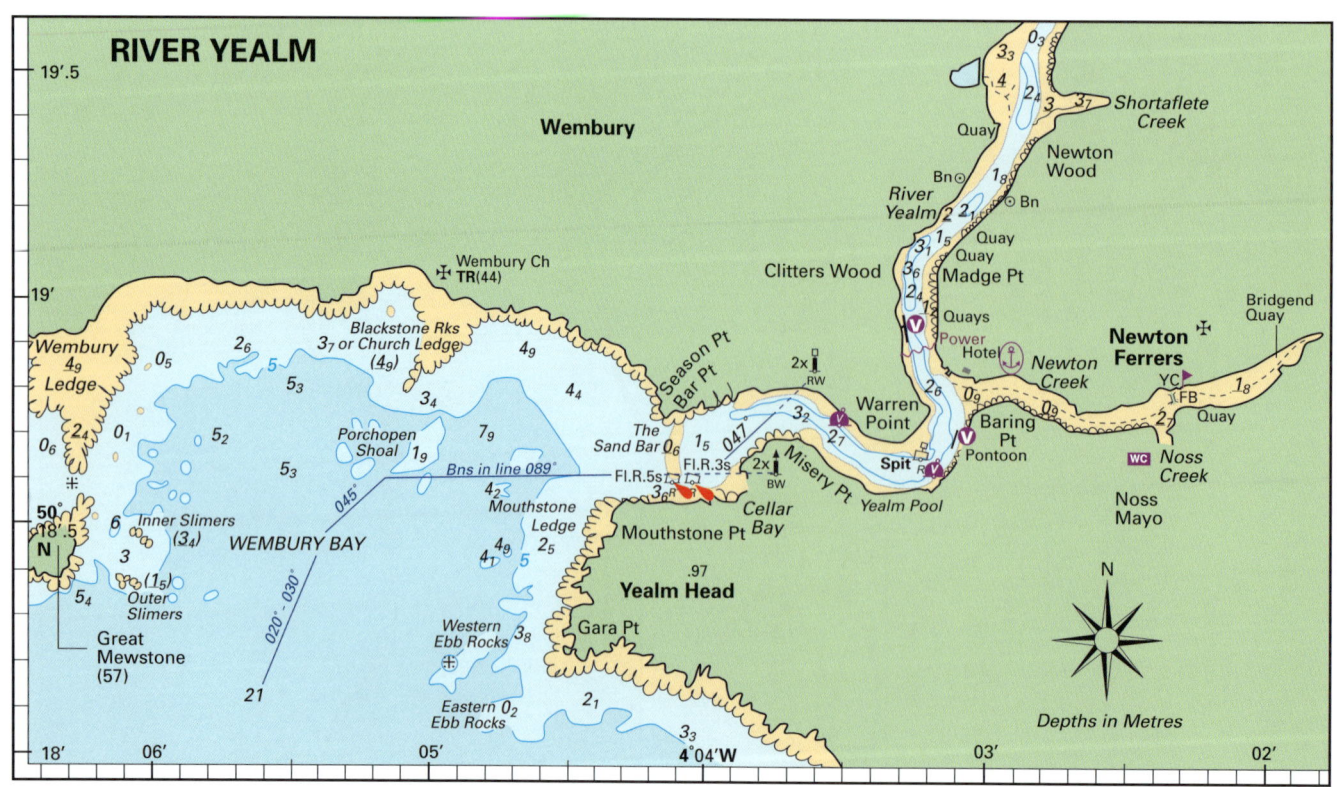

82 • West Country Pilot

Wembury Bay

Great Mewstone marks the E side of Plymouth Sound and the entrance to the Yealm

First set of leading marks in the entrance above Cellar Bay. Note the PHMs marking the end of the bar

Second set of leading marks

the leading line before deviating S round two PHMs which do clear the sandbar. Small yellow buoys mark the approximate seaward extent of the bar and the 6kn speed limit. The gap between the PHMs and the shore is narrow and, although there is room for two average sized vessels to pass in normal conditions, larger craft may need to stand off until the passage is clear. Turn NE after the second PHM on to a second leading line marked by white beacons with red vertical stripes on the shore ahead. A good anchorage for shoal draught is at Cellar Bay to starboard, perfectly sheltered in winds from SE to NE with room for several boats. Seagrass is encroaching here so future restrictions cannot be ruled out. The channel on the transit is shallow with 0.9m or less at LWS. As the river opens up, there is another anchorage inside the sandbar which is suitable in winds between NE and NW, but do not block the channel and stay far enough off the bar to avoid being pushed on by the ebb. It is more suitable for neap tides. The channel then deepens as it turns SE under the cliff and the moorings come into view.

The first large mooring in mid-stream has a long pick-up and is for visiting craft between 12m and 18m (max 25T combined). Continue following the moorings towards the starboard shore and then round to port. Be sure to leave a red PHM to port – it can be difficult to identify amongst the moorings. As the bend in

The first mooring in the Yealm is for larger craft

The main visitors' pontoon in the Yealm

the river eases temporarily there are three further visitors' moorings for up to three vessels each (max 12m and 25T combined). Moorings marked 'A' lining the channel can also be used if no tender or notice is attached and sufficient swinging room exists. Do not pick up any other moorings without permission from the HM. Just upstream of the moorings is an island pontoon for visitors with up to 2m draught. The tide runs diagonally across the line of this pontoon which can make mooring difficult but there are usually other berthed vessels or the HM if assistance is needed. The main river continues round to port and runs past the harbour office with a landing pontoon extending from the shore and Newton Creek forks off E. In the mouth of the creek there are a couple of small day craft moorings for visitors staying ashore

The main channel looking downstream from abeam the second visitors' pontoon

The tranquil upper reaches of the River Yealm are on a private estate

HM Office and landing pontoon

which must be pre-booked. Leave the SHM ('Office') to starboard. Continuing N, the deeper water is towards the port bank and another visitors' pontoon is located 0.25M above the fork in about 1.5m LAT. The moorings end 100m or so upstream at the start of an old oyster bed before resuming in the upper reaches on a private estate. These moorings are all private, as is the foreshore, but a few are occasionally available to visitors, *strictly by arrangement with the HM.*

NEWTON FERRERS

Newton Creek dries to its mouth but the villages of Newton Ferrers and Noss Mayo can be reached on the tide by vessels of moderate draught or by tender. The deepest channel initially follows the N bank, crossing gently to the S bank from the halfway point of the first reach, before resuming mid-channel where Noss Creek forks off S. Both creeks have a pedestrian causeway (known as a Voss) just above the junction. Noss Creek is only suitable for tenders but larger craft can continue in Newton Creek to reach Bridgend Quay 0.3M further up, where it is possible to dry out. Consult the HM before doing so.

Most craft will opt to stay afloat on one of the pontoons or moorings and can land in several places in a tender. The first is at Parish Steps (also called Kilpatrick Steps) on the shore adjacent to the downstream end of the main visitors' pontoon and is also the nearest to the visitors' moorings, which is worth noting if rowing since the tidal stream can exceed 2kn. Wide Slip is the next landing site (although it is not a slip!) on the S side of the mouth of Newton Creek where a long painter is required. The main landing is at the

Newton Creek

8 RIVER YEALM

Newton and Noss are linked by causeways

River Yealm essential information

Clubs
Yealm Yacht Club ☎01752 872232

Visitors' Berths
Island pontoons and moorings. Pre-book >13.5m/25T

Additional Berthing
None

Water Taxi
Local ferry/water taxi (limited hours)

Webcams
www.westernchannelobservatory.org.uk
www.bovisand.com

Water
HM pontoon, Newton Ferrers

Victuals
Newton Hill, Newton Ferrers

Nearest Large Supermarket
Plymouth (by bus)

pontoon below the harbour office and facilities block leaving the hammerhead clear (for vessels collecting water, stores or crew for max 20 minutes), or on the beach either side of the pontoon. It is also possible to land at Warren Point on the W shore opposite the main visitors' pontoon keeping the ferry landing clear. The ferry operates a limited service between Wide Slip, the pontoon and Warren Point.

In the villages it is possible to land in a tender about HW±2 at the village slip opposite Noss Creek, at the Yealm Yacht Club slip or at either of two pubs in Noss Creek. Facilities for launching and recovery from trailers are limited so it is best to seek HM advice. Vessels anchored near Cellar Bay should land on the beach and secure above the tide line as appropriate. From here it is a pleasant walk of about 40 minutes to Noss Mayo.

Shoreside

Toilets and showers are available (code lock) by the HM office at the landing pontoon, and at the yacht club when open which is 1M from the pontoon. Buses to Plymouth stop at the Harbour Office and village green.

Newton Ferrers is good for victualling with a small food store, chemist, café/deli and a post office/store which has a small range of deli, bakery and fresh produce. There is a pub, a bistro at the yacht club and two further pubs at Noss Mayo.

Looking across to Noss Mayo from Newton Hill

Yealm YC slipway

The quay at the Swan Inn, Noss Mayo

Plymouth Sound

Shag Stone in the E entrance should be given a wide berth

Plymouth Sound approaches

From offshore or a channel crossing, stay 1M off Eddystone Rocks (Lt.Ho. Fl(2)10s41m17M/Iso.R.10s28m8M) then shape a course towards the Sound. Beware Hand Deeps 3M NW of Eddystone, least charted depth 7m, marked by a WCM. Seas break here in bad weather. A yellow meteorological buoy (L4) is usually stationed 5M SSW of the breakwater.

Vessels approaching from E should keep 0.5M offshore in the vicinity of Hilsea Point and maintain this offing until clear of the Great Mew Stone at Wembury Bay.

From W, Rame Head can be passed fairly close to in favourable conditions but otherwise stay 1M off to avoid a patch of overfalls. The tide can be strong here so it is helpful to time the approach for a favourable E tidal stream which is from approximately HWP -0240. Aim for Draystone Ledge PHM unless heading for the River Yealm.

The Western Channel entrance is the deepest and easiest to navigate. From a waypoint in the vicinity of Draystone PHM (Fl(2)R.5s) steer NNE if bound for Plymouth leaving Knap SHM (Fl.G.5s) to starboard and keeping about 100m off the end of the breakwater (see photo p.80). Vessels intending to anchor in Cawsand Bay on the W side of Plymouth Sound can steer N from Draystone PHM and follow the coast into the bay. At night, the white sector of the sectored light at Maker Point (Fl(2)WRG.10s16m11/6M) leads between Draystone PHM and Knap SHM. Monitor VHF Ch14 by day or night to ascertain traffic movements.

Unless there is no commercial traffic, it is prudent for leisure craft to steer N from Draystone PHM on the white/red edge of the directional light until the next PHM (Queen's Ground Fl(2)R.10s) bears NE and then alter course towards it. This keeps mostly clear of the deep channel. Beyond the breakwater the IRPCS 'narrow channel' rules apply.

The Eastern Channel entrance is narrower and significantly more exposed in weather with a W component to the point where it is dangerous for small craft in gales. From a position due S of the beacon on the E end of the breakwater, steer N to leave East Tinker ECM (Q(3)10s) close to port before passing E of the beacon at least 100m off. Vessels approaching from the Yealm, or along the coast from E should stay well clear of the Great Mew Stone and aim for East Tinker ECM to avoid the rocks at Shag Stone (small unlit beacon). At night, remain in the white sector of the beacon (LFl.WR.10s9m8/6M) which clears both hazards. A further sectored light at Staddon Point (Oc.WRG.10s15m8/5M) provides an alternative approach W of Tinker shoal. Where the red sectors of the two directional lights meet, alter course to starboard temporarily to clear the breakwater and resume a N course once inside, leaving West Staddon WCM beacon (Q(9)15s6m3M) to starboard.

Keep clear of Bovisand Pier which is to starboard just past West Staddon WCM and is used by divers day and night. Sizeable fishing vessels use the Eastern Channel, but other commercial traffic generally uses the deeper Western Channel.

The beacon at the E end of the breakwater with Fort Bovisand right

8 RIVER YEALM

Cawsand Bay

W of the breakwater, Cawsand Bay has been used as a waiting anchorage by trading ships since their inception and is still used by coasters today, along with large numbers of yachts and small craft. Its situation in the lee of Rame Head gives good shelter from winds between SW and NW, but is subject to SW swell refracting around the headland.

Anchor anywhere clear of the moorings noting that the S shore is very steep-to. The holding is generally good on fine sand, where heavy chain is an advantage. In SW winds, a position along this shore just outside the charted danger zone may result in greater protection from swell. In W or NW winds, there is good shelter off the twin villages of Kingsand and Cawsand, N of the moorings. On summer weekends, the bay is packed with craft of all sizes and the NW side is usually quieter, but more exposed to swell unless the wind is NW or N.

Landing is easiest on the mostly shingle beach at Cawsand which has a shallower gradient. Keep clear of the area used by the ferry from Plymouth which is usually marked by a flag. It is also possible to land at Kingsand Beach although this is steeper. While this does not usually present a problem when landing, it can make for an interesting spectacle when trying to launch into the swell. There is a small slipway at Cawsand where launching and recovery may be possible. Kingsand has a small store and a couple of pubs.

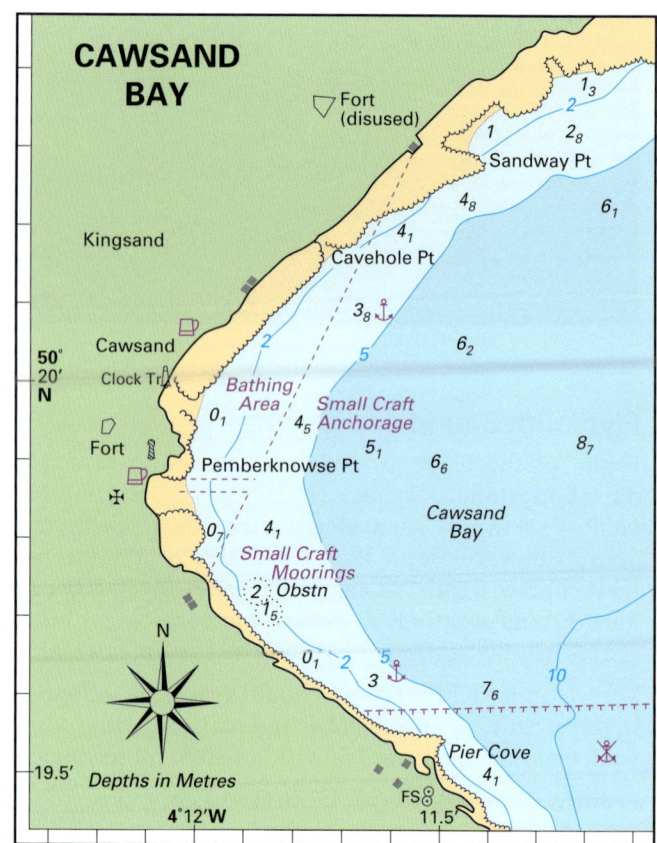

The Cawsand Bay anchorage gets very busy in summer, but quiet in late season

Cawsand Bay

Cawsand Beach where the ferry from Plymouth lands

Polhawn Cove

This is a very good anchorage in E and NE winds in the lee of Rame Head with added protection from swell provided by Queener Point just S. Enter from between SW and NW giving a diving area (HMS *Scylla*) marked by a PHM a wide berth, and sound in to a suitable depth off the beach. The holding is good and landing can be made on the beach. The cove has become increasingly popular with local small craft since a seagrass bed in Jennycliff Bay was established but it is rare for there not to be sufficient space. Remaining overnight should not present a problem since there is clear water through which to exit if conditions change. Anchoring also appears feasible along the coast in NE winds, as far as the charted danger area at Tregantle Fort.

Polhawn Cove W of Rame Head

A tricky but delightful small anchorage between Rame Head and Queener Point

9 PLYMOUTH
THE CATTEWATER & HAMOAZE

Approaching Plymouth

Harbour Master's Office
VHF 14 'Longroom' and 'Cattewater Harbour'
KHM Longroom House, RM Stonehouse, Plymouth PL1 3RT
☎ 01752 836953
Cattewater HM 2 The Barbican, Plymouth PL1 2LR
☎ 01752 665934

The city of Plymouth is steeped in maritime history with excellent road and rail connections and numerous attractions ashore. A major yachting centre, there are five large marinas and four smaller ones, together with multiple other mooring options. It is also home to HM Naval Base at Devonport which is one of the largest in Western Europe. A sizeable marine trades sector caters for repairs to craft of all kinds. The university has become a leading institution for maritime and climate studies.

Landmarks

Refer to the previous chapter for landmarks in the approaches. Within the Sound, once clear of the breakwater in the Western Channel, Drake's Island with a signal station is ahead with Smeaton's Tower (a former Eddystone lighthouse) in a green area beyond. Mountbatten breakwater is in the NE corner and three conspicuous blocks of flats are inland NW.

Main hazards

As with most busy ports the main channels are clear with any dangers marked by buoys or beacons, so the major hazard is traffic, especially naval. A moving prohibited zone is enforced 250m ahead and 100m abeam and astern of all naval vessels *and* any associated auxiliary/civilian craft such as tugs, police launches and crew transfer vessels (jolly boats). In practice, this means it is not advisable for leisure craft to transit the channel between Drakes Island and the Plymouth shore when any large naval vessel is entering or leaving port. Such vessels are often anchored in the area just N of the breakwater.

Smeaton's Tower and the war memorials on Plymouth Hoe

In the Hamoaze, vessels are not allowed to navigate within 50m of *any* naval installation or operation. The entire area (including vessel movements in the Sound) is monitored with high resolution cameras by a military appointed HM and patrolled continuously by a combination of MOD Police launches and small fast military craft. Requests from the HM or these vessels to follow a particular course of action are always polite and seamanlike. They are also compulsory, backed by the use of armed force if necessary. Do not deviate from their instructions under any circumstances as to do so may be deemed a security risk. Note the entire harbour can be locked down if necessary.

Commercial vessels including large ferries operate day and night from Millbay Docks, immediately N of Drakes Island, and the Cattewater. A sizeable fishing fleet operates from within Sutton Harbour and from Victoria Dock, at the seaward end of the conspicuous fuel depot in the Cattewater.

There are numerous deep holes in the channel between The Bridge (see below) and the ferry slipway at Edgecumbe, 0.5M N. Strong eddies and tide rips are created, sufficient to temporarily overwhelm some autopilots so hand steering is advised. The Bridge is the only navigable channel between Drake's Island and the Cornish shore.

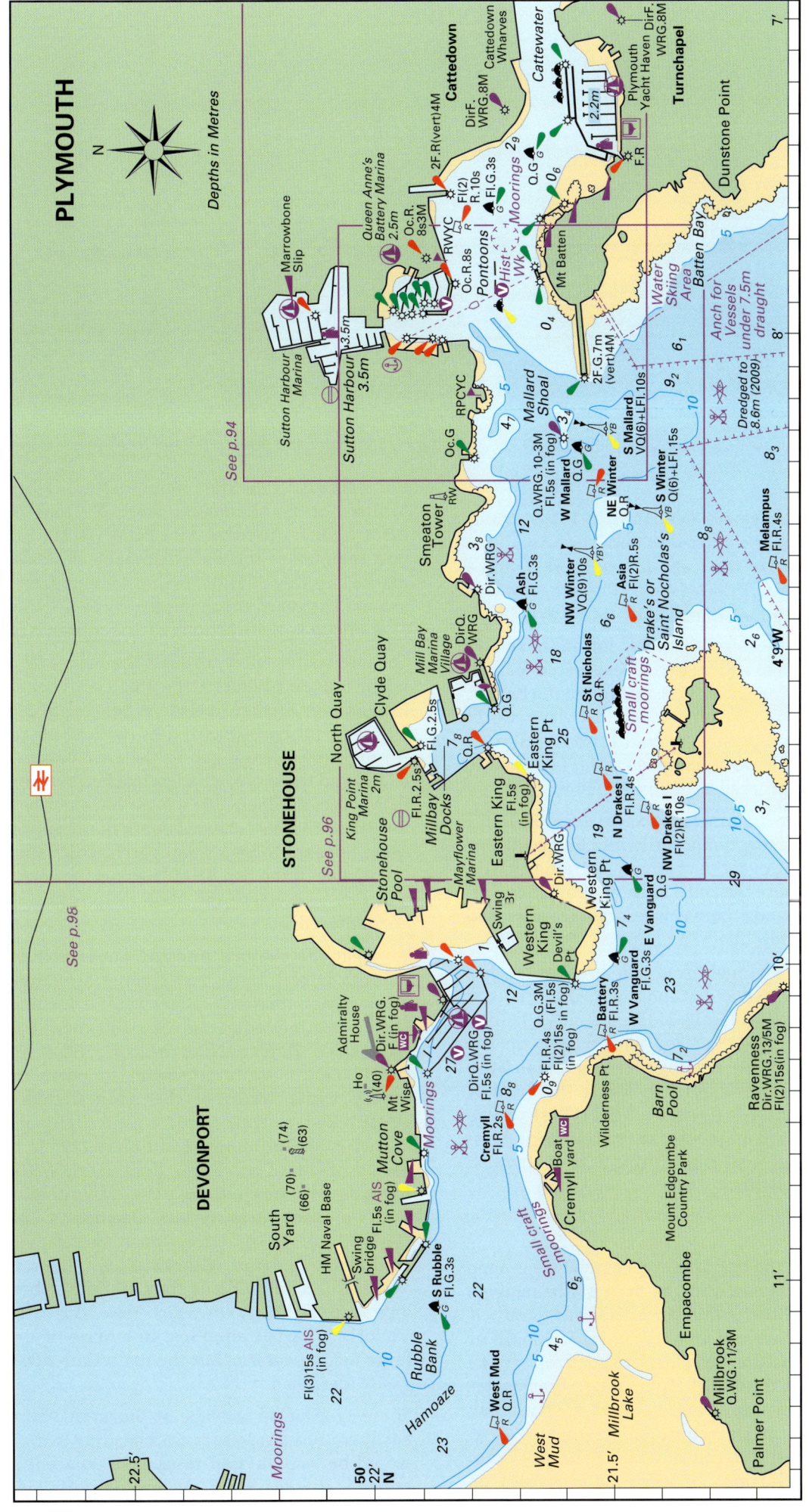

9 PLYMOUTH

The heart of Plymouth with ferry pontoons left, Queen Anne's Battery Marina right and Sutton Harbour lock left of centre

Approaches

The outer approaches are described in the previous chapter. There are two entrances to the city area - the main deep channel at the E end (Smeaton Pass) and a narrow channel W of Drakes Island (The Bridge) which is suitable for yachts and small craft except at LWS.

From the main Western Channel entrance, vessels which do not need to adhere to the deep water channel can steer 035° for Smeaton Pass or 015° for The Bridge. To avoid commercial traffic using the deep water channel, stay W of Queens Ground PHM (Fl(2)R.10s) then steer 045° to leave Melampus PHM (Fl.R.4s) close to starboard and proceed as in 'Entry' below.

From the Eastern Channel entrance steer 000° for Smeaton Pass, moving temporarily into Jennycliff Bay to starboard in the event of commercial traffic, or 315° for The Bridge. There is a small anchorage at Jennycliff, sheltered in E winds, between a large seagrass bed (marked with yellow buoys) and a SHM ('Fylrix').

The deep water channel from the breakwater has directional lights visible day and night. The first is at Withyhedge (Dir.WRG.13m13/5M) on about 071° then Mallard (Q.WRG.10/3M) paired with a light on the shore (Oc.G.1.3s11m3M) forming a leading line on 349°. All the main lights show quick yellow in the event of power failure and in fog a white light (Fl.5s) can be shown from Mallard on request to the HM. The lateral buoys are all lit but some can be difficult to distinguish against the shore lights.

Entry

The E entrance to the city area at Smeaton Pass is deep but the buoyage is confusing as most of the dangers it marks are of little significance to leisure craft. If heading for the Barbican area in central Plymouth or the Cattewater, the simplest plan is to just keep several boat lengths from the end of Mountbatten breakwater (2F.G.7m4M) then steer NNE towards a wavebreak with a forest of masts behind before turning N at the entrance to the Barbican channel or 100° into the Cattewater skirting the large mooring area on the starboard side after Mountbatten. If heading for Millbay or the Hamoaze, steer N from Melampus PHM (Fl.R.4s) to leave Asia PHM (Fl(2)R.5s) close to port then follow the main channel N of Drakes Island, marked by three PHMs, before looping first S then N around Vanguard shoal, marked by two SHMs. Beware of traffic in both directions as this corner is blind.

The alternative entry through The Bridge W of Drakes Island is a useful shortcut for small craft heading to the Hamoaze or further upriver. A bearing of 327° on the leftmost of three blocks of flats (with a blue roof) leads through the narrow gap in the reef between Drakes Island and the shore, which is marked by two PHM and SHM beacons. Their tide gauges have not been visible for years. The least charted depth in the gap is 1.3m but there appears to be a small patch which just dries at LAT between the two SHM beacons. Beware of eddies and tide rips where the main deep water channel is encountered.

At night the channel into the Cattewater is marked by both lateral buoys and leading/directional lights. From Mountbatten breakwater leading lights (both FBu(intens)) lead 026°30' then Oc.R.8s on 049° until Fishers Nose beacon Fl(3)R.10s4M) on the Plymouth shore is abeam to port. Then steer in the white sector of the main Cattedown light (Dir.F.WRG) on 102° until a 2F.R light at Victoria Wharf is abeam to port and finally 129° in the white sector of the Turnchapel light (Dir.F.WRG.49m8M) towards the marina on the Mountbatten shore with a back transit on Deadman's Bay PHM (Fl(2)R.10s). In practice, most vessels can follow the lateral buoyage without issue. The main lights are useful as a guide as they stand out better from any shore lighting. On which note, the 2F.R. light at Victoria Wharf is often lost in a blaze of lights from large fishing vessels, but the main Cattedown light is easily identified.

There is a lot of buoyage at Smeaton Pass which is easily confused so leisure craft heading to the Hamoaze would be well advised to use the adjacent Asia Pass which is simpler. Steer 000° from the Melampus PHM

Sutton Lock with Sutton Harbour beyond

(Fl.R.4s) until in the white sector of the Millbay light (Dir.Q.WRG.12m13/8M) on 325°. Then turn W on 270° on the light at Western King (Dir.WRG.14m13/5M) for a short distance followed by 225° on Ravenness light (Dir.WRG.13/5M) and finally Mount Wise (Dir.WRG.7m13/5M) on 343° towards Mayflower Marina. On exit it is easier to follow the lateral buoyage until abeam the Ravenness light then steer 048°30' on Millbay (Dir.Q.WRG.12m13/8M), 090° on Mallard (Q.W) for approximately 200m as far as St Nicholas PHM and finally 115° to Asia PHM (Fl(2)R.5s).

The Bridge is simpler at first glance, with just two sets of lateral beacons. From seaward, No.1 (Q.G), No.2 (Q.R), No.3 (Fl(3)G.10s) and No.4 (Fl(4)R.10s) after which a course of 315° will intersect the white sector of the Mount Wise light (Dir.WRG.7m13/5M) on 343°. The eddies and tide rips mentioned above present an additional challenge which some vessels may prefer to avoid at night.

Barbican

Barbican is right in the city centre. There are two marinas with limited space for visitors. The first is Queen Anne's Battery Marina (MDL), known as QAB, to starboard opposite the local ferry and trip boat pontoon, with an entrance at the end of a wave break. Turn sharp to starboard around the end of the wavebreak and there are a few spaces on the linear pontoon to starboard. The second is Sutton Harbour (Indep) occupying the main part of a locked basin at the end of the short channel.

The lock operates day and night. Proceed straight ahead past the fuel berth on leaving the lock, ignoring two small areas of pontoons to port and a further one to starboard by the fish quay. Berths may be available for visitors but there are none dedicated, so booking must be made in advance before transiting the lock.

The N segment of the ferry/trip boat pontoon has short stay berths alongside and there is a landing pontoon behind the S end for tenders and small craft, with steps straight into the heart of historic Plymouth. Keep a sharp lookout for other traffic when leaving this berth and proceed slowly.

QAB Marina entrance with fuel berth front left

The visitors' berths at QAB

Landing pontoon for tenders right next to the Barbican

9 PLYMOUTH

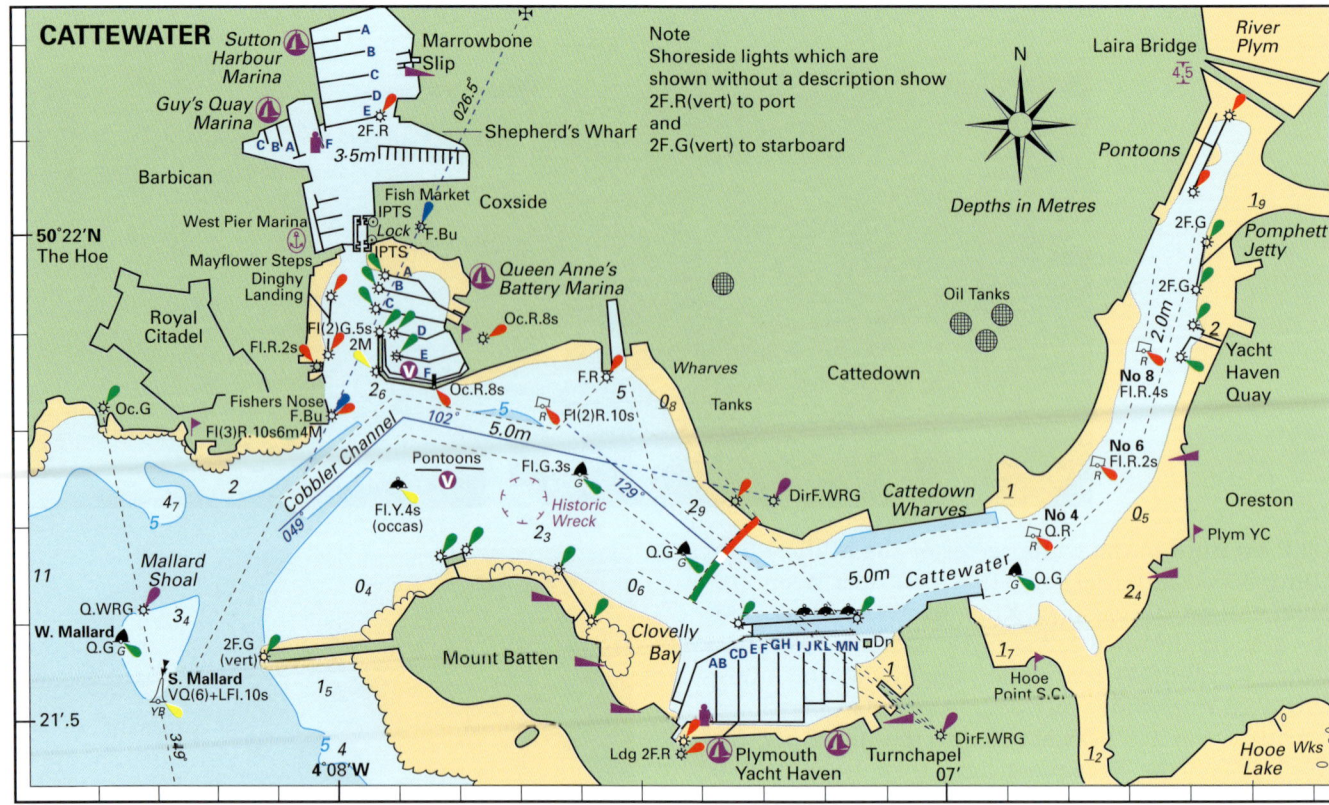

Cattewater

The Cattewater is the navigable part of the River Plym. It is mostly commercial, with its own HM, but has some good facilities for leisure craft. Moorings extend from the area immediately inside Mountbatten breakwater around the headland and all the way to Plymouth Yacht Haven on the S shore. Some moorings in this area are for visitors, administered either by the HM or the Royal Western Yacht Club, based at QAB Marina. The HM has also installed two large pontoons for visitors on the channel side of the moorings which are capable of taking substantial craft, but note they are particularly exposed to SW winds. On the shore behind the moorings is a large water sports centre at Mountbatten with its own jetty and sizeable slipways. A passenger ferry links Mountbatten and Barbican with a frequent service until late evening. Just upstream of the first PHM is Victoria Dock which is used by coasters on one side and large fishing vessels on the other. When the coasters arrive or depart, it is sometimes necessary for the fishing vessels to move and stand off temporarily, so keep to the edge of the moorings.

Beyond Mountbatten is Plymouth Yacht Haven (Yacht Havens) at Turnchapel where some large support vessels such as tugs and rescue craft are also moored. There are no longer dedicated visitors' berths but space is often available (see facilities). The entrance is at the end of two long linear pontoons, rounding the inner one and leaving a large concrete dolphin to port. Arrange berthing in advance. Just upstream is a wharf catering for larger craft up to about 50m LOA and 5m draught.

The river continues E then NE with commercial docks to port and a line of trot moorings for local boats off Plymstock to starboard, between which the channel is dredged to 2m. Above here is a dry stack facility

HM visitors' pontoons in the Cattewater and moorings beyond

Plymouth Yacht Haven at Turnchapel

and waiting pontoons for motor boats, operated by Plymouth Yacht Haven. The pontoons can be used as an overflow for the main marina although the immediate vicinity is somewhat industrial. A commercial jetty for aggregates is above the dry stack opposite the last commercial wharf, beyond which is a private marina and boatyard with an extensive laying up area. A road bridge restricts further access but the area beyond it is used by sailing dinghies and water skiers when the tide is in.

The dry stack facility for motor vessels at Plymstock

The landing slip at Turnchapel. It is quicker by dinghy from the E end of the marina

Laira Bridge is the limit of navigation for most craft

9 PLYMOUTH

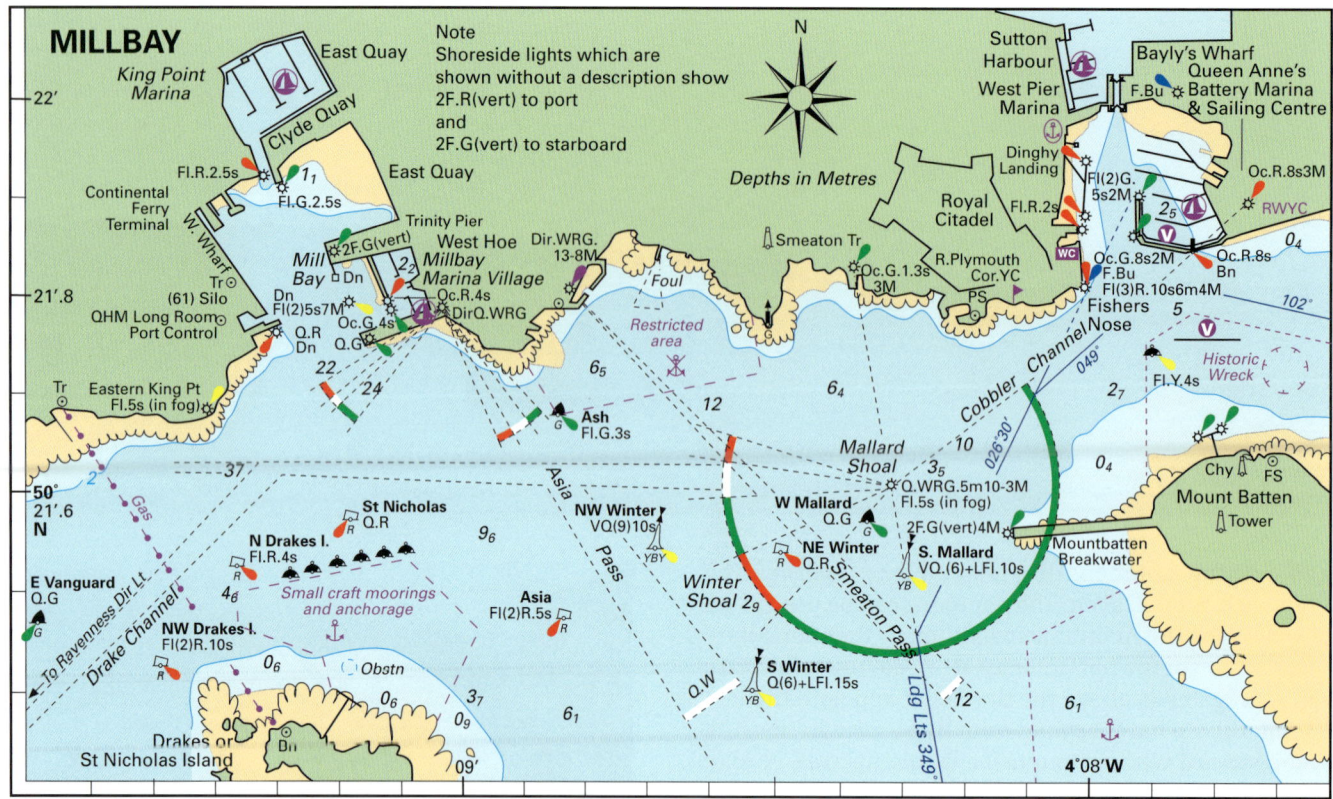

Central waterfront

For years there was a traditional anchorage off Plymouth Hoe below Smeaton's Tower, but this area is now protected and is no longer available. There are several moorings immediately N of Drakes Island which can be used by visitors although there is considerable wash from passing traffic. Millbay Dock is opposite, used by large ferries, and the IPTS signals must be followed if heading for the new King Point Marina (Indep) in a former locked basin, where visitors' berths may be available. Opposite the ferry berth is a small private marina with no visitors' berths.

Looking E over Cremyll Narrows towards Drakes Island *Jane Russell*

Barn Pool is an attractive anchorage but very steep-to and the S half is foul ground

Central waterfront

Millbay docks with the entrance to King Point Marina far right

The Bridge joins the main channel just past Drakes Island and there is an anchorage at Barn Pool to port, which can be used with care. The seabed is very steep-to, but at neaps it is possible to tuck well in out of any tide with good shelter from winds between SW and NW. Avoid a charted obstruction (7.2m) and wreck (8.8m) and note that foul patches are found, especially in the S half. A tripping line is a sensible precaution. Land on the beach where there is a ruined slipway.

Entrance to King Point Marina

King Point Marina

9 PLYMOUTH

Hamoaze

Above Barn Pool, stick to the main channel as Stonehouse Pool comes abeam to starboard, dominated by the large Mayflower Marina (Transeurope) with plenty of space for visitors. A small dock at Royal William Yard where the fortified wall ends is private, but customers of their retail and hospitality outlets can land at the pontoons within in tenders/RIBs. There are also several slipways in Stonehouse Pool but keep clear of the ferry berth. A small boatyard is located adjacent to the marina accessed behind the upstream end of the pontoons.

The river turns briefly W at the marina, then N. The Naval Base comprises the entirety of the Plymouth shore above the boatyard and one commercial slipway, to just below the bridges at Saltash and all other vessels must keep at least 50m off. In particular, beware of being swept towards the dock inside South Rubble SHM (Fl.G.3s) by the flood tide.

On the Cornwall shore opposite, there is a good anchorage clear of the moorings off Cremyll, near the entrance to Millbrook Lake. Visitors can sometimes use a mooring here via the marina at Torpoint which owns them. The same company also owns a drying marina at Southdown just inside Millbrook Lake where space may be available. Three small orange buoys (similar to fishing floats) mark the deepest water with access to the marina approximately HW±2 for moderate draught vessels. Further in there is a boatyard specialising in multihulls. The creek dries in excess of 3m above the marina but a slipway at Millbrook village can be reached by tender near HW.

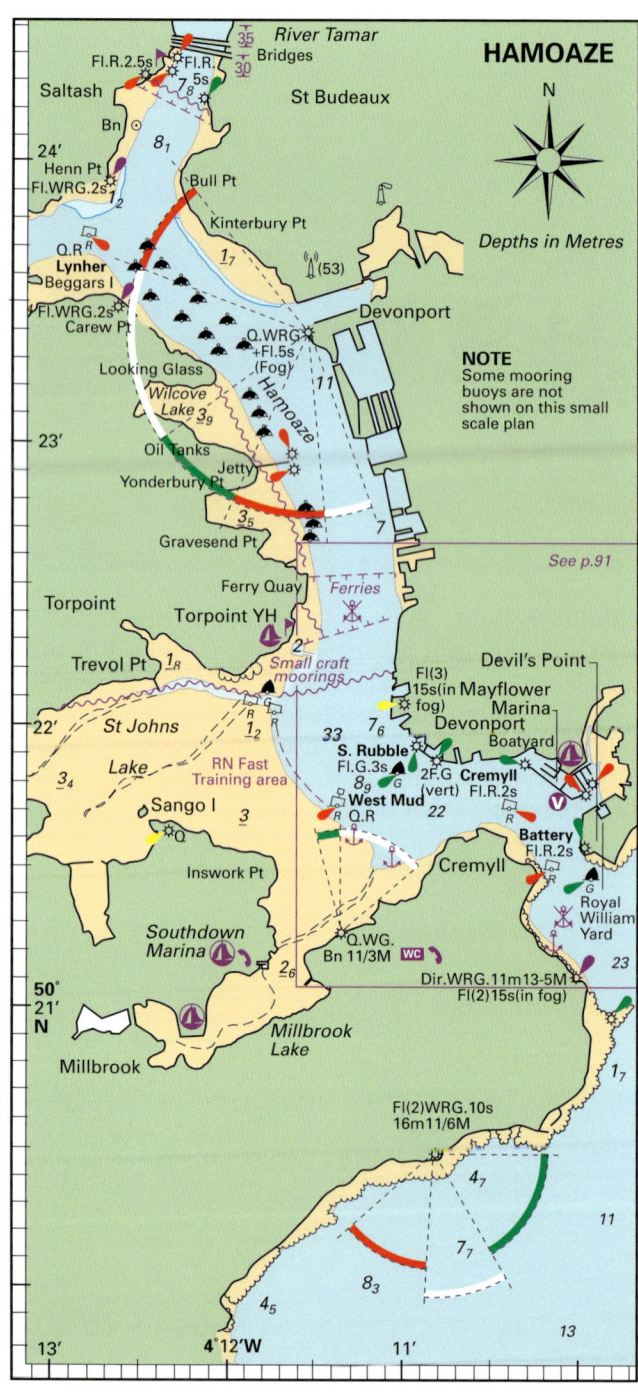

Southdown Marina 'channel marker'

Southdown Marina

98 • West Country Pilot

Hamoaze

HM Naval Base at Devonport

Torpoint ferries have right of way

US Navy cable laying ship *Zeus*

The German warship *Oldenburg* heads out on a NATO exercise

Continuing N, West Mud PHM (Q.R) marks an extensive bank which is very steep-to, and four unlit yellow buoys mark the centre of a training area used by the MOD for fast craft manoeuvres. Just above the last yellow buoy a narrow buoyed channel leads off to port. This ultimately leads to a MOD facility with restricted access, but between the third and fourth pairs of lateral marks a drying creek leads to a sizeable laying up yard and repair facility, under the same ownership as the marinas mentioned above. Finally, there is a small marina at Torpoint situated in an old ballast pound, making it literally bombproof. Visitors' space is sometimes available, along with swinging moorings and alongside quay berths, the latter of which dry out.

Shoreside

All the marinas and most of the yacht clubs have showers and toilets. The HM has a toilet and shower facility on Commercial Wharf, adjacent to the Barbican Steps landing pontoon. This is the nearest to the island pontoons and moorings. The moorings off Cremyll are part of the marina group on that side of the channel and their facilities can be used. There are no public facilities for those at anchor, so the best plan is a short stop at one of the marinas. There are chandleries at QAB, Mayflower and Plymouth Yacht Haven marinas.

Plymouth has a large pedestrian shopping area a short walk from the Barbican Steps, including supermarkets, and a large covered market. Eating options are varied and mostly concentrated around the Barbican. On the Turnchapel shore (Plymouth Yacht Haven), there is a convenience store at Hooe (10 min walk) or a small shopping precinct with butcher, chemist and food store at Plymstock (10 min bus trip). However, since the Mountbatten ferry runs until late in the summer, it is as easy to reach Plymouth. There are several places to eat at Turnchapel and Mountbatten.

Torpoint Marina

9 PLYMOUTH

King Point Marina is within walking distance of the city centre but Mayflower Marina is further away and best reached by bus or taxi, especially if carrying shopping or kit. There are several restaurants and retail outlets at Royal William Yard just opposite Mayflower Marina. On the Cornwall side of the Tamar, the nearest shops are at Torpoint where there is a food store.

The city has excellent road, rail and bus connections making it ideal for crew changes. All trains to Cornwall stop at Plymouth and Dartmoor is within easy reach by bus. Local ferries link Plymouth with Mountbatten, Cawsand and Edgecumbe, and there is a cross channel ferry to France and Spain.

Plymouth is home to the National Marine Aquarium

Local attractions

The many and varied attractions and places to visit are too numerous to list but chief among them is the National Marine Aquarium (by Sutton Harbour) and other notable places include the Barbican and Citadel, the old lighthouse on the Hoe, Royal William Yard and historic houses at Saltram, Antony and Mount Edgecumbe, the latter two on the Cornwall side. For entertainment there are two cinema complexes and a theatre.

Plymouth essential information

Clubs
Royal Plymouth Corinthian Yacht Club ☎07920 233621
Royal Western Yacht Club of England ☎01752 660077
Plym Yacht Club ☎01752 404991
Torpoint Mosquito Sailing Club ☎01752 812508

Local Information
The Barbican, Plymouth

Visitors' Berths
Island pontoons & moorings at Cattewater Entrance
Short stay pontoon at Mayflower Steps

Additional Berthing
Plymouth Yacht Haven (Yacht Havens) VHF 80
☎01752 404231
Queen Anne's Battery Marina (MDL) VHF 80
☎01752 671142
Sutton Harbour Marina (Indep) VHF 12 (Lock)
☎01752 204702
King Point Marina (Indep) VHF 80 ☎01752 424297
Mayflower Marina (Transeurope) VHF 80
☎01752 556633

Webcams
www.westwardshippingnews.com

Water
At marinas

Fuel
At marinas (except King Point)

Gas
From chandlers at all marinas

Chandlery
At all marinas (except King Point)
Gael Force, Fish Dock, Sutton Harbour

Victuals
Numerous shops in pedestrian precinct, Plymouth
Small shopping parade at Plymstock

Nearest Large Supermarket
N end of pedestrian precinct

Laundry
Union Street & Notte Street, Plymouth

Repairs
Mountbatten Boatshed, Turnchapel
Blagdons, adjacent to Mayflower Marina
Mashfords, Cremyll (large craft)
Voyager, Southdown
Huggins Bros, Torpoint

Engineers
Elite Marine Services, Turnchapel
Marine Engineering Looe, Plymouth

Riggers
Allspars, QAB; Hemisphere, Turnchapel; Eurospars, Mayflower

Electronics
PR Systems, Mayflower Marina; Marine Electronics Plymouth, Turnchapel

Sailmakers
Ullman; Swift, Plympton; Armada, Plymstock; Highwater, Plymouth; Watts, Torpoint; Westaway, Ivybridge (via marinas)

Car Hire
Numerous, including all major brands in city centre.

Transport
Mainline rail station with national and local services.
Buses to all local areas including Dartmoor.

Plymouth

Narrow streets leading down to the harbour

Smeaton's Tower on the Hoe

Defence of the Realm

For as long as would be invaders have threatened, ships have set out from Plymouth to counter them, the naval dockyard being established in 1512 to protect the fleet based in Sutton Pool. As part of this, defences on St Nicholas Island (now Drake's Island) were also strengthened.

Sir Francis Drake put to sea at the head of the fleet in 1588 to defeat the Spanish Armada, allegedly holding off long enough to complete a game of bowls. The first beacon lit to signal the victory was on St Michael's Mount (see chapter 18).

The first naval dockyard on the Devonport site opened in 1690 and expanded considerably during the 18th century (although it was only named Devonport from 1824). Heavy bombing occurred in WWII including an intense period of 59 raids known as the Plymouth Blitz. Much of the city was destroyed and has been rebuilt. Fast forward to the present day, and Plymouth is the largest operational naval base in Western Europe, serving not only the Royal Navy but vessels from other NATO member countries on a regular basis. Occasional open days are held which are well worth it if you happen to be in port.

Plymouth is also home to the Royal Marine Commandos. Several yachts anchored at Dandy Hole (including the author) were rudely awoken by gunfire before dawn one morning as a group of landing craft screamed through on a training exercise. There is never a dull moment in Plymouth.

Evening race fleet leaving Cobbler Channel into Plymouth Sound

Jane Russell

10 RIVER TAMAR
INCLUDING RIVER LYNHER

The point where the River Lynher branches off at Wearde Quay (far left), with the bridges at Saltash in the distance

Once past Plymouth, the Tamar and its main tributaries provide a quieter place to explore and some good spots in which to take shelter if the weather interferes with a passage. The Tamar itself is navigable for some distance with craft drawing up to 2m able to reach Calstock, about 8M inland. The largest town is Saltash, on the Cornwall side of the famous Tamar road and rail bridges.

Landmarks

It is those bridges which dominate in an otherwise rural landscape. With clearances above MHWS of 30m (rail) and 35m (road), the support towers are visible when passing the naval dockyard heading upstream and soon after passing Cargreen heading downstream. A low rail bridge spans the River Tavy near to its mouth and an impressive railway viaduct crosses the Tamar at Calstock. There are smaller railway viaducts crossing the rivers Lynher and Tiddy near St Germans.

Main hazards

Chain ferries (usually three) cross the river above Torpoint and have priority. Other craft should pass a reasonable distance astern. This can sometimes involve waiting for a suitable gap whilst one ferry has passed and the others are still loading or unloading. At the lower end of this area, there are still military restrictions to be observed, including a number of large unlit mooring buoys on both sides of the river between Torpoint and Saltash, off the mouth of the Lynher and a refuelling jetty just above the chain ferries off Yonderbury Point.

Unattended and unlit vessels may be encountered at anchor in the River Lynher at Dandy Hole. Above Saltash, the Tamar is shallow, albeit with many deeper pools, and the Tavy dries completely. A lot of debris may be encountered during spring tides in the upper reaches, especially in the Tamar.

Fallen trees make the upper reaches a challenge

Plenty of detritus on springs

102 • West Country Pilot

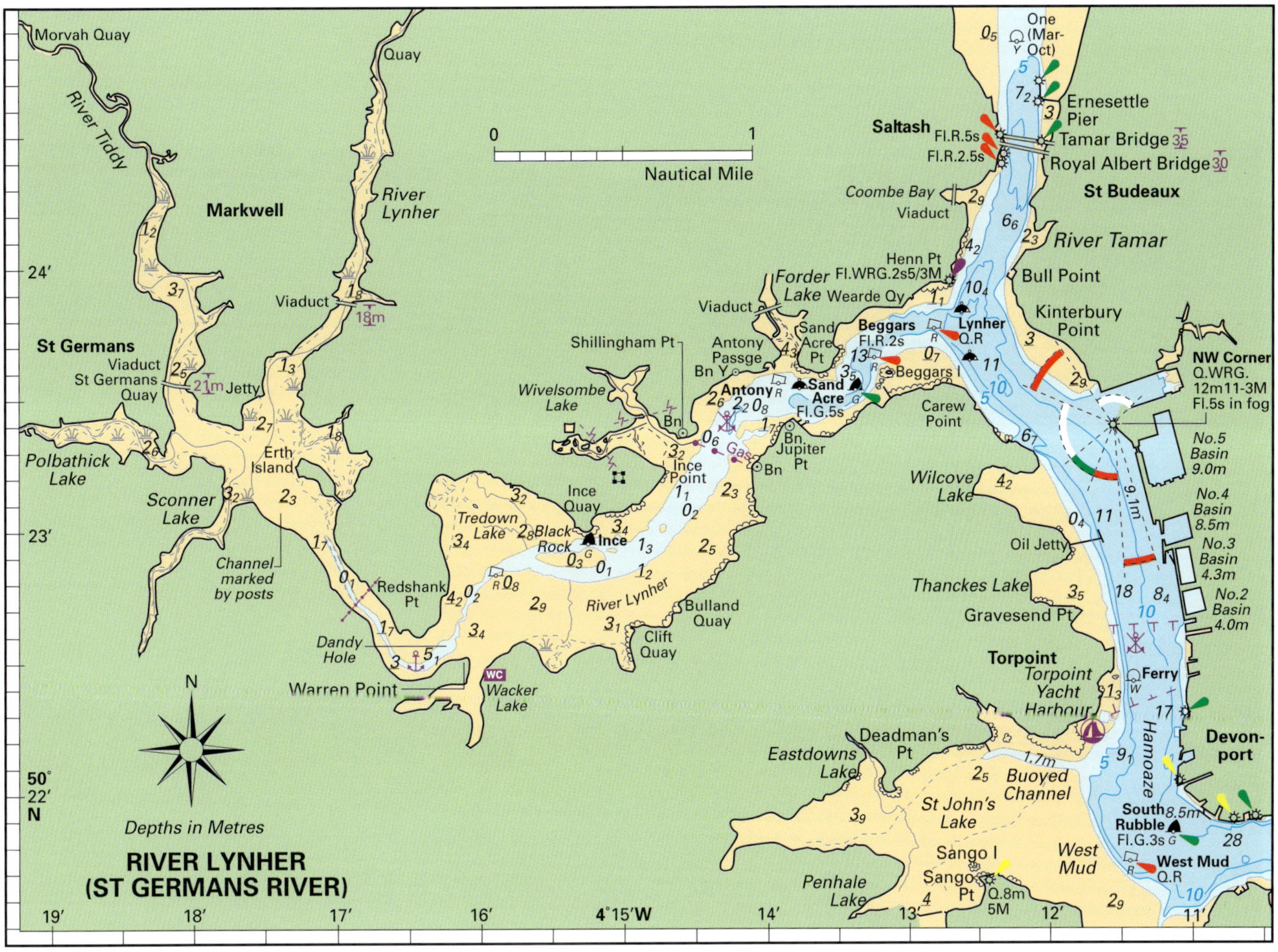

River Lynher

Approaches & entry

The approaches are described in the previous two chapters, and the channel past the naval base and ferries is obvious. At night, there are additional sectored lights covering the deep water channel at NW Corner (Q.WRG.12m.11/3M) and Henn Point (Fl.WRG.2s.5/3M). Outbound, there are sectored lights at Carew Point (Fl.WRG.2s.5m.5/4M) and Millbrook (Q.WG.11m.11/3M). In practice, there is sufficient illumination from the shore to identify the channel. Above the chain ferries, keep clear of the military refuelling jetty which is being rebuilt and extended.

MOD refuelling jetty N of Torpoint

River Lynher

The Lynher (or St Germans River) branches off W approximately 1M above the fuel jetty and is entered between the Lynher PHM (Q.R) and a small group of private trot moorings off Wearde Quay.

There are numerous unlit mooring buoys in the approaches which are in frequent use by the naval base, so the restrictions mentioned previously apply if any naval ships or support vessels are in attendance. Numerous drying creeks and inlets ('lakes') are a haven for wildlife, but only suitable for tenders.

Sand Acre Bay just upstream of the Wearde Quay moorings provides a comfortable anchorage in N or NW winds (and W for vessels which can take the ground). There are, however, numerous foul patches and a few wrecks so a tripping line is advisable. Continue SW leaving Beggar Island PHM to port and Sand Acre Point SHM to starboard before turning W. The pontoons and moorings on the S side are part of a naval training facility and access is restricted. Continue W, leaving a small naval training ship (HMS *Brecon*) at least 50m to port, towards Antony PHM which is unlit and difficult to spot, but the adjacent line of moorings is in deep water. This buoy can be ignored above half-tide by all but deep draught vessels. Upstream of the moorings, or after heading W from HMS *Brecon*, a yellow beacon on each shore marks a power cable and the start of a no anchoring zone.

10 RIVER TAMAR

Sand Acre Bay

River Lynher with HMS *Brecon* centre

Head SW from here for approximately 0.5M passing a beacon just E of Wivelscombe Lake marking a gas pipeline. After the beacon, it is possible to anchor again with depths up to 3m as far as Ince Castle, which is conspicuous on the bank. This part of the river is quite open so more suited to light winds, although Ince Point (below the castle) provides some protection from the NW.

The river now becomes very shallow and most craft will need to wait until half-tide to proceed. The deepest water is initially towards the Ince Castle shore where there is an unlit SHM (Ince) with a couple of adjacent moorings and a private slipway. Leave the buoy to starboard and aim for a small PHM approximately 0.5M distant bearing just S of W. This buoy is on the edge of a mud bank so leave it a boat length or so to port and turn slowly onto a bearing of about 220°, keeping a careful eye on the depth, until inside the tree covered Warren Point on the port side. There is a deep pool here, close under the trees at Dandy Hole, with good holding and shelter between SE and SW. The river turns NW here and virtually dries, but there is just enough water at neaps for shoal draught craft to anchor and stay afloat as far as the power lines 0.3M further on.

Dandy Hole

Looking upstream from Dandy Hole

The junction of the rivers Lynher (ahead) and Tiddy (left)

ST GERMANS

The winding channel above the power lines is marked by lateral beacons and a few small buoys, and it is best to seek advice from the sailing club or boatyards if planning to head upstream in keeled vessels. The channel heads initially NW and divides at a PHM (*see photo above*) which must be left to *starboard* if heading for St Germans as the Lynher heads N, marked by posts to a boatyard beyond a railway viaduct. It can be explored almost to Notter Bridge by tender.

The river Tiddy meanders W towards the quay at St Germans, now marked by small lateral buoys. It is sometimes possible to moor alongside the quay by arrangement with the sailing club or boatyard. Otherwise, land at the sailing club pontoon at the start of three rows of trot moorings, or a slipway just upstream of the trots. The Tiddy continues under the conspicuous viaduct as far as Tideford, which can potentially be reached by tender and even small day craft. There may be debris after flooding, so seek local advice beforehand. Polbathic Lake leads S from St Germans Quay, marked by posts, to a small boatyard and on to the village of Polbathic. Moderate draught vessels up to about 10m LOA can reach the yard with care (check with the yard) and tenders can reach the village near HW.

River Lynher lateral mark

Quay SC slipway

The railway viaduct at St Germans

Coombe Bay viaduct below Saltash

SALTASH

Back in the Tamar, the main naval port area finishes above a small dock at Bull Point, and moorings line both sides of the channel. They are owned by sailing clubs on each bank and one may occasionally be available via the clubs for visiting craft. There are slipways on both sides immediately below the impressive railway bridge. The sailing club at Saltash has a landing pontoon and the one on the Plymouth side has a further slipway. The tide runs very fast in this stretch, and can exceed 5kn in some conditions. There is sufficient room for two vessels to pass each other on either side of the central pier of the railway bridge although the majority of traffic transits W of it.

Above the bridges, the landscape almost immediately becomes rural and the sound of wildlife can again be heard. To starboard is another military facility and jetty, which other vessels must keep at least 50m away from. Opposite on the Saltash shore is Jubilee Pontoon with a few visitors' spaces. A seasonal passenger ferry operates from here to Royal William Yard in Plymouth. The river then widens to about 0.75M with a central channel of about 0.25M, marked by small SHM buoys, of which the first two are lit. Following the removal of a number of large commercial moorings, in light winds it is now possible to anchor anywhere in this stretch, clear of the local moorings. Note there are several wrecks along the channel edge, and dinghy racing takes place on some days between two yellow buoys adjacent to the moorings.

Saltash SC pontoon

The old ferry slipway below the Tamar bridge

Tamar River SC pontoon and slip

River Tavy, Cargreen & Weir Quay

Tamar bridges from N

River Tavy entrance

River Tavy, Cargreen & Weir Quay

Just after the third SHM, a drying patch in mid-channel (avoidable by aiming straight for the fourth SHM) marks the entrance of the Tavy which also dries. Opposite here, there is a neap tide anchorage in the lee of Neal Point which has good holding and is sheltered from NW winds. The Tavy heads ENE towards two yellow buoys giving advanced warning of a power line 9.1m above MHWS and a rail bridge 7.2m above MHWS. Combined with the rise of tide required, these effectively bar access to masted craft and all but small motor vessels with minimal air draught (there being as little as 1.7m clearance under the railway bridge at MHWS). Such craft can continue favouring the starboard bank after the bridge and passing under another (higher) power line before heading roughly N towards Bere Ferrers. A gutway leading to the village quay is occasionally marked by a post or a withy, but if this is missing simply aim straight up the line of the quay wall, noting the mud bank upstream of the gutway only just covers.

Neal Point anchorage

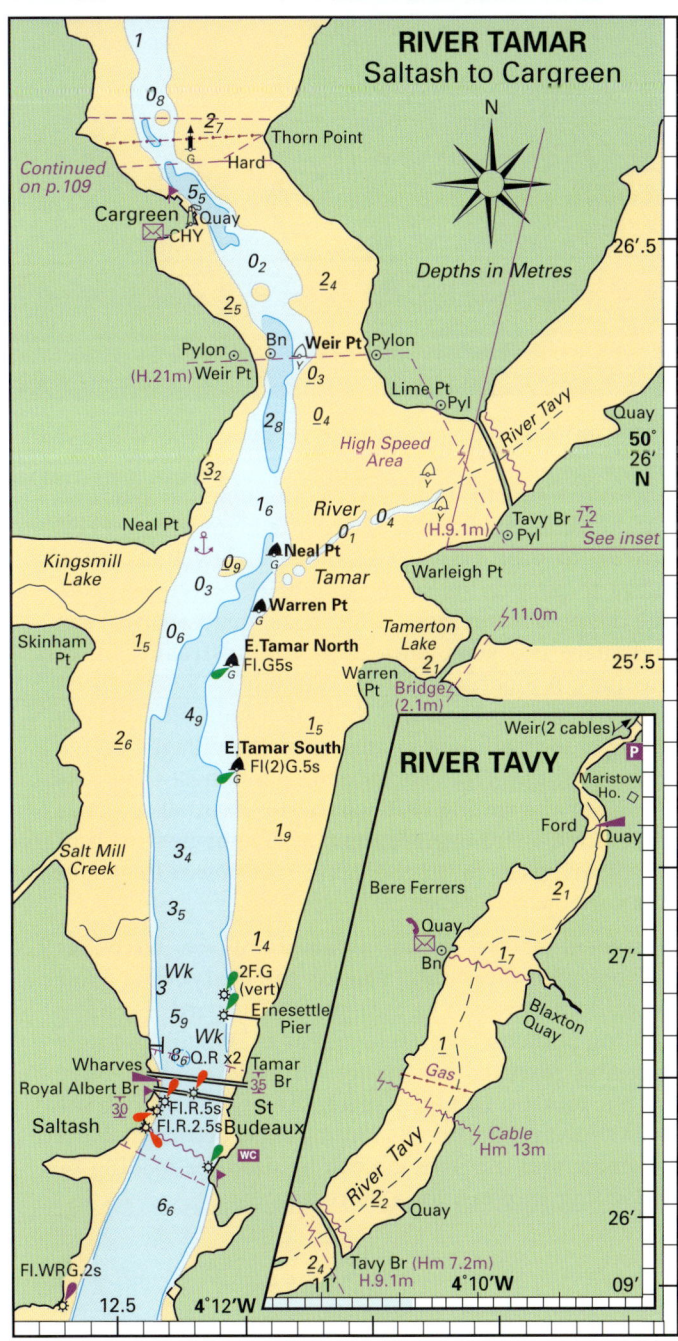

The moorings off Cargreen

The SHM marking a mud bank off Cargreen can be hard to spot

Above the fourth Tamar SHM, the channel narrows and becomes shallow in places. Steer towards a PHM beacon to pass between it and a yellow buoy, then curve to port to follow the line of the moorings NW. The deepest water runs close to the quay at Cargreen and there is a steep slipway at the upstream end of the quay. A mooring may occasionally be available via the sailing club here and there is a half-tide slipway at the club itself, just upstream of the village. Keep a look out for a SHM beacon hidden amongst the boats abeam of the sailing club where the channel resumes a N course. There is more room to anchor upstream of the moorings as far as the next set of power lines, but it is very open and the tide is strong.

Upstream of the power lines there are moorings belonging to the sailing club or the boatyard at Weir Quay, both of which have slipways. The yard also has a landing pontoon accessible except at LWS and a single mooring reserved for visitors. This is a white buoy with a pick-up in mid-stream, directly abeam of the yard slipway. Additional moorings may occasionally be available and the pontoon can be used for loading or unloading, but only for a short stay.

Upper Tamar

Proceeding upriver from Weir Quay requires sufficient rise of tide and for most craft this will be above half-tide, especially if intending to return downstream. A note of caution is also necessary regarding anchorages. There are any number of deeper holes in the river bed and a seemingly equal number of theories as to how they got there. One such theory relates to stray bombs from WWII. Although feasible, it seems improbable and no skipper would consider anchoring in them if that were the case. An alternative is that scour holes have formed on corners where the current has 'corkscrewed' as the river meanders. This might have some merit since many of the corners have deeper pools, but does not explain holes elsewhere. A more plausible explanation is that the frequent use of these places by trading vessels in olden days, when there was much industrial activity, has loosened the river bed, which has then washed out. Whatever the actual reason, local advice is not to drop anchor directly in the holes since the holding is definitely not as good, and the additional scope required may well result in a visit to the bank when the tide turns. Most of the river bed is a hard, almost shale-like material so heavy chain

Upper Tamar

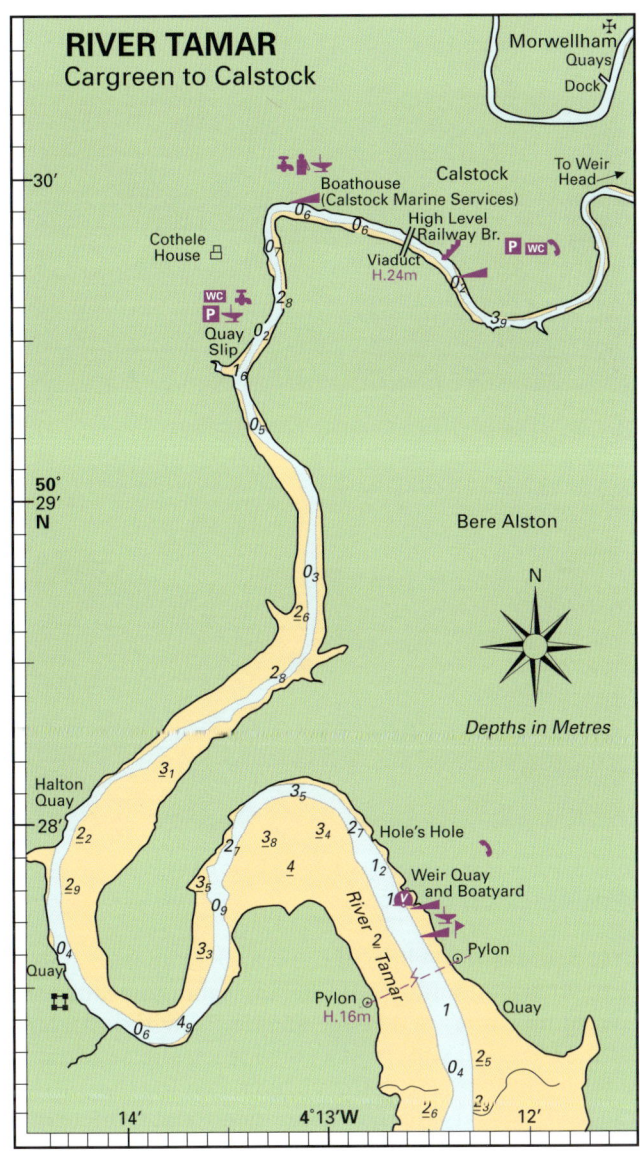

Pentillie Castle peeps through the trees

Pentillie Quay

The tiny chapel at Halton Quay

is a good idea, as is the use of an anchor chum (running weight). In the extreme upper reaches, locals suggest anchoring fore and aft.

Just upstream of the Weir Quay moorings there is a short stretch before the river turns back on itself where there is room for a few boats to anchor. A further line of moorings is laid along the outside of the bend in the deepest water and the channel turns S by a small slipway. Once inside the bank to port there a few more moorings and then a quiet anchorage between two holes protected from most winds, but especially those between SW and SE. The channel hugs the outside of the bend as it continues to turn back towards N with Pentillie Castle visible in the trees, and another spot is about 250m below Pentillie Quay. In fact, vessels frequently anchor in the stretch around this large bend which has very good protection from the prevailing winds.

The river straightens again at Pentillie Quay on the port bank, and continues NE until abeam a small chapel, which looks like an old signal box. From here, head towards a large patch of reeds in the distance, slowly crossing the river to be close under the starboard bank just below the reed bed which is actually the mouth of a small creek. The river then curves N with the deepest water about one third distance off the starboard bank (note a beacon at South Ward Farm shown on some charts is no longer there). Resume mid-stream at the farm where a horse (shoal) has developed across the river, favouring the port bank until the quay and buildings at Cothele Quay come in to view, at which point aim towards them. It is possible to land here

West Country Pilot • 109

Vessels can stop at Cothele Quay near the top of the tide

Calstock Boatyard has moorings and facilities

Final approaches to Calstock

A potential quiet anchorage front right. The chimney in the distance really is that crooked!

but do not use any moorings as their maintenance is uncertain. Instead, either tie up alongside the bank if draught permits, anchor below the quay or upstream of a small dock, using a tripping line for the latter in case of old mooring tackle.

Keep to the outside of the first bend above Cothele Quay then close the port shore about 100m before the river turns very sharply to starboard. The tide runs hard here so make due allowance to avoid being pushed on to the staging at the corner. A line of moorings now shows the best water between here and the spectacular railway viaduct ahead. The small boatyard at Calstock may be able to provide a mooring (between April and October only). Alternatively, having passed under the viaduct, it is possible to anchor off the village in approximately 2m, where a chum would be advisable to reduce the swinging circle, or a kedge anchor. Dinghies can land at the boatyard slip, or at a small steep slip adjacent to a ferry pontoon above the viaduct, leaving the outside clear. The boatyard has some deep water moorings 200m further on which may be available to visitors.

Passage beyond Calstock depends on the type of vessel and the risk appetite of the skipper. In theory, boats of moderate draught and up to about 9m LOA could reach Morwelham Quay 2.5M further upstream, and shoal draught a further 1.5M to Gunnislake Weir which is some 12M inland from Plymouth Sound. In reality

Looking back towards the anchorage at Calstock with the largest of the Tamar viaducts

Upper Tamar

The second potential anchorage about a mile below Morwellham Quay

though, there are sufficient barriers in the form of overhanging trees and sunken branches to deter all but the most eager explorers. That said, the first couple of miles may be suitable for some, and it is a pleasant trip in the tender on the tide.

The moorings above Calstock continue as far as the next bend passing a couple of houses with private landing stages, where the deepest water is again on the outside. A deepish pool begins just above here and continues around a long bend to port as far as a conspicuous house on the bank at the next bend. Anchoring fore and aft along this stretch should not present too much of a problem, draught permitting, although larger vessels may need to warp about in order to depart. The river turns sharply to starboard at the house and about halfway along the next reach is a potential shoal draught anchorage abeam a stone Celtic cross in the bushes on the shore. At the next bend, the river turns N again and there is a straight reach NNW alongside a tramway and disused mining works on the starboard bank. The depth appears fairly consistent and this may also suit shoal draught craft to anchor. This is probably now the limit of navigation for all but very small craft, as some trees have slipped down the bank after the next bend which would almost certainly deter any yachts. Small motor boats and RIBs might continue the final 0.5M to Morwelham Quay but the risk of debris is increasing. Until these hazards are cleared any further adventure requires a rigid tender to reach Gunnislake Weir, which is achievable on the tide from Calstock. Inflatable craft (including boards) may be at risk.

Shoreside

Facilities are somewhat more limited in this largely rural area. Toilets and showers are available at Weir Quay and Calstock boatyards and also Saltash Sailing Club. There is a food store and a butcher at Saltash, and a small store/post office at St Germans about 0.75M from the quay. Both boatyards on the Upper Tamar have cafés.

Rivers Tamar & Lynher essential information

Clubs
Quay Sailing Club, St Germans ☎01503 230877
Saltash Sailing Club ☎01752 845988
Tamar River Sailing Club ☎01752 362741
Cargreen Yacht Club
Weir Quay Sailing Club

Additional Berthing
Weir Quay Boatyard ☎01822 840474
Calstock Boatyard ☎01822 834559
Jubilee Pontoon, Saltash ☎01752 844846 / 07377 682698 (weekends)

Water Taxi
Boatyard launches

Water
Taps at St Germans Quay, Saltash SC, Weir Quay BY, Calstock BY

Chandlery
Weir Quay BY

Victuals
Limited supplies at St Germans and Saltash

Nearest Large Supermarket
Plymouth City Centre

Repairs
Boatyards at St Germans, Weir Quay and Calstock

Engineers
Enquire at yards

Car Hire
Nearest Plymouth (by train from St. Germans, Saltash, Calstock).

Transport
Trains to Plymouth from Saltash, St. Germans, Calstock.

Local attractions

St Germans Priory is a well preserved church in the heart of the village with Port Eliot gardens nearby. Cothele is a short walk from Calstock and Morwelham Quay can be reached by tender. The Tamar AONB lies on the western edge of Dartmoor.

Historic Morwelham Quay with the water wheel far left. It now has its own hydro electric station

West Country Pilot • 111

11 LOOE & POLPERRO
TALLAND BAY

Harbour Master's Office
VHF 14 'Looe Harbour' (occas.)
Harbour Office, The Quay, East Looe PL13 1DX
☎ 01503 262839 / ☎ 07484 086605

The small fishing ports of Looe and Polperro are often described as typically Cornish, featuring on many a chocolate box and jigsaw puzzle. Looe has a rail connection to the main line at Liskeard, but the local road network and restricted parking at both locations make them challenging for launching and recovery from trailers.

Looe Island from SW

Landmarks

Looe Island (45m) is distinctive when on passage along the coast, but less so from offshore. A communications mast is just W of Polperro, and measured mile markers W of Looe are identifiable from a reasonable distance off.

Main hazards

Both harbours dry and have narrow entrances. They are only tenable in offshore winds with low, or no swell. At Looe, a reef between the shore and Looe Island prevents access and extends SE of the island. Within the harbour the tides run hard and it is very busy when the fishing fleets dock. At Polperro, which is busy with trip boats in the season, a rock with least charted depth 1m lies close to the entrance almost on the direct approach line.

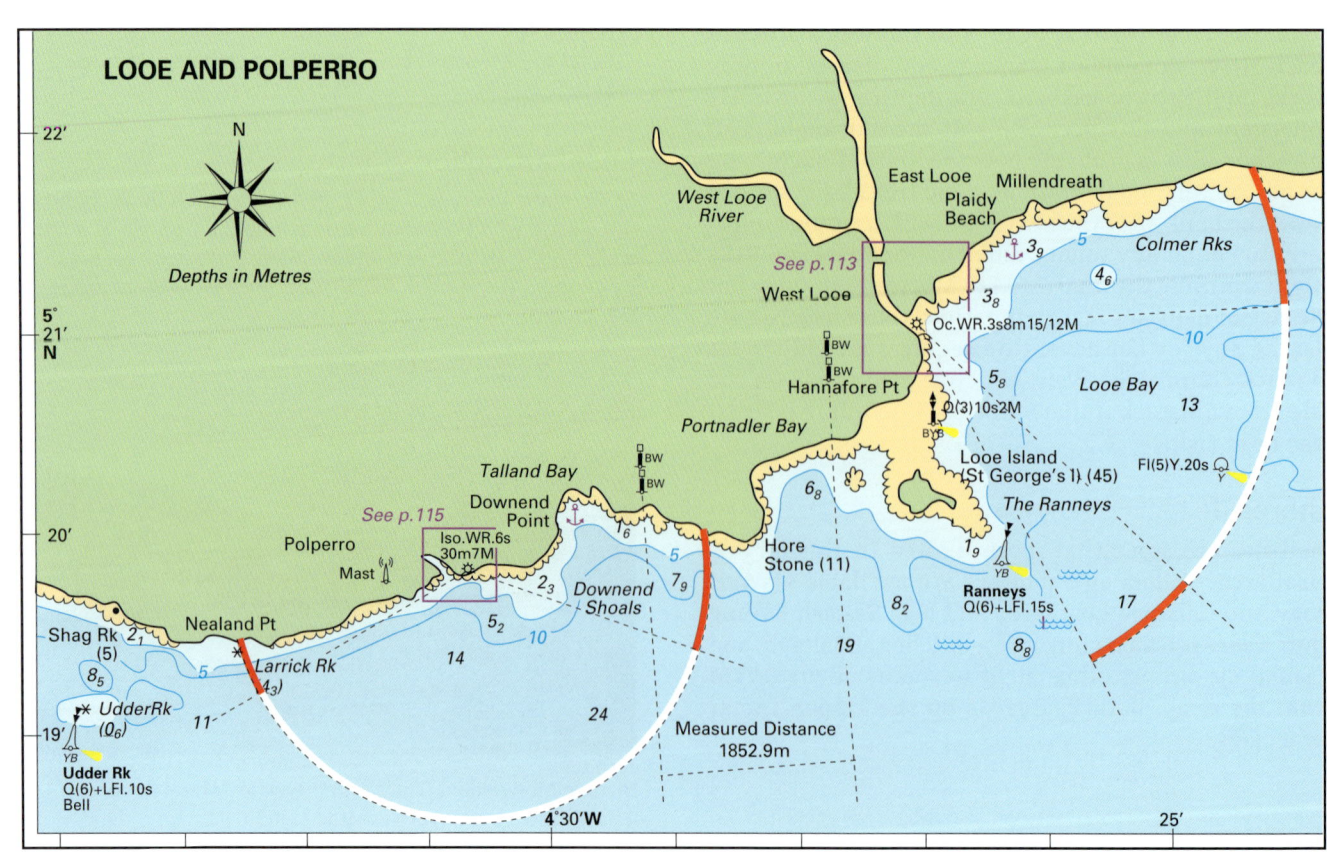

112 • West Country Pilot

LOOE

The traditional fishing town of Looe lies halfway between Rame Head and Fowey and is still a busy fishing port for smaller vessels.

Approaches

Looe is open from E, but from S or W aim to pass to seaward of The Ranneys SCM (Q(6)+LFl.15s) by several boat lengths. Overfalls can sometimes be encountered here but the effect is minimal in offshore winds. A yellow wave measurement buoy (Fl(5)Y.20s), 1.5M ESE of the harbour entrance is a useful waypoint.

At night, there is a light on the pier head at Looe (Oc.WR.3s.8m.15/12M) with the white sector covering clear water.

Entry

Steer WNW from the wave measurement buoy towards the pier head or, having cleared The Ranneys SCM, steer N until in the white sector of the pier head light, or the pier head bears WNW. There is an anchorage under high cliffs with good holding on sand near Plaidy Beach, 0.5M NE of the pier head (note this is in a red sector of the pier light which covers a rock (least charted depth 4.6m) further out. The beaches are mostly fringed with rocks except at Millendreath, where it is possible to land adjacent to a lido. Smaller craft and those with shoal draught may prefer a spot

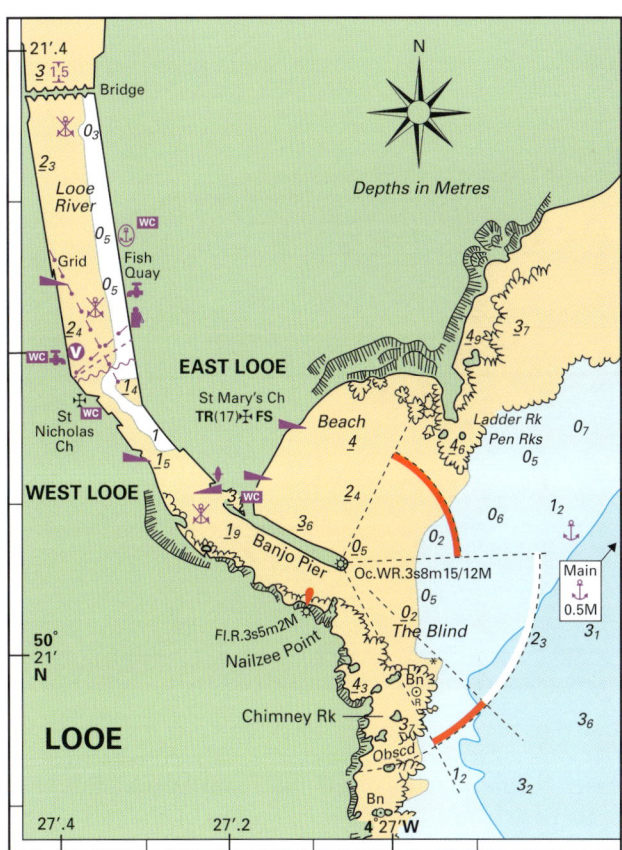

Looe Harbour

Looe Harbour Commissioners

11 LOOE & POLPERRO

Looe Harbour

The visitors' berth at Looe - fender board essential

closer to the pier head off the main beach. The best tactic here is to anchor *just on the line* of the red sector of the harbour light outside the buoyed swimming area (the marker buoys are on the surf line at LW). Tenders can land on the beach at either end.

Use a proper anchor light (2M visibility) at both locations due to frequent traffic.

Although possible to enter or leave the harbour earlier, it is preferable to wait until slack HW. The only visitors' berth dries to approximately 3.4m, giving a depth of just 0.8m at MHWN and 2.0m at MHWS, and the flood tide runs up the centre of the narrow harbour creating a counter current down both sides, which makes mooring a challenge except at the top of the tide. After checking with the HM that there is space, enter between mid-stream and the pier head keeping a sharp look out. The marked visitors' berth is situated to port upstream of the church, adjacent to a fisherman's shelter. Rafting is common so strong shore lines are necessary. Leisure craft are not allowed to moor on East Quay except when directed by the HM.

Shoreside

Showers and toilets are housed in a shelter on the quay adjacent to the visitors' berth.

There is a food store at East Looe and plenty of fresh seafood sellers, a chemist and a couple of bakeries. There is also a convenience store and a bakery at West Looe.

A branch line connects East Looe to the main line at Liskeard.

Looe essential information

Clubs
Looe Sailing Club ☏01503 262559

Local Information
The Millpool

Visitors' Berths
Quayside (dries)

Additional Berthing
None

Webcams
www.theoldbridgehousehotel.co.uk

Water
Tap on quay

Fuel
East Quay (contact HM)

Gas
Looe Service Station

Chandlery
Looe Chandlery, Millpool

Victuals
Fore St

Nearest Large Supermarket
Liskeard (by train)

Repairs
Norman Pearn

Engineers
Black Dog, Portlooe

Scrubbing Posts
West Quay

Car Hire
Nearest Plymouth City Centre

POLPERRO

Harbour Master's Office
VHF 17 'Polperro Harbour' (occas.)
Mawdsley's Store Room, The Warren, Polperro
PL13 2RB
☎ 01503 272423

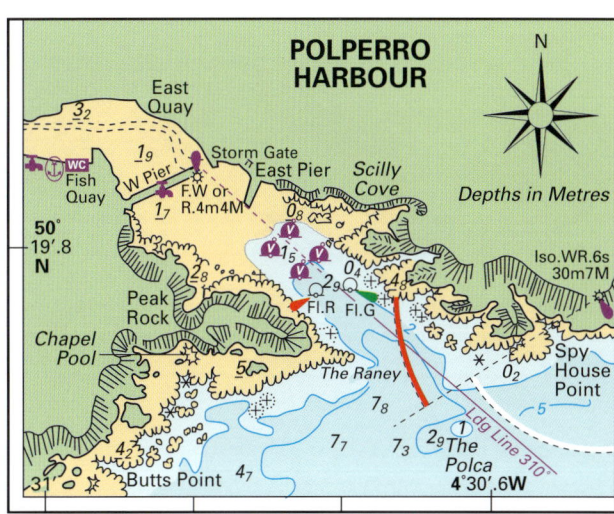

Polperro is a very attractive fishing village with a narrow street leading down the side of a stream to the traditional harbour.

From seaward, in particular from SE, Polperro appears as a collection of white painted houses in a cleft on the coast, and sailing along the coast from Fowey it can hardly be seen until right outside the narrow entrance.

Approaches

From W or SW the approach to Polperro is clear, except for Udder Rock 2M E, which is marked by a SCM (VQ(6)+LFl.10s) and is only an issue if approaching along the coast (from Fowey for example). There is also a light at the entrance to Polperro, Spyglass Point (Iso.WR.6s30m7M), but night entry is not a serious proposition for most craft.

Polperro from seaward

The light on Spyglass Point

The landing points can be used when the trip boats have finished, but pull the tender up the main beach

Polperro Harbour entrance

Entry

Although the harbour entrance faces SE, it is best to approach from S to avoid The Polca, a rock which has a charted depth of 1m and lies just outside the harbour on a direct approach from SE. However, with sufficient rise of tide a transit from seaward can be formed by aligning the ends of the inner harbour walls on about 310° using binoculars. Check with the HM that there is space before entering.

Six mooring buoys are laid in the outer harbour. In recent years, port and starboard lights have been attached to the outer two during the summer months. In the past, when trawlers were active at the harbour, the local advice has been to moor fore and aft (NW/SE) between two moorings. This implies space for four boats, but several things conspire to make this impractical for small craft. First, the moorings are a considerable distance apart, requiring long lines which would inevitably end up submerged, thus creating a hazard to other craft and swimmers. Second, the two inner moorings on the port side, and the inner one to starboard are often reserved for trip boats, so they may not always be available to visitors. It should also be noted that most of the moorings are close enough to the rocks either side to be unsuitable for larger vessels. In summary, vessels up to about 9m should be able to moor to a single buoy out of season without issue, but check first with the HM. During the peak season and school holidays this may not be the case, as only three moorings are potentially available. At any time, vessels larger than about 9m should stick with the advice to

Moorings at Polperro. The 'causeway' is a sewer pipe

Polperro Harbour near HW

moor fore and aft with tight lines incorporating a compensator, or anchor off in settled weather. Tenders can land at the beach and when the trip boats have finished for the day, there are half-tide and low water landing points fashioned out of the rock. Do not land at the apparent walkway on the E side. It is a sewer channel with no access to the village.

Small craft can access the inner harbour from about LW±2 on average tides with HM permission. The visitors' berth alongside East Quay shown on some charts is no longer in use following installation of a power cable across the harbour. Within the harbour, vessels are generally moored E/W and at the extreme W end there is a slipway, but note that access with a trailer is virtually impossible down the narrow streets.

Shoreside

The only facilities at Polperro are public (pay) toilets. There are two small food stores (one of which sells ice), a baker and a chemist together with a wide variety of places to eat. The village is remote, and only accessible from a car park on the outskirts from where there is a bus to Looe and Liskeard.

Local attractions

The stretch of coast between Looe and Polperro is very popular with walkers. In the summer, some of the local trip boats offer single journeys between the two ports for walkers. The salt water pool at Polperro, Chapel Pool, is well hidden, accessed by steep steps from the coast path just W of the village. It would be unsafe in onshore swell once awash though, but a perfect suntrap in N winds. Attractions include the Old Guildhall Museum at Looe and Polperro has a model village.

Talland Bay

This small bay lies in an indent in the coast approximately 2M W of Looe Island and 1M ENE of Polperro. It is a good anchorage in winds from W to NE, although in W winds the swell may work in. Sound in from SSE to anchor in 2-3m on sand in the centre of the bay. Rocks fringe the bay but there are two possible landing places on the E beach above about half-tide, and with care on the main beach in the corner of the bay at most states of the tide. It is a pleasant walk along the coast path to Polperro from here.

In settled conditions an overnight stop should not present a problem since the exit is straightforward and shelter off Looe is within an hour, or Fowey is around 6M W if onshore wind or swell develops.

Talland Bay anchorage. Measured mile markers right

Chapel Pool (*right*) is reached by an interesting route

12 FOWEY

Harbour Master's Office
VHF 12 'Fowey Harbour Radio'
Harbour Office, Albert Quay, Fowey PL23 1AJ
☎ 01726 832471
NCI Polruan VHF 65 ☎ 01726 254057

Fowey is a deepwater commercial port primarily exporting china clay. Facilities for leisure craft are excellent, although alongside berthing is limited. The harbour is accessible day and night at all states of the tide and in almost any conditions. The town is characterised by narrow streets and many old buildings and is popular with tourists, including from visiting cruise ships, being the nearest port to the renowned Eden Project.

Landmarks

A 104m high red/white day mark is on top of Gribbin Head W of the harbour entrance. Just E, a conspicuous house and NCI station are visible, but not from close under the cliff, so the harbour entrance is unsighted approaching from E.

Main hazards

Cannis Rock is 1.5M SSW of the harbour entrance, marked by a SCM (Q(6)+LFl.15s). Just under 3M E, Udder Rock is also marked with a SCM (VQ(6)+LFl.10s). Within the harbour, commercial shipping movements are usually accompanied by harbour patrol launches. There is a ferry between Caffa Mill and Bodinnick approximately 1M upstream of the entrance which has priority over other vessels. In strong winds between SW and SE the entrance can be extremely challenging and may not be manageable for small craft. The only potential anchorages in the harbour dry out.

Gribbin Head daymark

The main Fowey lighthouse

Approaches

From E, leave Udder Rock SCM to starboard and steer approximately 280° towards the main lighthouse at the harbour entrance. 1M from the entrance is Lantic

Cannis Rock SCM outside Fowey

Approaching Fowey from SW

118 • West Country Pilot

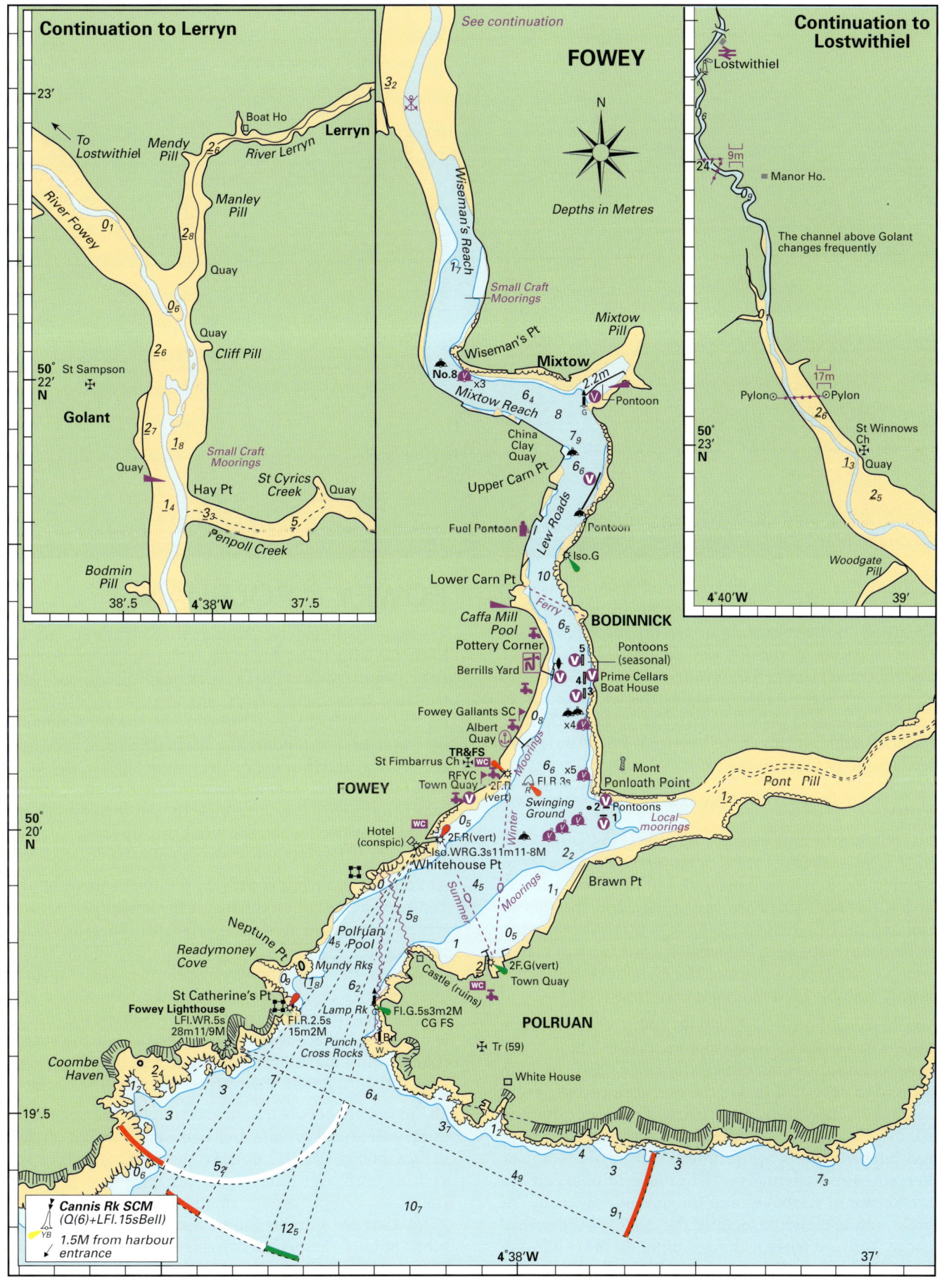

12 FOWEY

Fowey entrance (top right), with Polridmouth (left)
Susan Hemmin

Bay which is a good anchorage in offshore winds with a wide sandy beach, but beware of an isolated rock (charted) in the centre. It also offers some protection from E winds if tucked well in, but is exposed to ambient swell. From S or SW, leave Cannis Rock SCM to port and steer 030°. At night, the white sector of the lighthouse (LFl.WR.5s28m11/9M) clears both these hazards and an inner light (Iso.WRG.3s11m11/8M) leads directly to the entrance.

Entry

Just outside the entrance about halfway to Cannis Rock SCM is an anchorage at Polridmouth Cove in the lee of Gribbin Head. It is well protected in winds between W and N but both sides are very rocky, and there is an isolated rock in about 1.5m dead centre. Most vessels will anchor outside it, but smaller craft can work their way further in with caution. The many rocks suggest it is only suitable for a temporary daytime stop.

The harbour entrance is about 200m wide between Punch Cross Rocks to starboard, marked by a small beacon, and the ruins of St Catherine's Castle on high ground to port. Just inside the entrance bathing areas at Readymoney Cove, Boy's/Girl's Cove opposite and slightly further on at Whitehouse, are marked by dark red buoys. Vessels are prohibited from these zones. Remain in mid-channel until the castle ruins at Polruan are abeam to starboard and the harbour opens up. At night, stay in the white sector of the inner light described above. To assist when leaving at night there are lights at Lamp Rock on the Polruan shore (Fl.G.5s3m2M) and at St Catherine's Castle on the Fowey side (Fl.R.2.5s15m12M).

FOWEY & POLRUAN

The majority of moorings are on the Polruan side of the harbour with those for visitors concentrated around the entrance to Pont Pill (a creek heading E inland) and the area immediately N. Most shoreside facilities are on the opposite side of the river at Fowey, reachable by water taxi or tender. The harbour byelaws require *all* vessels under way to carry appropriate lights at night *including tenders* which must display an all round white light. All the moorings in the lower harbour suffer from swell when the wind gets up from S or SW, when a position further upstream may be preferable.

At Polruan there is a short stay pontoon (max 1 hour). Tenders can be left on the inside for longer periods but it is often crowded. A passenger ferry linking the village to Fowey operates from the adjacent quay. Immediately upstream, the larger pontoons belong to the shipyard. The facilities block here was closed during Covid and the yard currently has no plans to reinstate it. There is a slipway adjacent to the ferry steps, but the access roads would make launching and recovery by trailer very difficult. Better alternatives are identified below.

The moorings between here and roughly the end of the quay wall are all private, but there are four flat topped yellow buoys (V2-V5) outside the local moorings for visiting craft over 15m. Where the local moorings end there is a series of orange small boat moorings marked 'SBM' that are suitable for smaller day craft. The main block of blue visitors' moorings is at the mouth of Pont Pill which leads E off the main river channel and most are suitable for vessels up to about 15m. They can get cosy in some conditions, so fenders on the quarters are

Fowey & Polruan

Fowey with Town Quay (left) and Albert Quay (right) *Susan Hemmin*

advisable. All the yellow trot moorings in Pont Pill are private. A refuse and recycling pontoon is located on the southernmost trot (most visitors' pontoons also have refuse and recycling bins). Two large pontoons on the most northerly trots are for visiting craft where rafting is the norm. Pont Pill can be explored by tender although the quay at the head of the creek is private. Vessels can anchor above the trots and dry out, but only with prior permission from the HM, and charges are the same as for a mooring so the practice is infrequent! Immediately upstream of Pont Pill there is another block of blue visitors' moorings but the max LOA here is 10m. It is a shorter dinghy ride across to Fowey except when cruise ships visit, since they moor outside this area. Three further pontoons are positioned above the moorings, where again rafting is the norm. Rallies are usually accommodated here, on Pontoon 4, adjacent to a boathouse on the shore.

As mentioned earlier, most facilities are on the Fowey side of the river. Best practice in a tender is to cross the river at right angles and select the most convenient

The main block of visitors' moorings is at the mouth of Pont Pill

12 FOWEY

The lower harbour at Fowey. Visitors' moorings are far left with RFYC landing pontoon for tenders in the foreground

landing point, making due allowance for the tide on the return trip. If this means moving up or down river, manoeuvre on one side of the river or the other, rather than crossing at a wide angle. Note that movements may be barred or restricted when commercial shipping is underway.

The available landing sites are as follows, listed from seaward. The Royal Fowey Yacht Club is opposite Pont Pill and the main block of visitors' moorings. There is a dinghy pontoon of temporary construction with ladder access to the club. Town Quay is used by ferries, trip boats and the water taxi and should be kept clear. A seasonal short stay pontoon (max 1 hour) is next to the HM office at Albert Quay and is the most convenient for victualling. Tenders and small craft can tie up on the inside for a maximum of 12 hours, but do not obstruct HM craft moored on the downstream side by the access ramp. 100m further on, Fowey Gallants Sailing Club does have step access from the water at most states of the tide, but the distance saved and increased risk means Albert Quay will always be preferable. Finally, opposite Pontoon 5, Berrills Yard is another short stay pontoon (max 1 hour) adjacent to the lifeboat station, with space for tenders on the inside. However, it is also possible to moor on the outside of this pontoon overnight *from 1600 to 0800 only*. Rafting is permitted.

Susan Hemmin

Berrills Yard pontoon, Fowey

Coaster traffic is frequent at Fowey

BODINNICK & PENMARLAM

The slipway at Bodinnick is private and used by the car ferry crossing to Caffa Mill on the Fowey side of the river. Although it looks like a chain ferry, it is in fact self-propelled and restricted in its ability to manoeuvre. Other vessels should keep well clear, especially at springs and during periods of strong winds or restricted visibility. Just below Caffa Mill there is a wide slipway and adjacent car park which is the best place for launching and recovery, and just above is a self service fuel pontoon available 24 hours.

The main dock area now begins on the W bank and on the E side are trot moorings, mostly used by fishing vessels and the ferry. Above here before the next bend is a long linear pontoon mostly for local boats, but a 100m stretch on the outside of the upstream end is allocated to visitors. This position (Gridiron) is somewhat quieter than the lower harbour, unless a ship is loading, and offers some protection from swell.

The river turns 90° to port with a small creek, Mixtow Pill, continuing a short distance N. In the creek are two linear pontoons linked to the shore. The S side of the first pontoon is allocated to visitors and tenders can land at an adjacent, shore linked plastic pontoon, or by the access ramp/slipway, which is convenient if moored on the Gridiron pontoon. There are HM facilities here and launching/recovery is possible from the slipway by arrangement, although it is steep compared with Caffa Mill. A twenty minute walk across the field and down a road leads to Bodinnick and the ferry.

Continuing upstream towards the next bend, the last of the commercial wharves is to port and some private moorings and a pontoon to starboard. Red training vessels for deep sea diving are moored here along with harbour tugs and workboats. At the bend, where the river turns N, there are three blue visitors' moorings in deep water which can take two or three boats each depending on size. The third one (nearest the railway) is probably best suited to vessels under 10m due to its proximity to the bank. Wiseman's Pool is the area above the bend where the moorings are all private, although one is sometimes available via the HM. Note some charts show visitors' moorings here which is incorrect.

Ferryside, opposite Fowey

Upriver

Above Wiseman's Pool the river largely dries but it is very attractive and can be explored on the tide by most vessels as far as Golant, and with shoal draught to St Winnow 1.5M further upstream. Tenders can reach Lerryn around HW±2 and the more adventurous (without masts) might make it as far as Lostwithiel on a good tide.

The channel runs N alongside a railway line into a 0.5M gap between the end of the Wiseman's Pool moorings and the next block of moorings below Golant. This is a salmon fishing area and anchoring is not permitted (it would be risky if it was since the bottom is uneven). Penpoll Creek on the E side opposite a private staging can be explored by tender for about 1M. The moorings off Golant all dry out but there is the odd gap where it may be possible to anchor and dry out, again with prior permission from the HM. Tenders can land at a slipway at the downstream end of the village.

Upstream the river forks with the River Lerryn to starboard where the village slipway can be reached about HW±2 in a tender. The River Fowey continues NW, the channel meandering from side to side several times before reaching the slipway at St Winnow,

The gap above Wiseman's Pool with the Golant moorings beyond

12 FOWEY

Upstream approaching Lerryn

adjacent to a conspicuous church. There is a boatyard here capable of taking moderate sized craft with shoal draught. The twisting channel above Golant should only be attempted with local knowledge from the HM or after inspection around LW.

Leaving St Winnow, the shallow channel crosses to the opposite bank passing under a power line (17m clearance at MHWS) before resuming the centre as the river abruptly narrows and heads N once more for approximately 0.5M. It then begins meandering again passing a sewage works, then a silo before encountering a much lower power cable (4.8m clearance at MHWS) and an even lower rail bridge on the outskirts of Lostwithiel. After a final turn NNE, there is a short, straight section to the road bridge, where it is possible to land on the W bank but do not linger long.

Shoreside

Toilets and showers are available at both yacht clubs in Fowey and also at Penmarlam Boatyard (Mixtow). The facilities block at C Toms Boatyard in Polruan is now closed. There is a good range of shops including a small general store which has ice, butcher/deli, two bakers and a chemist. The yard at Mixtow has a small chandlery and a café. There are many places to eat in Fowey and two pubs at Polruan. The pub at Bodinnick is a 1M walk from Penmarlam. There are also pubs upstream at Lerryn and Golant.

Although china clay comes in by rail, there is no station at Fowey. The nearest is at Par and a regular bus service between Fowey and St Austell stops there. There is a local ferry to Mevagissey.

Fowey essential information

Clubs
Royal Fowey Yacht Club
☎01726 833573
Fowey Gallants Sailing Club
☎01726 832335

Visitors' Berths
Pontoons (2 shore linked) and moorings

Additional Berthing
None

Water Taxi
VHF 06 'Fowey Water Taxi'
☎07774 906730

Webcams
www.rfyc-fowey.org.uk

Water
Albert Quay, Berrills Yard and Penmarlam pontoons

Fuel
Self service facility S of docks

Gas
Penmarlam Quay Café

Chandlery
Mixtow Marine, Penmarlam

Victuals
Fore St, Fowey

Nearest Large Supermarket
St Austell (by bus)

Repairs
C Toms, Polruan
St Winnow Yachts
Kim Furniss

Engineers
Consult HM & Port Guide

Sailmakers
Sailshape, Fowey & Lostwithiel

Car Hire
Nearest St Austell (by bus)

Transport
Bus to Par for trains to Penzance, Plymouth, London.

Fowey's streets are narrow

Fowey River class dinghies

Local attractions

Fowey is the closest port to the renowned Eden Project in an old china clay pit on the outskirts of St Austell. There is a centre dedicated to author Daphne du Maurier who lived for a time at 'Ferryside', the prominent house in Bodinnick by the ferry slip. Many sites in and around Fowey appeared in, or were the inspiration for places in her works, and also those of Kenneth Grahame and Arthur Quiller Couch. The church at St Winnow is worth visiting by dinghy.

There are many fine walks around Fowey, including Hall Walk which is a circular route around Pont Pill using the ferries to complete the loop. There are also pleasant walks out to the daymark on Gribbin Head, along the Saints Way to Polkerris and between Lerryn and St Winnow.

Literary Fowey

Fowey and Polruan, with their attractive pastel cottages in terraces on the steep sided banks of the river, have inspired many writers, both resident and those for whom it was simply inspiration.

Among them, Kenneth Grahame is said to have been inspired to write the 'Wayfarers All' chapter of *The Wind in the Willows* based on his time by the river here. He was married at St Fimbarrus church in the town and the nearby Fowey Hall Hotel is one of a number of buildings Grahame is believed to have based Toad Hall on. It overlooks the harbour from a high vantage point. Grahame may have met another famous writer there, Arthur Quiller Couch ('Q'). Although best known for the *Oxford Book of English Verse*, he was also a novelist of some repute and Fowey is undoubtedly 'Troy Town'. There is a monument to Quiller Couch about 1M from Bodinnick along Hall Walk and a memorial stone in Truro Cathedral (see chapter 15).

But it is the romantic novelist Daphne du Maurier with whom Fowey is synonymous, with a literary centre dedicated to her life and works. A du Maurier festival is held in the town annually in May. She was born and brought up in London but the family bought Ferryside at Bodinnick in the 1920s as a holiday home and she wrote her first novel there. She moved to Menabilly on the nearby Gribbin peninsula after marrying and the house is said to be the inspiration for Mandalay in her novel *Rebecca*. There are many local sites connected with her books: Polridmouth, Tom's Boatyard at Polruan (on the site of Slade's) and Lanteglos church (where she was married). One notable exception is Frenchman's Creek on the Helford (see chapter 16), although a dinghy trip up the River Fowey reveals a couple of promising alternative candidates as some inspiration for the location.

13 MEVAGISSEY
& ST AUSTELL BAY

St Austell Bay looking towards Gribbin Head

Harbour Master's Office
VHF 14 'Mevagissey Harbour'
Harbour Office, Mevagissey PL26 6QQ
☎ 01726 843305 / 07422 968878
NCI Charlestown VHF 65 ☎ 01726 817068

Although not strictly correct geographically, St Austell Bay describes here the area between Fowey and Dodman Point. It is sheltered from the prevailing weather and has a number of good anchorages which are often missed by boats on passage to and from Fowey, but forms an ideal cruising ground in the right conditions, especially for smaller craft. The main harbour is at Mevagissey, a traditional and working fishing port.

Landmarks

The most prominent landmarks are the rounded headland of Dodman Point itself, and the red/white day mark on Gribbin Head near the entrance to Fowey. Within the bay, the china clay driers at Par are visible from some distance as an industrial complex. Commercial traffic has ceased at the port here. There is a conspicuous white house on Chapel Point 1M SE of Mevagissey.

Main hazards

Gwineas Rocks, 2M NE of Dodman Point are marked with an ECM (Q(3).10s) which should be passed to seaward at night or if heading for anchorages in the N of the bay. Note also the ECM is *SE* of the rocks so maintain an appropriate course until safely clear of the actual hazard. There are many fishing floats in the vicinity. In daylight, it is possible to pass inshore of the rocks if heading for Mevagissey after rounding Dodman Point.

Two large marine farms have been constructed in the bay, which has made passages between the anchorages difficult. One is on the direct track between Fowey and Mevagissey and a course deviation is now required to pass outside it. The second is off Little Gerrans Point SSE of Charlestown and consists of two blocks of floats and lines, the second block being around half the size of the main block but at an angle of some 30° from it, and positioned such that the corners of the two blocks meet with no gap to pass between them. There is a proposal for a third block S of the existing two.

The whole area should be avoided in winds between S and E (Polkerris is suitable in E winds, but not if prolonged when swell will work in).

Approaches

From E it is possible to head directly for Mevagissey in clear water. From Fowey, leave Cannis SCM (Q(6)+LFl.15s) to starboard then steer 235° to clear the marine farm before making a final approach on 250°. From S, or after rounding Dodman Point, leave Gwineas ECM to port and steer N until the lighthouse on the pier head is visible clear of Chapel Point, then

Gwineas ECM with the eponymous rocks beyond

Mevagissey

MEVAGISSEY & ST AUSTELL BAY

Depths in Metres

Mevagissey Harbour entrance

13 MEVAGISSEY BAY

Gorran Haven (far left) from the Gwineas ECM

head WNW towards the harbour. Alternatively, head NE about half the distance (1M) from Dodman Point to Gwineas ECM then head N behind the rocks past the anchorage at Gorran Haven before following the coast around Chapel Point keeping at least 0.25M off. At night, go outside the Gwineas ECM.

Entry

Visitors' berths are limited so call ahead to establish if there is space. Close the main pier head from E until 200m off then slowly move to a position NE of the entrance with a clear view in before proceeding. Stay SE of North Pier at all times as there are some nasty rocks adjacent to it. There are plans to reinforce this area with rock armour. Enter between the pier heads keeping a wary eye out for angling activity. At night keep the lighthouse (Fl(2)10s9m12M) between 250° and 300°. Do not attempt to enter the harbour in fog, in E winds of more than 10kn, or for at least 24 hours after prolonged E weather or storms.

MEVAGISSEY

This is primarily a fishing port but with some facilities for leisure craft in the outer harbour, where trots are laid E/W. Inside North Pier are two trot moorings for small craft (e.g. RIBs and day craft). On the S side of the harbour is a longer trot with space for up to five vessels, or up to ten rafted, where there is about 1.2m LAT.

Visitors' trot moorings at Mevagissey

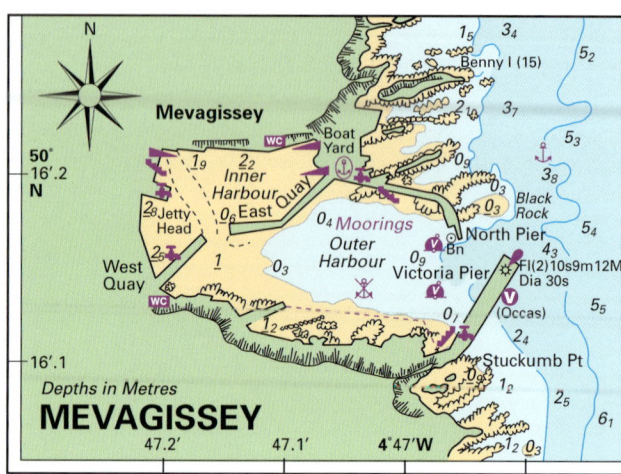

With permission, a short stop can be made alongside Lighthouse Quay (Victoria Pier) by the middle steps. At the HM's discretion, yachts may be allowed to tie up on the outside of Victoria Pier in settled conditions during busy periods, but permission *must* be sought in advance. Tenders should land at the steps in the centre of North Pier. The inner harbour is only for local boats and dries out. There are two slipways in the inner harbour, but the narrow streets make launching and recovery from a trailer somewhat difficult. Given the tidal restrictions, it may be preferable to launch and recover at Fowey where the slipway has all tide access.

If preferred, or when the trots are full, it is possible to anchor NE of North Pier in about 4m LAT although this position is subject to wash from passing vessels. Portmellon Cove (*see overview plan p.127*), 0.5M S of the harbour entrance is a better prospect, with good holding on sand and easy landing on the gently sloping beach at the village. Both are protected from W and SW winds although SW swell can be refracted by two minor headlands either side of the Gwineas producing rolly conditions. This can be partly mitigated by moving slightly further towards Chapel Point or to Ropehaven (see below).

1M N of Mevagissey, Pentewan Sands is a very popular beach affording a good anchorage in W and NW winds, but avoid a cable just S of the centre of the beach. The remains of an old harbour at the mouth of the St Austell River are at the N end of the beach providing a good landing place.

Polkerris

Mevagissey essential information

Clubs
Pentewan Sands Sailing Club
Porthpean Sailing Club

Local Information
Jetty St

Visitors' Berths
Fore & aft mooring buoys

Additional berthing
None

Webcams
www.mevagisseyharbour.co.uk
www.porthpeansc.co.uk

Water
Tap on quay in inner harbour

Fuel
Commercial **only** via HM

Victuals
Small stores around harbour

Nearest Large Supermarket
St Austell (by bus)

Laundry
Clifden Rd, St Austell

Repairs
Contact HM

Scrubbing Posts
Inner Harbour

Car Hire
St Austell (by bus)

Transport
Bus to St Austell for trains to Penzance, Plymouth, London

St Austell Bay

As mentioned above, transiting this area is challenging due to the position of large marine farms off Little Gerrans Point. Although marked, they are difficult to see until close to. At night the light characteristics of the yellow buoys marking them are all the same, and navigation through the area should be undertaken with extreme caution, or avoided altogether.

The anchorage at Polkerris is the only place offering any protection from E or NE winds. It is also comfortable in lighter winds from N but in SE, or during prolonged E weather, swell works its way in around Gribbin Head and would make for a bumpy return to Fowey. Access is straightforward from between S and W, the only obstruction being Killyvarder Rock in the middle of the beach just WNW, marked with a green beacon. Anchor clear of the local moorings keeping outside the 1m contour to avoid a wreck approximately 200m due W of the end of the harbour wall. Small and shoal draught craft can enter the small harbour as can tenders for landing on the beach. It is possible to dry out here anchored fore and aft, taking care to avoid frape lines extending from the beach, which is very popular in summer.

Par Docks, at the W end of the beach at Par Sands is no longer used by shipping but the industrial complex is still active and leisure vessels should not enter. There have been suggestions of building a marina here for many years but there are no actual plans as yet. The beaches W of here are popular daytime anchorages.

CHARLESTOWN

On the other side of the bay is the historic former china clay port at Charlestown. There is a good anchorage here in winds between N and W, and off Duporth Beach just S of the harbour. Sadly, the locked harbour itself is no longer available for casual visitors, although longer term stays (min one month) can be arranged. Square riggers and other historic craft used for filming are based here and any transit of the lock has to coincide with another vessels movement. Tenders can land at several sets of steps in the outer harbour. The single

Topsail schooner *Anny of Charlestown* moored off the harbour. Note the huge marine farm in the bay

13 MEVAGISSEY BAY

Rocks S of Charlestown with Ropehaven anchorage in the distance

mooring buoy is for use by large sailing ships which frequently visit embarking crew by tender. At neaps, it is possible to anchor further in gaining additional protection from a reef and some large rocks adjacent either side of the harbour entrance.

S of Charlestown, the coastline begins a slow curve S and then SE. There are several beaches where anchoring is possible with due allowance for any rocky areas, most of which are close to the shore. The area is popular for kayaks and paddleboards. Just before reaching a small headland at Little Gerrans Point there is an extensive area of woodland and a large house with a long slipway and small artificial harbour. This is Ropehaven and there is a deeper anchorage off here in around 5m LAT. The shore is private but landing at three small shingle beaches just N seems to be permitted, although there is no further landward access from them. Crucially, this spot does not suffer from SW swell anything like as much as the rest of the bay, or indeed Portmellon and Gorran Haven, and is therefore the best anchoring option in SW winds.

Shoreside

The HM runs a toilet and shower facility on the quay at Mevagissey (keys from HM office) and there is a public toilet nearby. Most of the shops are aimed at the tourist trade but there is a convenience store, a greengrocer also selling local meat and dairy produce, a small deli and a chemist. Most eateries are cafés and pubs. At Gorran Haven there is a licensed shop with an adjacent café/bar.

Charlestown Harbour and historic trading vessels

Several landing places in the tidal outer harbour

Classic West Country anchorage at Gorran Haven

GORRAN HAVEN

This small fishing village is tucked in a coastal indent inside the Gwineas reef and gives very good protection from winds between W and N. It is also a convenient anchorage to await a fair tide at Dodman Point.

The beach is of hard sand and shelves very gently making it an ideal spot for vessels which can dry out. The tiny harbour is protected by a wall which makes landing in a tender easier. S of the harbour, the coast is steep-to and rocky. The only downside to this anchorage is that it suffers from SW swell being refracted round Dodman Point.

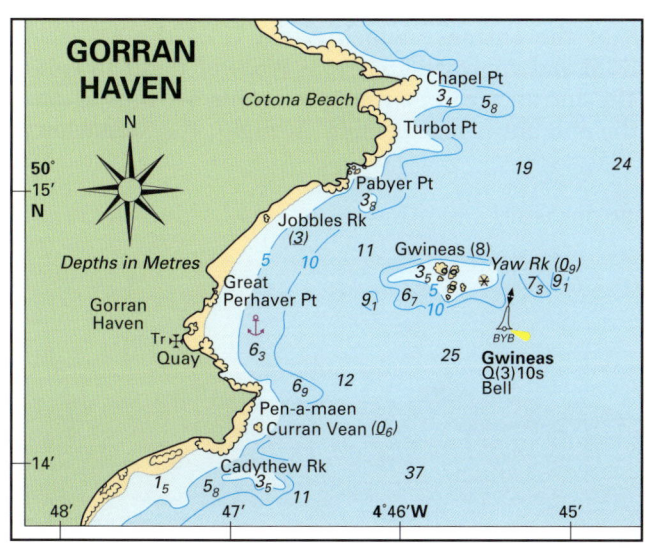

Local attractions

Mevagissey has a small museum charting the history of the port and a large model railway museum for enthusiasts near the harbour. The famous Lost Gardens of Heligan are within walking distance of the village and on the local bus route.

The Shipwreck Treasure museum is adjacent to Charlestown Harbour and has a fascinating collection of artefacts. Caerhays Castle is slightly further afield overlooking Veryan Bay and is home to the national magnolia collection if you happen to be visiting in early season

The Eden Project

In 1998, initially to some scepticism, construction of a multiple greenhouse complex began in an exhausted china clay pit near St Austell. The site was akin to a lunarscape following 160 years of mining. Despite major flooding of the site in the early stages, it officially opened to large acclaim in March 2001.

Two huge biomes form the hub of the site, each with thousands of specimens. They are constructed of a translucent plastic polymer shaped into individual 'pillows' set into a hexagonal framework which set a world record for the most scaffolding used in a single project at the time. The engineering alone is worth visiting for.

The 'rainforest' biome houses tropical plants from around the world whilst the 'Mediterranean' biome contains those from the temperate and arid climates of that region, and the outdoor spaces are given over to plants from other temperate areas and local flora. An education complex completes the set up.

In addition to its main function, the site has also featured in a number of films and hosts music concerts. It is the most popular visitor attraction in Cornwall. The nearest harbours are Fowey and Mevagissey, both of which have bus connections to the site.

West Country Pilot • 131

14 FALMOUTH
PENRYN & ST MAWES

Harbour Master's Office
VHF 12 'Falmouth Harbour Radio'
44 Arwenack Street, Falmouth TR11 3JQ
℡ 01326 213537
NCI Portscatho VHF 65 ℡ 01872 580180

St Anthony lighthouse

Falmouth is one of the largest natural harbours in the world with deep approaches and extensive facilities for all types of craft. It is a true port of refuge where entry is possible day and night in any weather and shelter can be found from any wind direction within a short distance, including at anchor. Vessels of moderate draught can reach the historic port of Truro on the tide, via some of the most attractive scenery anywhere in the region. Falmouth Bay just W of the entrance, Gerrans Bay just E and Veryan Bay on the Falmouth side of Dodman Point provide plentiful fair weather anchorages.

Landmarks

Pendennis Castle sits on a promontory on the W side of the entrance and is visible from S and SE. On a bright day, there may be plenty of reflection both from the glass of Falmouth Coastguard headquarters sited immediately below the castle, and from parked cars in a popular sightseeing position immediately below that. On the E side of the entrance sits St Anthony lighthouse (Iso.WR.15s22m12/9M) – note that the light is only visible between SW and SE. Approaching from E, the large satellite dishes at Goonhilly on the Lizard peninsula can be seen on a clear day until about 4M out, with an adjacent wind farm. An approximate initial course is to aim for the right hand edge of the wind farm from a position S of Dodman Point, with Gull Rock conspicuous to starboard at about half distance.

Main hazards

Approaching from S, the Manacles reef is marked by an ECM (Q(3).10s) and should be passed to seaward. The other major hazard is shipping. Falmouth Bay is busy with large commercial ships at anchor awaiting fuel or sailing orders. From E, beware of pot markers in the final stretch from Porthmellin Head staying a good 0.5M off at night. A wave energy test area lies 1.5M 155° from St Anthony lighthouse and is marked variously with cardinal buoys and special marks.

Approaches

The approach is in deep water so aim for a waypoint S of the entrance which is 4M N of the Manacles ECM and approximately 12M WSW of Dodman Point. The entrance can be rough in strong S winds against the ebb but is manageable. At night, the Manacles is

Black Rock, with Falmouth Coastguard above and Pendennis Castle on the hill

132 • West Country Pilot

Falmouth

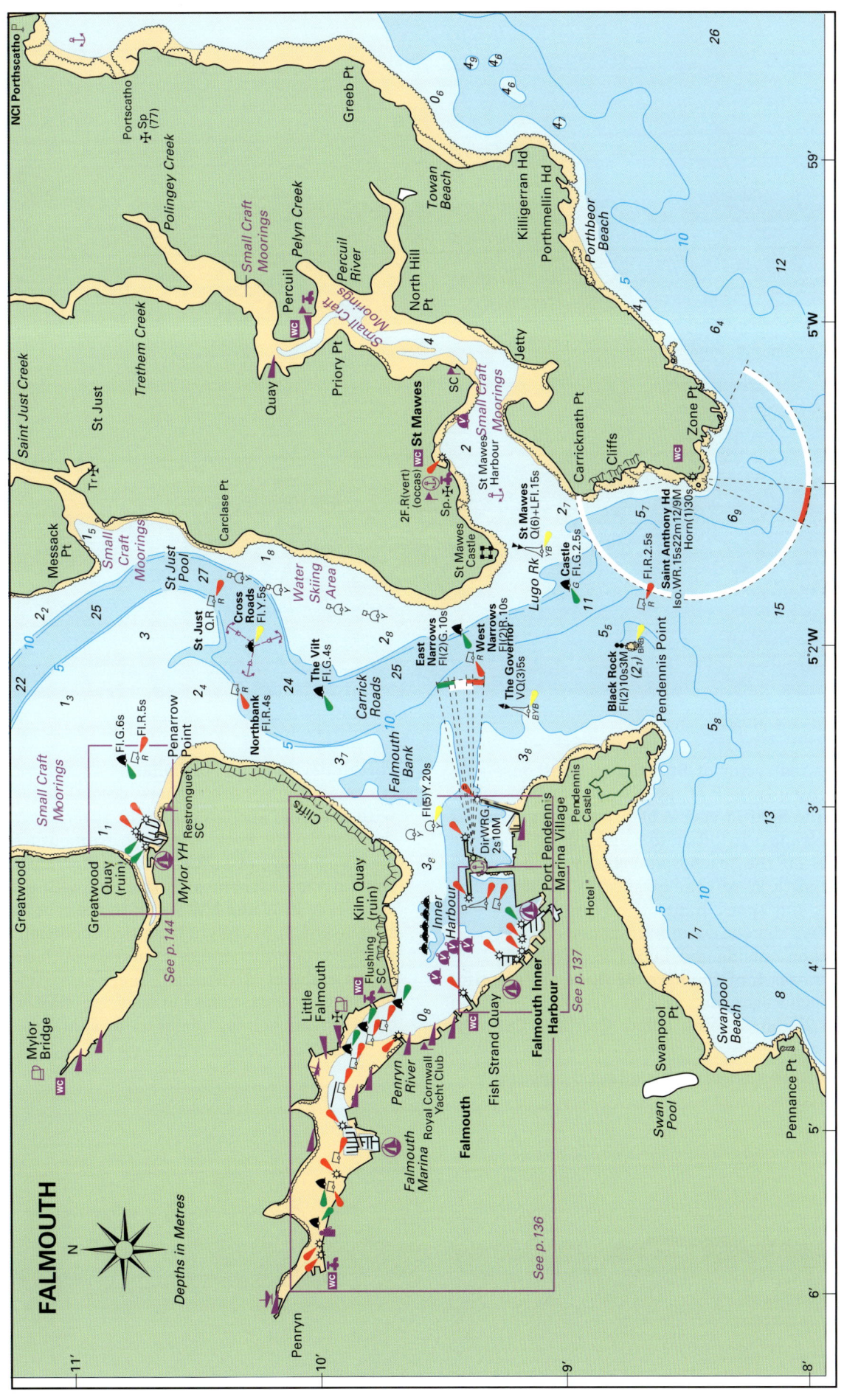

14 FALMOUTH

Approach to Falmouth from S

Swanpool Beach in Falmouth Bay

within the red sector of St Anthony lighthouse and, if approaching from E at night, wait until the white sector of the light is visible before shaping a course for the entrance. In offshore winds there are good anchorages off the beaches at Gyllingvase, Swanpool and Maenporth W of the entrance in Falmouth Bay. There is a 4kn speed limit off all the beaches and yellow buoys denote swimming zones and seagrass beds. Anchor outside the buoys in about 5m LAT. In the two bays E of the harbour there are plentiful daytime anchorages including at Hemmick Beach in the lee of Dodman Point, below Caerhays Castle at Porthluney Cove, at Portholland and at Portloe. There is a small drying harbour here, accessible for day craft with potential anchorages in the three coves between there and Gull Rock. Closer to Falmouth there is a good anchorage at Carne Beach in Gerrans Bay and a small drying harbour at Portscatho with a very good anchorage in W and NW winds in the cove just N. This spot is tenable overnight in settled conditions whereas all the other anchorages E of Falmouth are subject to the ambient WSW swell. There are a few visitors' moorings at Portscatho but they are mostly occupied by RIBs from holiday homes in the summer.

Portscatho, E of Falmouth on the Roseland peninsula

Falmouth

The beaches just inside the lighthouse are popular on sunny days with E winds

Gull Rock is about halfway between Dodman Point and Falmouth. This is from the inside passage

Entry

The entrance is around 1M wide but there is a major hazard almost in the centre. Black Rock with an associated reef running N/S is marked by an IDM (Fl(2)10s3M). Leisure craft can enter either side of Black Rock where the deeper East Channel is buoyed and used by large commercial vessels. This is the safest route at night but there is at least 6m in the channel W of Black Rock and the Governor ECM (VQ(3)5s) is a useful waypoint. The two channels meet just NE of this point. Keep a sharp lookout for ferries transiting between Falmouth and St Mawes and for bunkering coasters which sometimes use the West Channel. As you enter from seaward, there are two beaches to starboard which are popular daytime anchorages in the summer when the wind is E. The holding is variable though due to the amount of kelp so they cannot be recommended overnight, and a seagrass bed is encroaching from N.

Governor ECM is a useful waypoint in the West Channel

14 FALMOUTH

Approach to Falmouth Haven — *Jane Russell*

FALMOUTH

The final approach to Falmouth and the Penryn River skirts the edge of the docks. Beware of large vessel movements in this area. There is a good anchorage along the opposite shore off Trefusis Point in NW or N winds, but stay clear of any commercial mooring buoys which have substantial chains on the seabed. Once level with the end of the commercial docks, Port Pendennis Marina (Indep) with the conspicuous tower of the National Maritime Museum lies SSW, and Falmouth Haven (HM) is SW. If heading for the latter, aim initially towards Port Pendennis until reaching four large yellow buoys which mark the edge of the

The anchorage off Falmouth with Port Pendennis Marina and the National Maritime Museum left

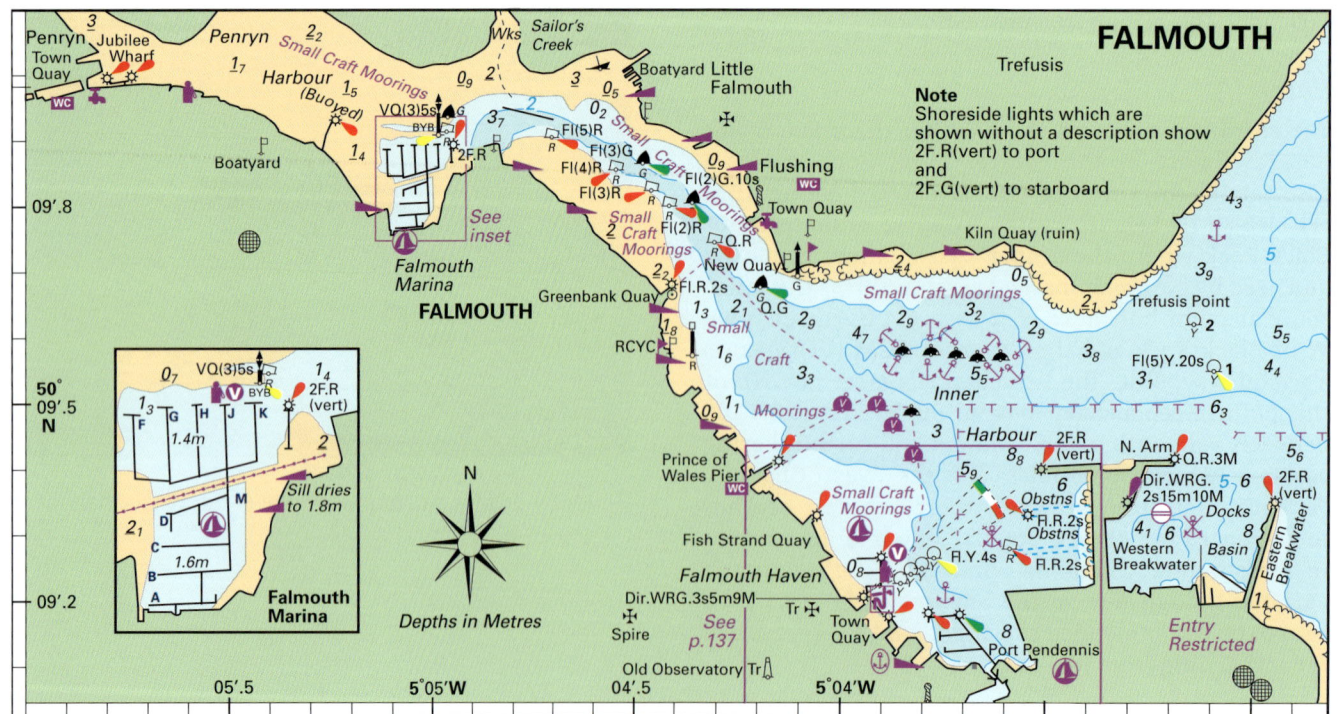

136 • West Country Pilot

Falmouth

Falmouth Harbour looking SE. Sailing cruise ship *Sea Cloud Spirit* is left of centre

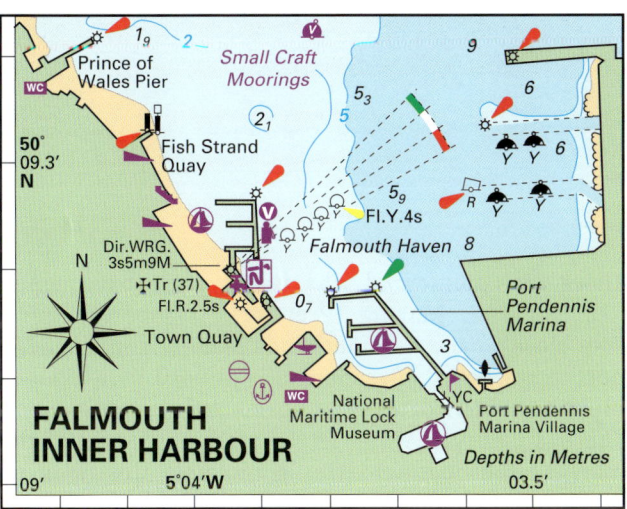

Approaching Falmouth Marina

anchorage area, and then turn SW leaving these to port. There is a directional beacon (Dir.WRG.3s5m9M) covering the final approach to Falmouth Haven with a least depth of 1.4m on the leading line (two orange triangles in transit).

The main anchorage lies between the four yellow buoys mentioned above and Port Pendennis. There are no other anchorages on the Falmouth side of the channel. A number of green visitors' moorings are provided by the HM (marked FHC) off Prince of Wales Pier (N of Falmouth Haven). The best landing places are at Falmouth Haven (if anchored) or the yacht club (if on a mooring). Avoid Custom House Quay and Prince of Wales Pier which are busy with ferries and trip boats. There is a large slipway beyond the anchorage at Grove Place for launch and recovery.

In strong NE winds this part of the harbour can be uncomfortable and St Mawes (see p.139) is a better option for craft which do not need to be alongside.

Shoreside

Showers and toilets can be found at all the marinas and yacht clubs. Falmouth and Penryn have all the shopping facilities of a large town including supermarkets and there are several chandleries. Both have many options for eating ashore.

All repairs can be catered for (from a paddleboard to something approaching 100,000 tons!) with many facilities centred on Commercial Road in Penryn.

There are rail stations at both Falmouth and Penryn, connecting to the main line at Truro. Regular ferries link Falmouth with St Mawes and Penryn with Flushing on the opposite bank. River cruises head upstream to Trelissick and Malpas, and across the bay to Helford.

West Country Pilot • 137

14 FALMOUTH

The quay at Flushing opposite Falmouth

Penryn River

Continuing NW, the Penryn River is buoyed and lit as far as the Penryn road bridge. The village of Flushing lies opposite Falmouth and the area between the two is densely packed with moorings, so it is best to stick to the main buoyed channel. At the upstream end of Flushing is a repair yard with substantial slipways. Just past here, as the main channel trends W, is an inlet known locally as Sailor's Creek with a variety of vessels moored along the bank and a small wintering yard just upstream.

There are commercial wharves to port above which lies Falmouth Marina (Premier). If mooring here, stay close to the hammerheads leaving a small ECM post to starboard. The marina is divided by a disused pipeline which dries leaving a dredged inner pool. There is plenty of water in the main outer part of the marina. The channel dries completely upstream of here but Freemans Wharf can be reached above about half-tide. Many ancillary marine services are found in Commercial Road, Penryn, which runs alongside the river.

Drying pontoons at Freemans Wharf

St Mawes Castle and the SCM marking Lugo Rock

ST MAWES & PERCUIL

St Mawes is closer to the entrance than Falmouth and lies to the E on the Roseland Peninsula. Sheltered in winds from N through E to S, it provides an excellent alternative if Falmouth is uncomfortable but is a pleasant destination in its own right. The harbour opens to starboard after passing Black Rock and before the Castle SHM; leave St Mawes SCM (Q(6)+LFl.15s), which marks Lugo Rock, to port. Depths range from 2.5-5m with good holding. There is a voluntary anchoring restriction close along the S shore protecting an area where the holding is poor due to an abundance of seagrass. S of the harbour wall, a start line and turning marks for racing are identified by

Slipway and landing steps in St Mawes harbour

St Mawes

Visitors' moorings with the entrance to the Percuil River beyond

orange buoys with flags arranged in a triangle, where anchoring is prohibited during racing. Contact the HM before anchoring in this vicinity. A number of green visitors' moorings lie in a line off the main beach just E of the harbour wall and there are large white moorings (prefixed 'O') W of Amsterdam Point which may also be available to visitors.

Above Amsterdam Point, the Percuil River briefly turns SE before heading NNE round a sweeping bend. Many moorings make it difficult to identify the deepest channel. The corner is overlooked by the impressive Place House and it is just possible to anchor clear of the moorings below the LWS mark which is somewhat sheltered from SW winds. The beach is private above the LW mark.

The Percuil River heads inland behind the town of St Mawes getting progressively shallower. There are many moorings but anchoring is not permitted for some distance due to the presence of oyster beds. The sailing club has a dinghy park and slipway at Stoneworks Quay on the E bank, where it is possible to land by dinghy at most states of the tide and use their facilities. As you continue N towards the hamlet of Percuil the river becomes very shallow, but the scenery is spectacular and worth exploring on the tide, or in a tender. The wooded Porth Creek heads E away from the main river which then forks below Percuil Boatyard with the main channel to port and Pelyn Creek to starboard. A good neap tide anchorage can be found here. Yachts can continue NW then E at Bosloggas following the line of moorings although bear in mind the channel dries. Trot moorings line both sides of the river here, ending where the river forks into two creeks. Shoal draught boats can stay afloat in this stretch and it is also possible to anchor again although you will dry out, but it is a beautiful spot.

Falmouth essential information

Clubs
Royal Cornwall Yacht Club ☎01326 312126
Flushing Sailing Club ☎01326 375980
St Mawes Sailing Club ☎01326 270686

Local Information
Prince of Wales Pier, Falmouth; The Square, St Mawes

Visitors' Berths
Falmouth Haven (HM) VHF 12; ☎01326 310991
Moorings Falmouth & St Mawes

Additional Berthing
Port Pendennis Marina (Indep) VHF 80; ☎01326 211211
Falmouth Marina (Premier) VHF 80; ☎01326 316620
Freemans Wharf

Water Taxi
RCYC launch

Webcams
www.royalcornwallyachtclub.org
www.falmouthharbour.co.uk

Water
At marinas

Fuel
Falmouth Haven & Falmouth Marina

Gas
Port Pendennis, Falmouth

Chandlery
Port Pendennis, Falmouth
Macsalvors, Penryn
Fal Chandlers, Falmouth Marina

Victuals
Church St & Killigrew St, Falmouth
King's Rd & The Square, St Mawes

Nearest Large Supermarket
Penryn, nr Falmouth Marina

Laundry
Killigrew St, Trelawney Rd & Polwhaveral Terrace, Falmouth

Repairs
Numerous yards in Penryn; Falmouth Boat Co, Flushing
Pendennis Shipyard (Superyachts); A&P Falmouth (Ships)
Polvarth BY, Freshwater BY, Percuil BY, all St Mawes

Engineers
Falmouth Harbour Marine Services
Simon Caddy; Robin Curnow, Penryn

Riggers
Allspars, Grove Place
A2, Falmouth Marina
Riggers-UK, Penryn

Electronics
BT Marine, Charity & Taylor

Sailmakers
SKB, Penryn,
Gaff Sails, Falmouth,
Penrose, Sailtech, Collins (outskirts)

Scrubbing Posts
Adjacent to Falmouth Haven. Contact HM

Car Hire
Penryn

Transport
Trains from Falmouth, Penryn to Truro for mainline. Ferry between Falmouth and Flushing/St Mawes.

Shoreside

Showers and toilets are available at St Mawes Sailing Club, adjacent to the quay, and at their dinghy park upriver. There is a food store, deli, bakery and wine merchant in the town together with several pubs and restaurants.

Local attractions

Ashore, Falmouth is home to a branch of the National Maritime Museum and the equally well known Falmouth Marine School, and is a frequent port of call for cruise liners and the tall ships. The narrow main street has many historic buildings linked to maritime history. Pendennis Castle and St Mawes Castle are open to the public.

Orders and oysters

Falmouth's geographic position as the first and last major port results in a wide variety of marine traffic as it has done for centuries, but some traditions continue.

'Falmouth for orders' is an instruction known to commercial seafarers worldwide. In the days of trading under sail, with limited communication, cargo skippers would not be sure of the final destination for their goods until they made landfall. By dint of its geographic position, Falmouth was the port of choice for most of Europe. In today's modern connected world, this still happens to an extent, although the action (or inaction) is now out in the bay rather than the Carrick Roads. Most ships at anchor in Falmouth Bay are there for refuelling, but some are awaiting instructions ('orders') whilst, during periods of slack trade, quite large vessels can be found laid up in the Fal off Tolverne.

Another tradition is oysters, for which Falmouth is famous. Every year from the end of September, large swathes of moorings are taken up as the oyster dredging season begins. Local byelaws dictate that this activity can only be carried out under sail or oar and between 0900 and 1500, which has the effect of conserving stocks whilst also maintaining the skills required. Gaff rigged Falmouth working boats are exclusively used and at weekends and during the summer months, they can be seen racing in full rig with incredible speed and agility in the Carrick Roads, at local regattas as far away as Fowey and in the bay. They are still built today (for dredging, racing or cruising) at the Gaffers and Luggers boatyard at Mylor (see chapter 15).

In late summer, there is often a cosmopolitan feel to the town itself, especially around Falmouth Haven and Port Pendennis where ensigns of many nations are seen as yachts preparing to depart mix with those arriving from far and wide. It is literally the ultimate destination.

Falmouth working boat at St Mawes

Sailing cruise ship *Sea Cloud Spirit* docked at Falmouth

15 TRURO
MYLOR, CARRICK ROADS & RIVER FAL

Harbour Master's Office
VHF 12 'Carrick', 'Carrick 3'
Harbour Office, Town Quay, Truro TR1 2HJ
☎ 01872 324216 / 07736 618509

The port of Truro, part of which is still active, is 10M from Black Rock at the entrance to Falmouth Harbour. Numerous creeks abundant with wildlife are ideal for exploring in small craft and there are multiple mooring options for larger boats (and some for large ships!). Truro is a small city reachable on the tide by moderate draught vessels and even deep keeled yachts can reach Malpas, which is a short bus ride, or an hour's leisurely walk, from the city centre.

Landmarks
From the Carrick Roads above Black Rock, Trelissick House is conspicuous in the distance where the channel narrows very abruptly. Truro Cathedral is always visible for the final 2M to the city.

Main hazards
If heading inland, be aware that it is very shallow outside the buoyed channel in places at low water, although the bottom is mostly mud. The channel itself is very deep, being a flooded glacial valley (ria). The final 3M stretch to Truro dries and there is a flood barrier 1M from the limit of navigation, where coasters

Trelissick House

still occasionally visit the adjacent commercial wharf. A chain ferry crosses the river about halfway up and has priority.

Approaches
Approach as for Falmouth (Chapter 14) and from abeam Falmouth Docks, the main buoyed channel continues NNW until The Vilt SHM (Fl.G.4s), then heads NE towards the hamlet of St Just.

St Just is a good anchorage in E winds where it is possible to land on the beach and follow the coast path to the village, or to St Mawes. The drying creek runs behind the village and there is a boatyard with a half-tide slipway, but with sufficient rise of tide it is possible to reach the village church.

Busy summer weekend on Carrick Roads

Truro

RIVER FAL AND TRURO RIVER

Depths in Metres

Truro Cathedral

West Country Pilot • 143

The forest of masts at Mylor

MYLOR

Opposite St Just is Mylor Yacht Harbour (Transeurope). The entrance channel is buoyed at its outer end and it is possible to head directly for the buoyage other than at LWS when it is safer to approach from S or SE. From the St Just PHM (Q.R), head NW with a back bearing on the conspicuous water tower between St Just and St Mawes. There is 2m at LAT for the most part on this line until very close to the entrance buoys where the depth reduces slightly. Alternatively, head due N from the big ship mooring ('Crossroads') in the middle of the main channel leaving the Northbank PHM (FlR.4s) to port, until the St Just PHM and the water tower are in transit SE. Then head for the marina channel markers.

The approach channel is dredged to 2m and the mooring buoys either side are red/green as appropriate. The marina has a large linear pontoon and several moorings for visitors and is a popular base from which to explore, as you can hire everything from a paddle board to a motor yacht. There are also three slipways in the immediate vicinity for launching and recovery. Mylor Creek (dries) heads W from the end of the marina approach channel where the entrance narrows.

Ultra low spring tide at Mylor Yacht Harbour

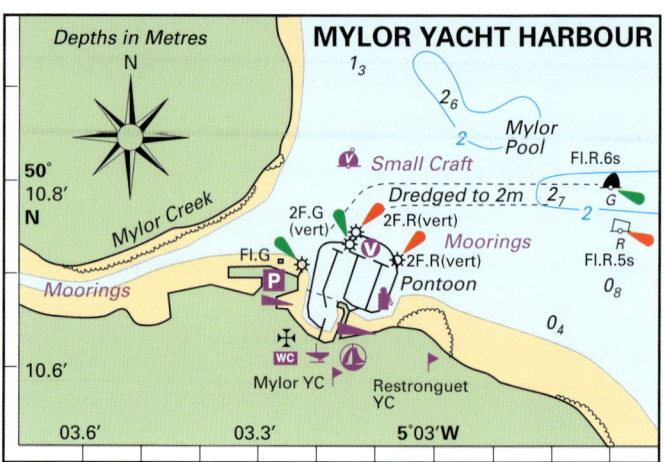

The deepest water is in the centre until the creek opens out around 0.25M past the marina. Thereafter the channel is close to the starboard bank until you reach the boatyards at Mylor Bridge at the head of the creek. The yards can be approached near HW. Mylor Creek Boatyard has a large slipway and several drying spaces along the beach, both of which may be available to visiting craft that can take the ground. Adjacent is the Gaffers & Luggers yard which continues the Mylor tradition of building and maintaining the Falmouth working boats for which the area is famous. It is feasible to moor alongside the quay opposite the yards very briefly to visit the village but it is preferable to come by dinghy from Mylor Yacht Harbour if planning to spend longer ashore.

Carrick Roads

After St Just, the buoyed channel swings sharply NW for the next mile or so towards Restronguet. The approach to Restronguet Creek is shallow (1.3m LAT) but it is possible to anchor off the entrance at neaps in W winds. Beware of Carick Carlys rock near the approach which is marked by NCM and SCM posts. They can be very difficult to identify in the evening sun. There are many moorings in the creek itself, which dries soon after the entrance. The pub to port has a drying pontoon for customers boats accessible from about half-tide. With a tender the creek can be explored well inland and the marshy upper reaches have a wide variety of wildlife. The first inlet to starboard is Penpol Creek where there is a boatyard and about 1M further on you reach the restored trading quay at Devoran. Above Devoran the creek becomes a marsh and the channel is no more than a gutway marked by the occasional bamboo pole. The limit of exploration is the bridge at Perranarworthal.

River Fal

Back in the Carrick Roads, the buoyed channel resumes a NE course from the Carick SHM (Fl(2)G.10s) past Pill Creek, which can be explored by dinghy, until Turnaware Point where the expanse of water narrows abruptly. Turnaware Bar, marked by a small SHM (Fl.G.5s), is hard shingle and should be avoided leaving the buoy to starboard. Local line fishermen work this area. The channel beyond here is deep and steep sided, bounded on both banks by scrub oak woods. To port is Channals Creek below Trelissick House which affords a good anchorage in winds between NW and NE. Unlike most of the remainder of the coast within the Carrick Roads, this corner is owned by the National Trust and so landing can be made from here as far as the pontoon at the King Harry ferry further upstream. To starboard after Turnaware Point is Turnaware Beach, which is a popular anchorage with some interesting remains of the preparation for the D-Day landings found ashore, and Tolcarne Creek. Although sheltered in winds from SE to SW, the bank is very steep-to and requires significant scope to anchor, since it is quite easy to drag down the bank into the deep channel which carries around 15m at this point. Opposite Tolcarne Creek is the first of four visitors' pontoons run by Truro Harbour Authority. The river heads N from here past the King Harry chain ferry which has right of way at all times – pass clear astern of it. Adjacent to the ferry

Channals Creek below Trelissick

King Harry ferry has right of way

on the port bank is the pontoon for Trelissick House. Dinghies can be moored on the inside and yachts can moor alongside briefly, or after the trip boats have finished for the day, to take on water. Above the ferry are large ship moorings, often with ships laid up.

Turnaware is a popular spot in S weather

15 TRURO

Commercial shipping is often laid up in the Fal

At the next corner as the river turns E is the combined entrance to Lamouth Creek and Cowlands Creek, popular with canoeists and paddle boarders. These drying creeks split just inside the entrance at Roundwood Quay with Lamouth Creek heading just S of W and Cowlands Creek NW. As you head up Cowlands Creek there is a picturesque inlet to starboard by the hamlet of Combe.

The main river runs a short distance E past Smugglers Cottage at Tolverne. There are a few moorings here including one for visiting yachts and a slipway for landing. It is possible to anchor on the outside of the bend near the entrance to Lamouth/Cowlands Creeks or along the Tolverne shore clear of the moorings but beware of a shallow patch near the upstream moorings.

At the next corner the channel divides. The large spit protruding from the bank to port used to see many groundings but is now marked with two PHMs. The River Fal continues E but dries soon after. There is enough water to anchor here, particularly at neaps, although there are several sunken concrete blocks marked by a yellow post. The drying channel hugs the N bank until a pair of inlets either side before heading towards the opposite bank. Shoal draught craft may be able to stay afloat as far as this point and those which can dry out might find a spot 0.5M further E where a hard on the S side is reached by a public footpath. Any further exploration is best done by dinghy and the village of Ruan Lanihorne can just be reached at HW through the marshy upper reaches, although the last stretch is barely more than a ditch in size.

Smugglers Cottage, Tolverne. The visitors' mooring is the yellow buoy extreme left

Yachts anchored in the Fal above Tolverne

The meandering final approach to Truro

TRURO

Just N of the entrance to the River Fal is the second Truro Harbour Authority visitors' pontoon and the main channel is the Truro River which heads N with two further PHMs marking the deepest water. If mooring on this pontoon, allow for the strong current which crosses it on a NW/SE axis. Maggoty Bank encroaches from starboard above the pontoon with a SHM (Fl.G.5s) at its extremity, before the channel curves NNE towards the next visitors' pontoon. The whole stretch is a very good anchorage in any winds other than direct N or S. As you pass the third pontoon the channel slowly curves NW and narrows as the depth reduces and the best water is along the line of larger moorings just to starboard of the centreline. Below Malpas, as the river divides again, is the final visitors' pontoon which can accommodate vessels up to 15m but only has 0.7m depth at LWS. Moor on the E side only. It is linked to the shore and the HM has a small boatyard here, and tenders from boats moored downstream can land near the shoreward end.

One branch of the river heads NE from here and can be explored by dinghy as far as the village of Tresillian. The other branch also dries but vessels of modest draught can reach Truro at HW as the channel is marked and still used by the occasional coaster (officially, craft drawing 4m can reach Lighterage Quay). Leave Malpas just after half-tide and follow the channel buoys, initially SW. Lambe Creek is immediately ahead and

Shore linked pontoon at Malpas

15 TRURO

Truro tidal barrier and waiting pontoon

Approaching the quays at Truro

the channel turns NW past two SHMs then more N towards a pair of PHMs in an area known as Sunny Corner where there are small craft on beach moorings and a slipway. Calenick Creek heads off W and what appears to be a large expanse of water is actually very shallow, but the creek itself can be entered further upstream. The channel remains close to the shore then curves W, slowly at first with the bend tightening as you round the next PHM heading towards the end of Lighterage Quay which is commercial. Halfway between the last PHM and the quay, is the entrance to Calenick Creek which heads inland for about a mile. Continuing to Truro, the channel hugs Lighterage Quay for its entire length until resuming midstream at the

Truro tidal barrier. This is normally open except when large spring tides occur or a surge is predicted. From here, the channel is no more than a gutway marked by unlit red/green posts, first along the E shore and then over to the W side where it remains for much of the rest of its length, only meandering for the last 0.25M or so. Contact the HM for berthing, which is normally in the most westerly of the three basins alongside a large supermarket or the quay opposite where there is power, water and basic facilities. The bottom here is soft mud and, if not planning to dry out, it is best to leave no later than HW.

HM moorings in the centre of the city

Truro

Truro essential information

Clubs
Mylor Yacht Club ☎01326 374391
Restronguet Sailing Club ☎07952 157316

Local Information
Boscawen St, Truro

Visitors' Berths
Island pontoons (1 shore linked) plus moorings
Alongside drying berths at Truro

Additional Berthing
Mylor Yacht Harbour VHF 80; ☎01326 372121
Mylor Creek Boatyard ☎01326 377366

Water Taxi
Mylor Water Taxi (at Yacht Harbour) VHF 08

Webcams
www.falriver.co.uk
www.mylor.com

Water
At marina and boatyards. Trelissick pontoon near King Harry

Fuel
Mylor Yacht Harbour

Gas
Mylor Chandlery
Truro Calor Centre

Chandlery
Mylor Chandlery and boatyards

Victuals
Mylor village & Truro

Nearest Large Supermarket
Penryn (by bus from Mylor); Truro

Laundry
Chapel Hill, Truro
Mylor Yacht Harbour

Repairs
Mylor Yacht Harbour (MarineTeam)
Cockwells; Gaffers & Luggers, Mylor Creek;
Pascoes Boatyard, St Just

Engineers
Mylor Yacht Harbour (MarineTeam)

Riggers
Mylor Chandlery & Rigging

Electronics
Mylor Yacht Harbour (MarineTeam)

Scrubbing Posts
Ask at boatyards

Car Hire
Penryn (nearest to Mylor); most brands in Truro

Transport
Trains from Truro to Plymouth, London, Penzance, Falmouth.

Shoreside

There are toilets and showers at Mylor Yacht Harbour and at Truro by the HM office. There are also facilities at Malpas and at Tolverne by the slipway.

Truro has a wide variety of shops including supermarkets and all supplies should be available. Mylor village is a half hour stroll from the marina and has a general store (with fresh bread and ice), post office/convenience store, a butcher and a fish shop.

There is a chandlery at Mylor Yacht Harbour, a café and a restaurant. There is also a company specialising in dinghies and boards.

St Just has a café opposite the church, about 1M from the anchorage, with St Mawes a 40 minute walk away.

Truro is the main transport hub for West Cornwall with a rail station on the main London-Penzance line. The branch line from Falmouth arrives here. There is a central bus station close to the HM office offering connections to most of the surrounding villages and the North Cornwall coast, including the airport at Newquay.

Local attractions

'The most beautiful churchyard on Earth', according to John Betjeman is at St Just and can be reached by tender on the tide. Mylor Harbour was once the smallest Royal Naval yard, and home to the notoriously tough HMS *Ganges* training school. There is a memorial to its attendees in the churchyard near the marina, and the ancient church is worth a visit.

Trelissick House and grounds overlooks the estuary. If anchored off Loe Beach, Turnaware or in Channals Creek, it is possible to land by tender on the beach 0.5M directly below the house and walk up the hill to visit. Anchored upstream, the best plan is to land on the inside of the ferry pontoon situated just below the King Harry chain ferry. Truro is a compact city, easily explored on foot, and can be reached by water, rail or road. Truro Cathedral is a fine example of gothic revival architecture, its three spires being a rarity.

Late evening at Turnaware

West Country Pilot • 149

16 HELFORD RIVER
PORTHALLOW & PORTHOUSTOCK

Harbour Master's Office
VHF 37 'Helford Moorings Officer' (*Note* no actual HM)
Ashfield, Porkellis, Helston TR13 0JR
☎ 01326 221265 / 07808 071485
NCI Nare Point VHF 65 ☎ 01326 755076

The Helford is a picturesque river off Falmouth Bay, and a popular cruising destination. The entrance is approximately 4M SW of Black Rock in Falmouth Harbour making it ideal for smaller craft based or launched at Falmouth. The river is navigable for some 4M inland as far as the quay at Gweek, which vessels drawing as much as 2m can reach on a spring tide.

Landmarks

From offshore, the landmarks near Falmouth described in Chapter 14 are good for the Helford. Closer to, Nare Point is low lying S of the entrance, identified by a NCI lookout. Rosemullion Head lies on the N side but is not particularly distinctive. From Falmouth, a cluster of houses located in Gillan Creek can be seen in most conditions bearing 210°.

Main hazards

The river is very exposed to E winds and swell. August Rock (also known as Gedges) lies just offshore between Rosemullion Head and the river entrance, and is marked by a seasonal SHM. During the winter,

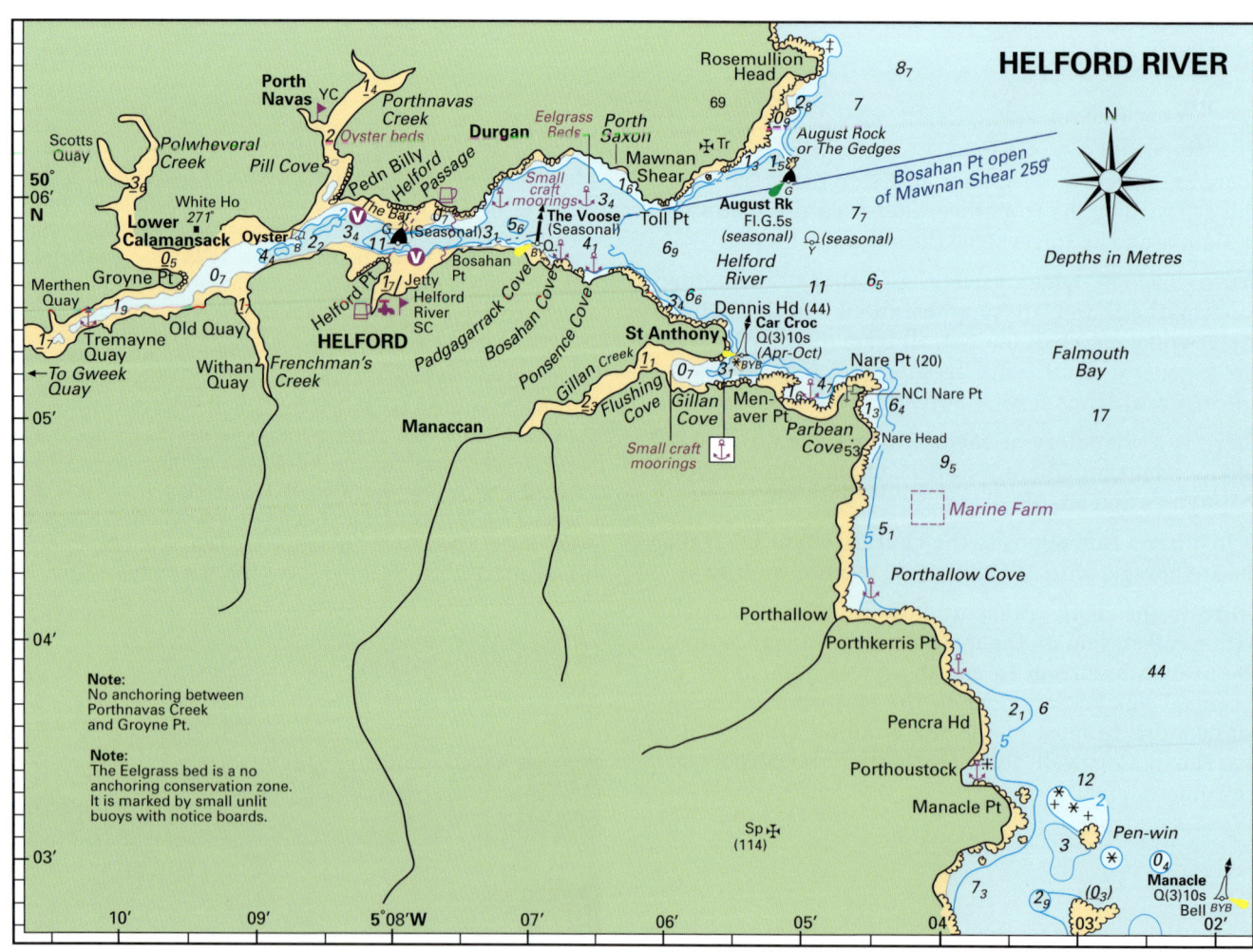

150 • West Country Pilot

Helford River

NCI Nare Point marks the S side of the entrance

August Rock SHM at the entrance to the Helford

when the buoy may not on station, a clearing bearing of approximately 260° can be formed by keeping Bosahan Point (just downstream of the moorings) open of Mawnan Shear (the first headland *inside* the river on the N side). An unmarked reef extends NE of Nare Point for some 300m. Within the river, a large mud bank is on the N side opposite the village of Helford marked by a small unlit SHM. This buoy can be difficult to distinguish from the surrounding moorings. Above Helford, there are old oyster beds in shallower water before the river dries beyond Tremayne Quay about 2M from the entrance. The creeks off the river all dry out, except the lower end of Porth Navas creek.

Approaches

Approach initially as for Falmouth (see Chapter 14) but if approaching from offshore steer NW from the Manacles ECM; from Dodman Point or along the coast continue on 240° past Falmouth; or, from Falmouth Harbour entrance, steer 210° to leave August Rock SHM to starboard.

Entry

Once the moorings 1M inside the entrance are in clear sight, steer due W until in the vicinity of the chosen anchorage or a position abeam the Voose NCM, just before the main block of moorings begins.

Anchorages on the north bank

Between Mawnan Shear and Durgan there is a sizeable seagrass bed, with a voluntary no anchoring zone inshore of an imaginary line joining the two headlands. It is additionally marked by three small white buoys positioned approximately 100m from the shore. Anchor anywhere outside the (extended) line of the buoys where the holding is generally good, but be aware that depths have been reported as being greater than the charted 3.5-4m LAT. Landing is possible on the beaches at Porth Saxon, which is roughly central, at Grebe at the inshore end of the anchorage which is slightly steeper, or at the hamlet of Durgan inshore of the local moorings which is the

Grebe anchorage

Durgan

16 HELFORD RIVER

most protected. A large, barrel shaped mooring here is often allocated for visitors and has a green pick up buoy.

W of the local moorings is another anchorage off the beach at Trebah at Polwigden Cove/Robin's Cove. This offers slightly better protection from W winds and the seabed appears to have a bit more mud mixed in with the sand than is the case downstream, which might improve holding. The beach at Trebah is private so landing involves a short trip in the tender to Durgan or upstream around a small headland to the beach at Passage Cove. In settled conditions it is feasible to cross the river by tender to the sailing club pontoons at Helford, although they dry (LW±2) at springs.

Note that neither of the anchorages described above offer protection in NE winds or swell, which tends to funnel into the river.

Anchorages on the south bank

The first potential anchorage is just inside Narc Point at Parbean Cove which is protected in winds from SE to SW. There is a cluster of local moorings but room for a couple of boats to anchor outside them. Day craft may be able to find a spot inshore of the moorings off the small beach. There are some small boulders on the seabed to avoid but the bottom can be seen in most conditions, and a tripping line can be deployed if unsure.

Just upstream is Gillan Creek which dries. There is a good potential anchorage off here for larger vessels outside the 5m contour. A rocky outcrop, Car Croc, sits in the centre of the approach. It is marked by a seasonal ECM but the mark often lies NE of the rock. It can be passed either side mid-way to the shore with due caution, the W side being the safer option. There are a couple of sandy patches at the entrance to the creek, the outer one in about 2.5m LAT and the inner perhaps only 1m, but adequate on neap tides for most craft. The outer harbour is fairly flat and offers potential for drying out clear of any moorings, with landing possible to starboard at St Anthony, where there is a slipway, or opposite at two small beaches by the mouth of the creek. A causeway crosses the creek just after it turns SW but shoal draught vessels can explore further on the tide. Seek local advice from the boatyard before attempting to dry out above the causeway.

The anchorages at Ponsence Cove and Bosahan Cove are almost exactly opposite those on the Durgan shore described above, and there is similarly more water reported here. Bosahan Cove is better for landing on the beach (identified by a boathouse), but leave sufficient swinging room to avoid the Voose, a jagged reef with a NCM. It is just over a 1M walk to Helford from here. There is a half-tide passage through the reef to the beach at Padgarrack Cove.

Parbean Cove offers some protection from SE winds

Gillan Creek with Car Croc ECM (left)

HELFORD

A large area of moorings is found off Helford village on the S bank. A number of these are for visitors and can take sizeable craft, with rafting the norm in peak summer. The visitors' moorings are all green and have very substantial chains. At times, private moorings are allocated to visitors when their owners are away and these are identified by having a green pick up buoy. The tide runs fast through the moorings so ensure the mooring chain is fast on a cleat or deck post.

Tenders can land at the sailing club, except at LWS±2 or at a permissive pontoon just upstream of the ferry landing slip where there is an honesty box.

Immediately upstream of the moorings is a small area for anchoring occasionally marked by buoys. There is only room for a few boats but it remains fairly popular.

Porth Navas Creek is N of the anchorage. The lower part is crowded with local moorings and anchoring is not permitted above the moorings due to the presence of oyster beds. The local yacht club may be able to arrange a drying berth or mooring in the inlet off the creek by the club, but otherwise the area is worth visiting by tender.

Ponsence Cove on the S side opposite Durgan

Bosahan Cove (with boathouse) and Voose NCM (right)

Porth Navas Creek and moorings

16 HELFORD RIVER

Peaceful anchorage at Tremayne Quay

GWEEK

Oyster beds are no longer laid in the river above Helford, but this section is now a Site of Special Scientific Interest (SSSI), and a local byelaw prohibiting anchoring remains in force. The area includes Frenchman's Creek of literary fame and, if exploring it by tender or small day craft, beware of submerged debris from fallen trees as well as the more obvious hazards above the water.

Above Groyne Point anchoring is possible again. Polwheveral Creek branches off W then N and is a quiet, attractive spot in which to dry out. Anchoring fore and aft is recommended to avoid ending up at a jaunty angle, especially further upstream. At neaps, shoal draught vessels can anchor inside Groyne Point in the mouth of the creek and stay afloat.

The main river continues WSW from Groyne Point and there is between 1m and 2m LAT on average as far as Tremayne Quay, with a few deeper pools. Due to the survey data being quite old, a depth sounder makes a better friend than a chart plotter in this area. Tremayne Quay is private but landing is permitted. Just past the boathouse at Tremayne the river dips very briefly S and there is a comfortable neap tide anchorage in this bight opposite Merthen Creek. The channel dries here.

The quay at the village of Gweek is the limit of navigation. The meandering channel is marked by lateral red/green buoys with creeks off either side suitable for exploring by tender. Approaching Gweek itself, the channel turns NW with a couple of small factories to port and an adjacent boatyard. Another small boatyard is located on the opposite bank. Any barges or shellfish frames anchored here, just below Gweek Quay, should be left to port and the quay approached fairly close to. There is a long narrow islet running practically the entire length of the quay which must be kept to starboard. The traditional yard is mainly for laying up but it might be possible to arrange an alongside drying berth, although it will likely be necessary to warp a vessel out on departure. Otherwise, if visiting by tender, leave no later than HW.

Helford River essential information

Clubs
Helford River Sailing Club ☎01326 231606
Port Navas Yacht Club ☎01326 340525

Visitors' Berths
Moorings

Additional Berthing
Gweek Classic Boatyard (drying quay)

Water Taxi
Helford Ferry VHF 37

Water
Helford River Sailing Club; Gweek Quay

Gas
Gweek Classic Boatyard

Chandlery
Gweek Classic Boatyard

Victuals
Limited supplies at Helford & Gweek

Nearest Large Supermarket
Penryn or Helston (bus from Gweek or Helford Passage)

Repairs
Gweek Classic Boatyard; River Boatyard, Gweek

Engineers
Cellar Marine, Porthallow

Car Hire
Nearest Falmouth/Penryn

Transport
Occasional buses

Shoreside

There are small stores at both Helford and Gweek and both villages have pubs. Showers and a laundry are available at Helford River Sailing Club.

Local attractions

The area in this chapter is rural with limited public transport. Glendurgan and Trebah gardens are near to the anchorages at Durgan, and a slightly longer walk from Helford Passage which is closer to the main visitors' moorings. There is also a foot ferry across the river.

Further upstream is the seal sanctuary at Gweek and at Gweek Quay Classic Boatyard, on the opposite bank, there is always an array of traditional vessels undergoing restoration.

Goonhilly Earth Station is on the Lizard peninsula, but it is easier to reach it from Falmouth or Truro.

Porthallow anchorage. Beware of discarded fishing tackle N

PORTHALLOW & PORTHOUSTOCK

These adjacent anchorages lie within Falmouth Bay around 1.5-2.5M S of the entrance to the Helford and are therefore included in this chapter.

Porthallow Cove should be approached on a course between S and WNW, taking care to avoid a marine farm about 0.5M out. This is a good anchorage protected by cliffs W and S. In addition, the Manacles reef beginning around 1M S helps dissipate the ambient swell, meaning this is one of a few places around Falmouth Bay where it is possible to anchor overnight in SW weather without suffering the usual effects of the swell. Anchor in the corner of the bay in about 3.5m LAT. There are reports of detritus on the seabed (fishing gear) so a tripping line may be advisable. The beach is shingle and fairly steep-to, but the absence of swell mitigates this. When landing, note that the upper part of the beach near the pub is used for car parking.

Just around the rocky headland is Porthkerris Cove which should be approached from NE. It is a pleasant daytime anchorage outside the few local moorings but is more exposed to SW swell (although not SW winds). A conspicuous lookout tower lies at the entrance to the cove and there is a small reef here, Drawna Rocks, most of which is always visible.

The final anchorage is a further 1M S at Porthoustock. This is situated right at the start of the Manacles reef and, as Porthkerris, is best approached from ENE. It is formed by a decent sized indent in the coast which affords additional protection from swell, but its proximity to the Manacles means it should not be considered as anything other than a temporary anchorage in daylight. Keep well clear of the granite quay fashioned from the rock which is used occasionally by coasters serving a local quarry. Expected shipping movements are published by Falmouth Harbour Authority.

Coasters occasionally load granite from the local quarry

Porthkerris

17 THE LIZARD PENINSULA
& PORTHLEVEN

Harbour Master's Office
Porthleven No VHF
3 Celtic House, Harbour Head,
Porthleven TR13 9HU
☎ 01326 574270

NCI Bass Point (Lizard) VHF 65 ☎ 01326 290212

Lizard Point is the S extremity of mainland Britain and a tidal gate in every sense of the phrase. A glance at a large scale chart shows vast numbers of rocks and shipwrecks, so many that a prudent navigator would immediately keep two miles off. In anything other than very settled conditions, that is exactly the right course of action. In light winds, low swell and good visibility however, there are plenty of spots to explore for experienced skippers, some tenable overnight.

156 • West Country Pilot

> The layout of this chapter is slightly different in that there are no general approach or entry headings, the relevant information being incorporated in each destination. Refer to the 'Headlands' section (p.14) for the strategy for rounding Lizard Point.

Landmarks

Lizard Point is an impressively large headland with a conspicuous octagonal lighthouse at the summit, together with white outbuildings and walls giving the impression of a fort. Bass Point just E has a former Lloyd's Signal Station and NCI lookout visible from E.

Main hazards

There are literally thousands of rocks between the Manacles and Loe Bar, the vast majority being within 0.5M of the shore. Approach any anchorage with an abundance of caution and maintain a good lookout as there are undoubtedly many uncharted rocks and it cannot be assumed that any charted information is accurate. 0.5M SSE of Cadgwith Cove, Craggan Rocks is an isolated shallow outcrop which should be avoided. Vrogue Rock (actually there are two) is about 0.25M off Bass Point and is not far below the surface, creating impressive eddies when the tidal stream gets going. The Boa is 2M WNW of Lizard Point and, although over 10m deep, creates a breaking sea in heavy weather, and rough conditions otherwise.

The Lizard has been dubbed the graveyard of ships. Hundreds of known wrecks are found in this area and new ones are being discovered all the time (orange markings on the rocks are just as likely to be rust from iron keels as algae blooms). Most will not present a hazard to small craft except potentially when anchoring, since the action of the sea can move substantial pieces of debris over time. To mitigate this, anchor only where the bottom can be seen.

Tide rips form at Lizard Point and other nearby minor headlands. In particular, Black Head (S of Coverack) produces overfalls in any strength of tide and should

The N end of the Manacles reef

Manacles ECM 4M S of Falmouth

be given a clearance of 1M or more in wind over tide conditions or if there is any significant swell.

Finally, the mobile phone signal in this area is between patchy and non-existent, so VHF is the best source of weather and sea state information, either from Bass Point NCI (VHF 65) or a passing vessel.

COVERACK

This tiny harbour and popular anchorage is just S of the Manacles, protected in winds from W to N. There is a prominent hotel building and the best approach is from due E. At first glance it also appears to be suitable in SW weather but this is not always the case. Several small headlands between here and Lizard Point refract the swell and in SW winds, anchored craft will be beam on to it making life pretty uncomfortable for anything except a short stop. The same can be true in W winds during the top half of the tide, especially if the wind

Coverack Cove

17 THE LIZARD PENINSULA

The harbour arm and slip aid landing at Coverack

is forecast to back. For an overnight stay, NW wind is the optimum. The holding is very good on sand with no dangers outside the 1m contour, and there is a slipway in the drying harbour for landing, protected by a curved harbour wall. Day craft might be able to creep in alongside but nothing larger.

Cadgwith Cove

Cadgwith is a small fishing village just over 1M N of Bass Point. Approach from SE taking care to avoid Boa Rock just right of centre, and anchor off in about 4m LAT. There is shelter in winds between W and N and, being closer to the Lizard, there are fewer headlands to refract the swell. Thus, when the wind is W, it is arguably a better prospect than Coverack. A rocky outcrop divides the harbour and the best place to land is where the local fishing boats are hauled up on the beach.

Local boats hauled up on the beach at Cadgwith

Cadgwith Cove

158 • West Country Pilot

Church Cove & Parn Voose Cove

Looking S towards Church Cove. Lizard lifeboat station is in the centre and Bass Point NCI on the headland above

Church Cove & Parn Voose Cove

Adjacent N of Lizard lifeboat station, it is possible to anchor off Church Cove or Parn Voose Cove in settled conditions. Unless ticking off a list of anchorages, the most likely purpose is to await a fair tide at the Lizard, for which they can be very useful. Parn Voose is the easier of the two approaching from due E and anchoring off the beach. Landing is a tricky affair in an inflatable tender since it is fairly rocky. Church Cove has a few small local moorings but is possible to anchor just S of a charted sewer outfall, the end of which is marked by a yellow buoy. There is little in the way of a beach here but an adventurous LW landing might be possible using the concrete casing of the sewer outfall. It is a quiet spot and the sight of an all weather lifeboat screaming down the launching ramp will be memorable.

Housel Bay

The most southerly anchorage on the UK mainland requires local knowledge and is only suitable for a temporary stop in daylight and in settled conditions. Heavy chain is essential, preferably with a chum.

Anchored in Housel Bay by Lizard Point lighthouse

West Country Pilot • 159

17 THE LIZARD PENINSULA

Housel Bay

Dragging anchor here is a one-way ticket to the tidal race or the rocks adding to the number of wrecks. If awaiting a fair tide, it is much safer to drop anchor in the places described above than to risk it here.

This small bay with a hotel on the cliff above is literally below the lighthouse. Anchor only in NW winds or light N as yachts will be on the wind for the return trip. Timing is critical so for a first visit aim to arrive as the channel ebb tide is easing around HWF-0330. The reason for this is that if an emergency arises, or the trip has to be abandoned, the tide will be running E from HWF-0300 and then N towards safety, rather than W into Mounts Bay. Approach only from E by closing the coast to about 200m off, in the vicinity of Bass Point, and passing inside Vrogue Rock (if it is too rough here then return up the coast). Abeam the signal station/NCI lookout follow the coast round maintaining the same offing and keeping a sharp lookout for fishing floats (these should be visible as the tide will be slack and it is worth making at least a mental note of their positions as they will likely be submerged on departure). Anchor in a suitable spot as to draught where the bottom is fine sand but beware of a rocky outcrop S of the hotel. If the timing is right, it will now be HWF-0300, giving a couple of hours to enjoy the experience or have a quick trip ashore, but note there is very little beach left near HW. Departure should be timed for HWF-0100 which will enable most craft to reach Coverack or clear the Manacles ECM before the strengthening tide turns S out of Falmouth Bay at around HWF+0300. Inevitably, vessels will end up punching the tide for the last hour or so to Falmouth or Helford, so an overnight stop at Coverack or an earlier departure might appeal. In any event, always leave with sufficient flood tide remaining to reach safety.

Kynance Cove

Kynance Cove is a well known and popular beauty spot around 2M NNW of Lizard Point. The bay is surrounded by rocks and the best approach is from due S between Lion Rock to starboard and Gull Rock to port. The green topped Asparagus Rock lies immediately N of Gull Rock. The Boa (see Hazards) is approximately 2M W. Due to the popularity of the beach, and the many rocks, boats tend to anchor near the entrance to the cove. It is rarely free from swell, which will find its

Kynance Cove with Asparagus Rock centre

way in even when the wind is E, so is only suitable for a temporary stop. As with Housel Bay, the thought of an anchor dragging here is sobering. Landing on the beach is made easier by the presence of large rocks which dissipate the swell but it is worth remembering that they will also mask any change in the direction of it whilst ashore.

Mullion Cove

The next anchorage is some 4M further up the coast and thus further from danger. This stretch of coast has many offlying rocks so stand out in deep water. Identified by a prominent hotel on the cliff, Mullion Cove is sheltered in winds from SE to NE with Mullion Island just offshore going some way to mitigating any swell from SE. Crucially, it can create a lee from the ambient WSW swell if the wind drops away, for example at dusk, making it a viable overnight stop in offshore winds and settled weather. In fact, this was the traditional waiting anchorage heading up channel in the days of trading under sail. Approach from NW and anchor anywhere suitable as to wind and swell, but note the seabed between Mullion Island and the closest point ashore is mainly rock. In E winds, a fair number of vessels will likely be anchored here.

The tiny harbour (Porth Mellin) is private but landing is permitted, either at the steps to port just inside, or on the beach. Larger vessels including yachts are allowed to tie up briefly for loading but it is not a very practical scenario.

Several potential daytime anchorages in E winds can be found just along the shore from Mullion at

The anchorage at Mullion Cove in the lee of the island

Porth Mellin, Mullion Cove on the Lizard

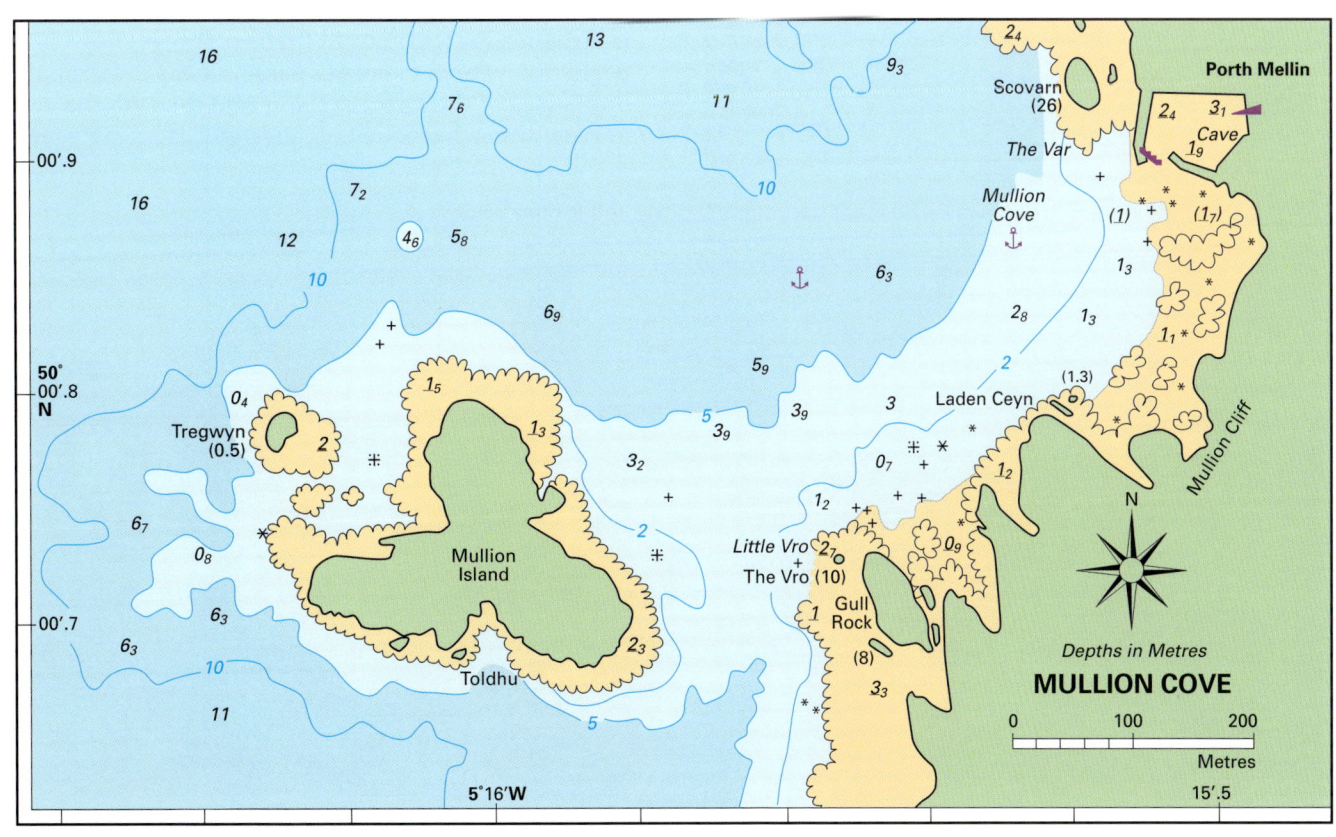

17 THE LIZARD PENINSULA

Polurrian Cove, Poldhu Cove and (Gunwalloe) Church Cove. All are best approached from W but beware of a charted obstruction between the latter two. There is a deep water anchorage off Loe Bar SSW of Loe Pool which is suitable for larger vessels, keeping clear of the charted historic wrecks nearby.

PORTHLEVEN

Porthleven is an active fishing harbour just NW of Loe Bar. A harbour wall extends SW and in fair weather has the appearance of a bright horizontal stripe along the shore when approaching from the direction of Lizard Point. There are reefs either side of the narrow entrance and within it as far as the outer harbour walls. The inner harbour dries by about the same extent as the reefs (2-2.5m) so they will be submerged on entry. Only enter the harbour in conditions of low swell/surf.

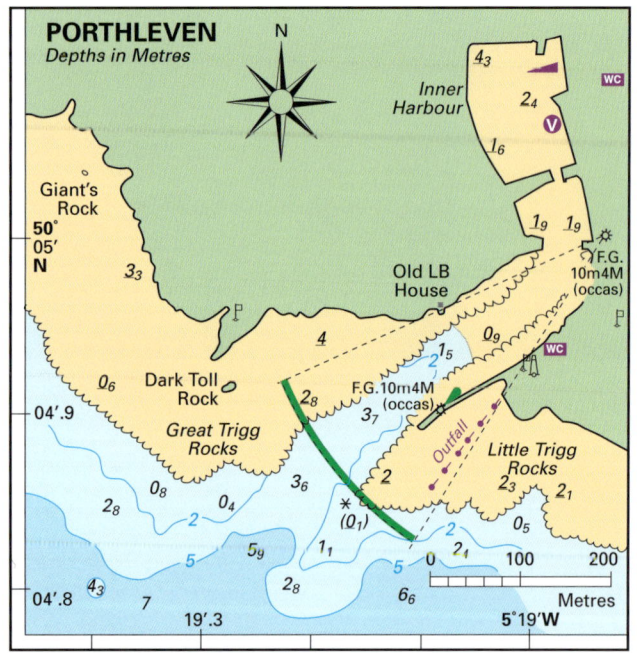

Surfing – yes, anchoring – no. Looking SE towards the Lizard

Approach initially with the old lifeboat house (W of the entrance) bearing 040°, altering course to 055° as soon as the harbour wall is reached. Proceed with caution keeping midway between the harbour wall and the shore to port as there is a nasty section of the reef drying 2.8m jutting out from the wall. Its position is on a line due S of the old lifeboat house. Once clear, begin a slow turn to port to pass midway between the buttresses of the outer harbour and through the very narrow inner harbour entrance at dead slow speed.

Approaching the outer harbour wall. The inner harbour is blocked off for the winter

Porthleven

Porthleven Harbour. Berthing is on the quay wall outside the pub, centre right

Slipway in the inner harbour

Porthleven essential information

Visitors' Berths
Drying quay wall

Additional Berthing
None

Webcams
www.theshipinnporthleven.co.uk
www.mullion-cove.co.uk

Water
Tap on quay

Victuals
Adjacent to harbour

Nearest Large Supermarket
Helston (by bus)

Engineers
Gordon Lake, Helston

Car Hire
Nearest Falmouth or Penzance

Although there are two lights marking the entrance, they do not form a transit to clear the reefs so entry at night should not be attempted without local knowledge.

Berthing is alongside the inner end of the quay to starboard, but contact the HM from outside the harbour to ascertain if there is space. The alternative is to anchor off the entrance where there are patches of sand S and SE of the harbour arm outside the reef. Note that depths here are at least 6m LAT and it is rarely free from swell. There is a slipway in inner harbour for landing with a tender or for launching and recovery.

Shoreside

The area covered in this chapter is remote with limited transport links. The largest town is Helston, about 2M inland from Porthleven.

Facilities are largely limited to public toilets, but there are small general stores at Coverack and Porthleven which also has a baker and fishmonger close to the harbour. There are cafés at most of the destinations listed and pubs or restaurants at Coverack, Cadgwith, Mullion and Porthleven. Exploring further afield should be undertaken from larger ports elsewhere.

18 PENZANCE & NEWLYN
ST MICHAEL'S MOUNT & MOUSEHOLE

Harbour Master's Office
VHF 12 'Newlyn Harbour',
22 Strand, Newlyn TR18 5HW
☎ 01736 362523
NCI Penzance VHF 65 ☎ 01736 367063
NCI Gwennap Head VHF 65 ☎ 01736 871351

Mounts Bay is bounded by Lizard Point to the E and Tater-du to the W. It is directly exposed to the ambient Atlantic swell with only limited respite in one corner where the twin ports of Newlyn and Penzance are located. The sea state in the bay is always more agitated than elsewhere, partly due to the swell but also the topography of the seabed. Newlyn is the only port with nominally 24 hour access, but in strong winds or high swell from E or SE small craft could easily be overwhelmed, and larger craft might only be able to enter at HW, so it cannot be considered completely safe.

The landscape gets more rugged the further west you go

St Michael's Mount from SW

Landmarks
The castle at St Michael's Mount is visible from about 5M out and lies 2M E of Penzance.

Main hazards
Mounts Bay is completely exposed to any weather with a S component and small craft would be well advised not to contemplate visiting in such conditions.

Newlyn is a major fishing port with everything from small pot boats to huge beam trawlers. As a result, there are fishing floats aplenty in Mounts Bay with clusters around the many rocks some of which are in very deep water. That said, they tend to be better marked than elsewhere with larger floats and more flags.

Closer to shore, there is a triangle of three dangerous rocks between 0.25M and 1M S of Cudden Point. A SCM marks the westernmost one, Mountamopus, and staying S of this latitude clears all three. About 0.5M S of Penzance and 0.75M NE of Newlyn, The Gear IDM (Fl(2)10s) should be passed at least 150m to seaward as there are also rocks and shallows inshore of it towards Penzance.

Low Lee ECM marks a rock with least charted depth 2.1m, between Mousehole and Newlyn. Leave this to port when approaching from offshore and continue towards the Gear IDM for a further 0.5M to clear another rock with least charted depth 2.3m. Above half-tide, these two dangers should not affect leisure craft.

The beaches in this corner of Mounts Bay look inviting but all have offlying reefs to some extent. Although small day craft may find their way in behind the reefs to anchor off the beaches, there is always a risk of becoming stranded.

Penzance & Newlyn

The ferry to the Isles of Scilly operates from a berth just outside the dock gates at Penzance, normally departing around 0930 and returning about 1900, subject to tides. Times vary on Saturdays. Small craft movements are suspended whilst the ferry is under way so be prepared to wait if these times coincide with the dock gate being open. The ferry usually operates from Easter until October.

Approaches

Low Lee ECM (Q(3)10s) is a good initial waypoint, being 16M NW from a position S of Lizard Point. From S or SW keep 0.5M offshore after passing the Runnel Stone SCM (Q(6)+LFl.15s) until reaching Low Lee. At night Tater-du lighthouse (Fl(3)15s34m12M) can be seen from the Lizard and all points offshore giving a rough guide if kept on the port bow. Its red sector (F.R.31m9M)) covers the Runnel Stone so keep in the white sector if approaching from SW. The white sector of the Penzance Harbour light (Fl.WR.5s11m17/12M) is theoretically visible from Lizard Point but is more useful closer in.

NEWLYN

For those seeking shelter, Newlyn is the most likely destination as it has the least restricted access of the harbours in this section and so it is listed first. Guidance for Penzance and the smaller harbours is given in the relevant sections below.

Dogs are prohibited from Newlyn Harbour, even if kept on board.

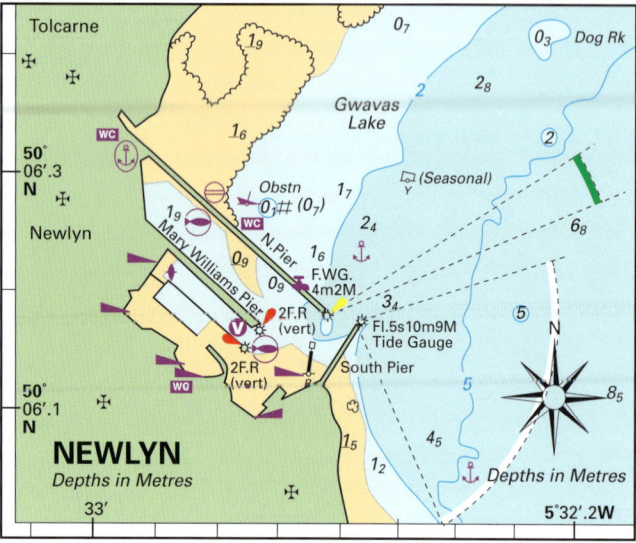

Visitors raft three abreast between the pontoons

Newlyn is one of the busiest fishing ports in the UK

From the vicinity of Low Lee ECM, contact HM Newlyn for berthing instructions as space is limited and the entrance partially blind to small craft. Once cleared to proceed, head NW to a position N of the entrance piers, where you will likely have been asked to call again. If it is necessary to wait there is good holding NNE of North Pier which is out of the main traffic area, or there are waiting buoys off Penzance Harbour 1M NE (*see p.167*). With permission to proceed, enter between the pier heads and turn to starboard as soon as the large central pier comes in to view, heading directly for the pontoons SW of it. The area outside the pontoons dries and may be marked by small red buoys (unlit). At night, remain in the white sector of the Penzance Harbour light until the Newlyn Harbour light on South Pier bears NW. *Note both of these lights have the same characteristics (Fl.5s).* From E, or after rounding Lizard Point, steer for Penzance until the main Newlyn approach light (F.WG.4m2M) is identified, then remain on the cusp of the green sector just to starboard of it.

Berth as directed which is usually on the first couple of fingers of the pontoons, deep draught on the near side closest to the central pier and shoal draught on the opposite side nearest the shore which may not be accessible at LWS. There is space for three boats between the fingers so some vessels might be rafted centrally between two others, or alongside a fishing vessel (although not one that is likely to move). The latter option is more likely for larger yachts.

Although fishing vessels (of all sizes) are given priority, it is very rare that leisure craft will be directed to Penzance or to anchor off, and certainly not in an emergency or bad weather.

Newlyn Harbour entrance

PENZANCE

Harbour Master's Office
VHF 12 'Penzance Harbour'
North Arm, Wharf Road, Penzance TR18 4AH
☎ 01736 366113

Penzance has a tidal harbour and an adjacent wet dock which make it a better prospect than Newlyn for a longer stay. The downside, at least of the wet dock, is that the access times do not fit with the tidal gates at either Lizard Point or Lands End and a temporary stop elsewhere will be required if on passage.

From Low Lee ECM steer N to leave The Gear IDM well to port continuing until the harbour entrance can be clearly seen. The dock gate usually opens from HW-2 to HW+1 with IPTS lights although they may only be shown for commercial vessel movements. There tends to be an exodus of craft when the dock gate first opens. Once inside the dock, visitors normally berth along the wall immediately to starboard, often rafted, but larger vessels may be given space elsewhere. A small cargo coaster operates from the harbour to the Isles of Scilly and all other movements are prohibited when it is manoeuvring.

The tidal harbour is accessible at half-tide for the majority of leisure craft, with space sometimes available on the wall to port just inside and occasionally a trot mooring may be available via the HM or the sailing club. There is a large slipway at the root of Albert Pier suitable for launching and recovery and a smaller one adjacent to the swing bridge which is better suited to tenders. At the end of Albert Pier, which forms the E wall of the tidal harbour, there are steps with near all tide access for tenders.

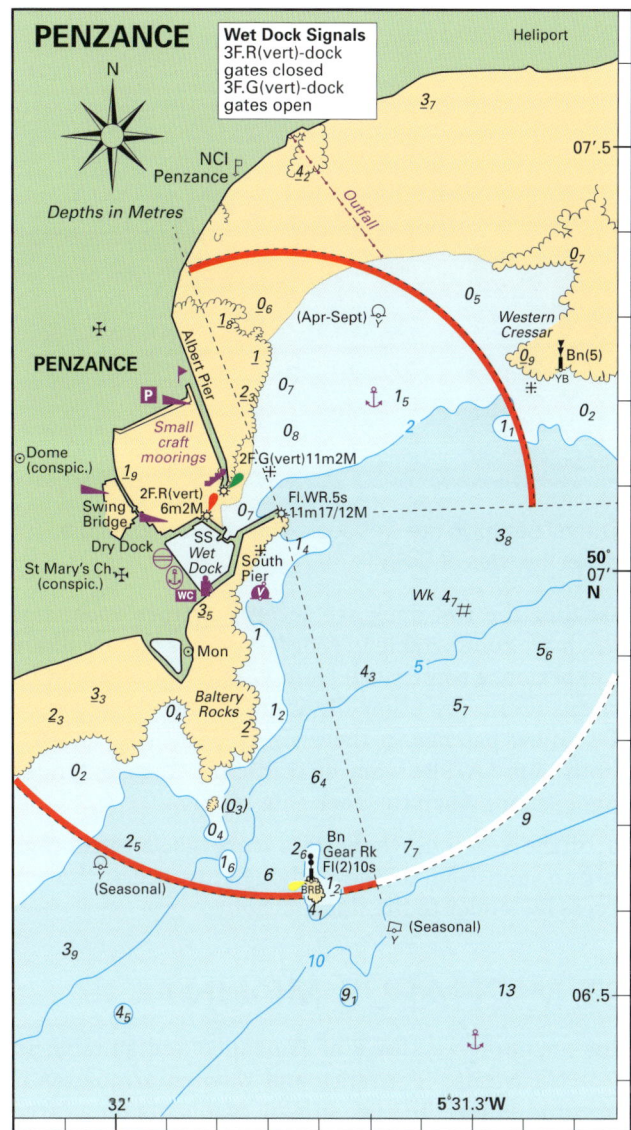

Late afternoon at Penzance Harbour

Chris Jones

18 PENZANCE & NEWLYN

Visitors' berths in the wet dock. The cargo ship far left serves the Isles of Scilly

Just S of the wet dock are several visitors' moorings which are comfortable in N or NW winds but are likely to experience some swell from W or SW and would be untenable in any other direction. There are a couple of shallow patches in the vicinity with least charted depth 1.4m LAT. Be wary of traffic if using the tender to get ashore when the dock gate is open.

In offshore winds there is a very good anchorage on fine sand NNE of the harbour entrance with easy access by tender to the tidal harbour.

ST MICHAEL'S MOUNT

This anchorage is 2M E of Penzance and suitable in N or NE winds - Penzance and Newlyn are better if the wind is NW. The prominent castle sits on a large island outcrop and the anchorage lies just W between the island and a reef, so there is also some protection from E winds and it is viable overnight if no swell has built up. The E side of the island should be avoided altogether and a causeway to the mainland prevents all but very shoal draught vessels from circumnavigating.

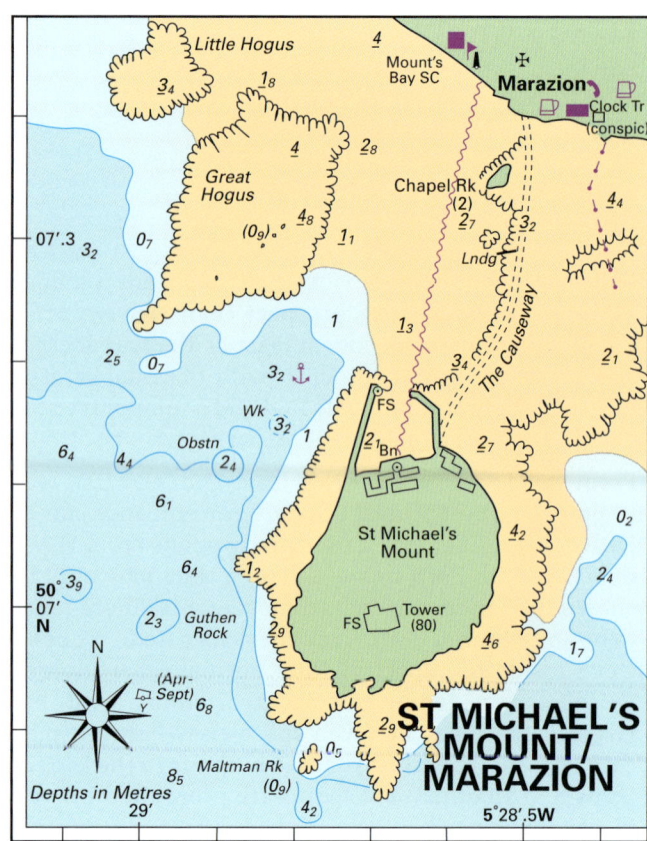

The tiny harbour facing the mainland is private and very busy during the day with small trip boats from the mainland. Small craft may be able to dry out with permission but this should only be attempted in very settled weather as the bottom is hard sand and any amount of swell could cause a boat to ground hard when lifting or settling. Landing in a tender from the anchorage is less of an issue and there is a slipway in one corner.

Enter from SW keeping Chapel Rock (2m) dead ahead and anchor as suitable to draught between the island and Hogus Rocks, a large unmarked reef just NW, but note the island side is rocky out to around 150m from the HW mark. In (light) E winds, a position abeam the

St Michael's Mount harbour entrance

168 • West Country Pilot

The main anchorage area for E winds in the lee of the harbour wall

Susan Hemmin

root of the harbour wall will mean less swell although it is deeper at approximately 5m LAT.

On neap tides it is possible to work further in but do not anchor directly N of the harbour entrance as power cables run between the island and the shore here.

St Michael's Mount

The island, with its fairy tale castle in the style of the larger Mont St Michel in Normandy, may have been settled from the 4th century BC, and is chronicled from at least the 1st century BC. The harbour was used for the export of tin mined on the North Cornwall coast and transported overland. Following a period as a pilgrimage site a Celtic monastery was established and a religious community grew up around it from the 8th to the early 11th century AD. In the mid 12th century AD, the island was gifted to the order of Benedictine monks at Mont St Michel in Normandy and construction started on a replica of the priory, which lasted until the dissolution by Henry VIII.

The St Aubyn family purchased the island in the mid 17th century as a family home and the harbour was redeveloped, becoming an important seaport until the extension of the railway to Penzance transferred maritime interest there and industry was reduced to local fishing. In Victorian times, a narrow-gauge tramway was constructed to move goods and supplies between the harbour and the main house, parts of which can be seen at the harbour end. It apparently is still used occasionally.

Today, the family is still in residence and have managed the island in partnership with the National Trust since 1964. The grounds and some of the rooms are open to the public and it is one of the most popular tourist destinations in Cornwall.

MOUSEHOLE

Mousehole is the last of the traditional Cornish harbours on the South Coast, situated about 1.5M S of Newlyn (2.5M from Penzance). St Clements Isle, a large granite outcrop, sits just E giving the approach and harbour entrance some protection in winds from that direction, but it is not large enough to prevent the swell. The gap between the N end of the island and the mainland is tiny so any approach should be made from S. Note the harbour is closed in the winter months.

There is a good anchorage on sand midway between the island and the shore in about 3m to 5m LAT. The anchor

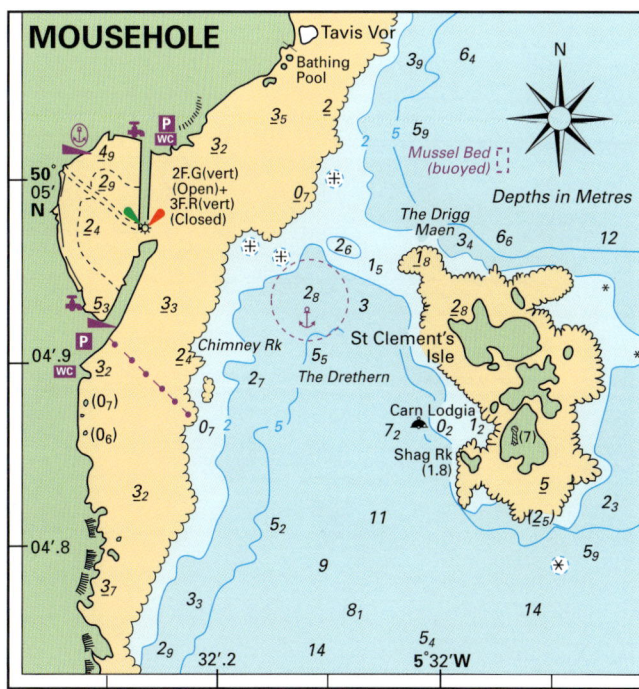

West Country Pilot • 169

18 PENZANCE & NEWLYN

The quay at Mousehole - the yacht is on the first visitors' berth

symbols on charts only denote a general area and there are some large, pebble like, boulders in places. Anchor only where the bottom is visible as clean sand and stay S of a line between the E extremity of the island and the pier heads.

The drying harbour can be entered around half-tide by vessels up to 9m with moderate draught. The two spaces nearest the beach ahead on the main wall are usually kept for visitors, drying out on firm sand. If landing by tender, aim for the beach at the root of either wall to avoid the shore lines of local boats.

Lamorna Cove

Protected by the headlands of Tater-du and Carn-du, this small cove is the last useable anchorage on the mainland, although not quite the final frontier (Porthcurno 4M W being the point at which numerous cables come ashore). It is sheltered from winds between NW and N and potentially NE if no swell has built up. Approach from between SW and SE then aim towards the centre of the beach and anchor off. The seabed shoals quite steeply despite the flat looking beach so conditions would need to be very settled to remain overnight. A small harbour arm provides some protection to a slipway in the corner of the cove which is the most suitable landing point.

Shoreside

There are showers and toilets at both Newlyn and Penzance harbours, a public toilet and shower at

Mousehole Harbour

Lamorna Cove

Wild day at Lamorna Cove

Local attractions

St Michael's Mount is a short bus trip from Penzance or Newlyn. Small ferries operate to the island from the village of Marazion or there is a pedestrian causeway if tide and weather conditions suit. Adjacent to Penzance Harbour, the Jubilee Pool is a preserved art deco lido open during the summer months. Two art galleries (Penlee House and Newlyn) showcase both historic and contemporary works including pieces from the 'Newlyn School'. Plant lovers will find sub-tropical displays at Penlee Park and Morrab Gardens in Penzance while Trengwainton and Tremenheere Sculpture Gardens are a short distance out of town. Slightly further afield is the Minack Theatre perched precariously on the cliff edge with performances throughout the summer months, and the PK Porthcurno Museum of Global Communications is close by. They are best visited by public transport as nearby Porthcurno Cove below has many cables on and beneath the seabed.

Mousehole close to the visitors' berths, and a toilet at St Michael's Mount.

Penzance has the best range of shops including several supermarkets just outside the town. There is a food store very close to the HM office at Newlyn and a small deli/store at Mousehole specialising in local produce.

Penzance is at the end of the main railway line from London, Exeter and Plymouth and there are frequent bus services to Newlyn. The ferry and cargo ships to the Isles of Scilly operate from here. Alternatively, there are (small aircraft) flights from Land's End airport, which is reached by bus or taxi, and helicopter flights from Penzance to Tresco.

The Minack perched on the cliff above Porthcurno Cove

Newlyn & Penzance essential information

Clubs
Mounts Bay Sailing Club ☎01736 710620
Penzance Sailing Club

Local Information
Station Rd, Penzance

Webcams
www.mbsc.org.uk
www.pzsc.org.uk

Visitors' Berths
Pontoons at Newlyn
Quay walls at Penzance (wet dock & drying)
Mousehole (drying)

Additional Berthing
None

Water
On Pontoons/quays

Fuel
Penzance at entrance to wet dock

Gas
Newline Chandlery, Newlyn

Chandlery
Newline Chandlery, Newlyn

Victuals
Market Jew St, Penzance; The Strand, Newlyn

Nearest Large Supermarket
Penzance outskirts (by bus)

Laundry
Tolver Rd, Penzance

Boatyard
Sandy Cove Boatyard, Newlyn
Fleetwood Marine Services, Penzance
Penzance Dry Dock (commercial/superyachts)

Engineers
SRC Marine, Newlyn
Penwith Marine Services, Penzance

Electronics
MJ Marine Electronics, Albert Pier, Penzance
Sirm UK, Newlyn

Sailmakers
Solo Sails, Newlyn

Car Hire
Three in Penzance

Transport
Trains from Penzance (by bus from Newlyn).
Ferry to Isles of Scilly (seasonal).

St Martin's Flats

ISLES OF SCILLY PASSAGE PLANNING

Scilly is a stunning destination, but one where the passage planning requires careful consideration, preparation and execution. Getting there involves a 60M passage from Falmouth (the nearest true port of refuge) or 35M from the W end of Mounts Bay. Vessels need to be largely self sufficient and skippers must have solid contingency plans, on which the crew are fully briefed. That includes the weather and sea state which changes frequently, and sometimes rapidly. The following information concentrates on the variable factors involved in passages between the mainland and the islands.

Critical factors

The primary consideration for any passage to Scilly is the requirement to *arrive in daylight, with enough time to anchor or find a mooring*. The only lit marks are in the approach to St Mary's where the harbour is only suitable in winds with an E component and is fully exposed to the ambient swell. Arriving and anchoring/mooring at night ought to be beyond the risk appetite of any small boat skipper. In fact, it is probably a safer option to undertake a night passage and arrive in the early morning, rather than risk a late evening arrival.

The next consideration is the actual intended anchorage. This is dictated by a combination of

Approaching Peninnis Head, St Mary's Scilly from E

conditions at the time, forecast conditions and available space. Since the latter is unlikely to be known until you arrive (especially in peak summer), it is best to have multiple options. The destinations listed at the end of this chapter are only those accessible at LW with deep draught. Note that St Helen's Pool has the best all round protection from swell (despite being more exposed to wind) and should always be on your list. For larger vessels, it may well be the preferred option.

Borough Beach nr Old Grimsby, Tresco

Isles of Scilly Passage Planning

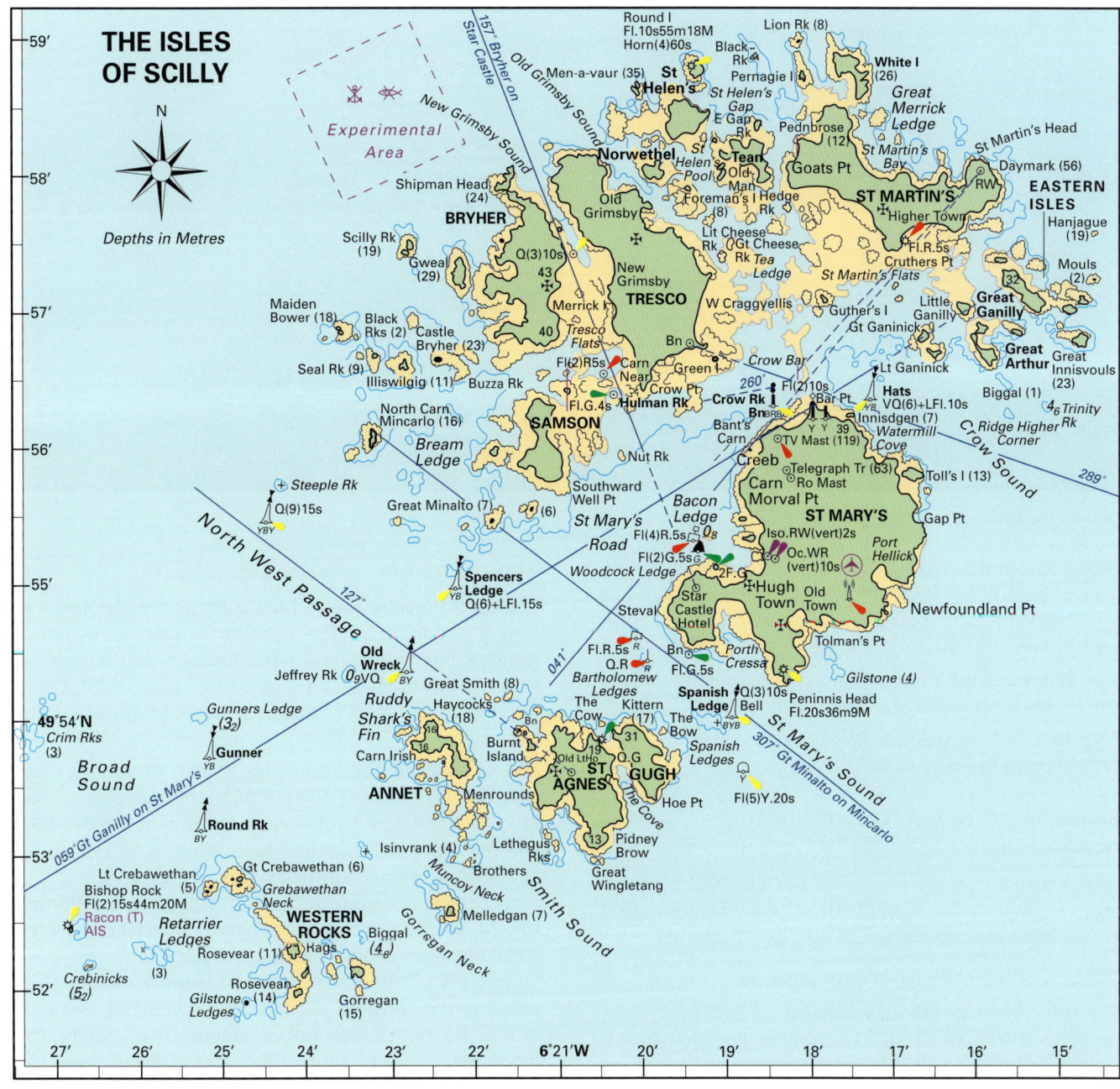

Lastly, plans should be made in advance for the return to the mainland. Note that prolonged E winds increase the sea state in the English Channel and, if a change to E or SE is forecast, swell from that direction may arrive up to 24 hours earlier. Rough weather from that quadrant makes Mounts Bay untenable and a passage to Falmouth beyond unpleasant, so consider the North Cornwall coast as an option.

Weather

The weather can, and often does, change quickly in Scilly, so a longer range forecast is needed in addition to that mentioned in the main passage planning section. Beyond three days, forecasts become more generalised so this is an instance where computer models (GFS being the most common available) can be useful to deduce trends. As mentioned previously, always use the full data sets (0000/1200 GMT) for long range forecasts. The generalised decimal coordinates for Scilly are '50.0, -6.3'; Mounts Bay is '50.0, -5.5' and Falmouth '50.0, -5.0' (these are quicker to enter than the actual coordinates and are accurate enough as the modelling is based on 80km squares, and neither the islands nor headlands are large enough to impact the model). Outbound, the most favourable wind direction is between N and SE, maximum 15kn. Light S winds are also an option, but tend to occur as a high pressure system declines E usually heralding something less settled.

It is also helpful to note and compare the actual conditions with the forecast, both in the lead up to departure and whilst there. Official observations are published from Culdrose (Airbase), Seven Stones (Light Vessel) and St Marys (Airport). Also record your own observations.

Tides

Tidal considerations are three-fold. First, there are tidal gates at Lizard Point and Land's End, the former

ISLES OF SCILLY

Green Bay, Bryher

being the most critical. Second, the tidal height on arrival is of importance and third, the tidal range has a material influence on the available space to anchor, once there.

The distances involved are considerably longer than the average day passage in this book:

Falmouth to Lizard Point 16M, then
Lizard Point to Scilly 44M
or
Lizard Point to Newlyn/Penzance 16M
Newlyn/Penzance to Scilly 35M

thus a direct passage from Falmouth is 60M and two legs via Mounts Bay is 67M with the sections roughly equal. Both are considered in the final summary.

Tidal Streams – direct passage

The tide turns W off Lizard Point at half-tide down (approx HWP+0300) so assuming a nominal 4-5kn boat speed gives a departure time from Falmouth or Helford close to local HW, and thus suitable even for those on a drying mooring. This gives a largely fair tide S past the Manacles and a small set SE between there and the Lizard. The direct course from a position 2M S of Lizard Point to Scilly is due W and the tide runs SW for the next two hours, then W for three hours. At the same nominal boat speed, this equates to a position 1-2M S of Wolf Rock lighthouse (or about 10M SSW of Land's End). From here, the remaining distance is around 20M but the tidal set will rotate through NW, N, NE and E over the subsequent four to five hours producing an overall set N at 5kn boat speed, but more like NE at 4kn and will be setting SE on arrival between about HWP+0100 and HWP+0200 (the latter being local HW+0100). Maintain a W course (which crosses the TSS off Land's End at right angles) until in the vicinity of the islands, and avoid punching the tide on the E side of the islands to reach the intended anchorage if there is a suitable down tide alternative.

Tidal Streams – via Mounts Bay

The directions as far as Lizard Point are the same as above. From there, the Newlyn/Penzance corner of Mounts Bay is 16M NW. This passage will largely be across the tide arriving around HWP-0500 (local LW+0130) and will require an offset to allow for the tidal stream.

For the second leg, leave the W end of Mounts Bay at HWP+0130 (local HW+0030), aiming to be at the Runnel Stone SCM (S of Gwennap Head) at HWP+0300. The Dock gate at Penzance opens from local HW-0200 to +0100 so it might be necessary to pick up a mooring or anchor for an hour or two if berthed here. Although the tide is initially contrary, there is a back eddy which runs close in along the shore from Lamorna Cove from HWP+0230, but head away from the shore after passing the Minack Theatre (Porthcurno) because it will be rough beyond Gwennap Head where the tides are unpredictable. Scilly is 28M WSW from the Runnel Stone SCM (but see below regarding course to steer) which is six to seven hours at the nominal boat speed used above. The tide sets SW for two hours, then strongly W, NW and N during the next three, before starting to turn NE about HWP-0230. The overall set for this passage is NW and the likelihood is that the tide will still be sluicing N on arrival around HWP-0300.

The need to cross the TSS off Land's End as near as practicable at right angles creates an additional complication for this route. Depending on boat speed and the tidal coefficient, steer an initial course of about 240°-250° and then turn W on 270° when Wolf Rock lighthouse bears due E or upon reaching the TSS, whichever occurs first. Keep a sharp lookout for vessels cutting the corner as they enter or leave the TSS. Resume the initial *compass* course once clear of the TSS with the tide setting N and enter the islands through Crow Sound. Faster boats will probably arrive off St Mary's Sound.

Return to the mainland

The tides are slightly less critical on the return trip and a daylight arrival is one of preference rather than necessity. However, the tides are also less helpful, being stronger and rotatory between Scilly and Mounts Bay, resulting in a shorter period of E tide in the Channel. Based on this, the conventional advice is to be S of the Runnel Stone with enough fair tide remaining to reach Mounts Bay or Lizard Point (respectively, this is HWP-0130 or HWP-0330 S of the Runnel Stone). But, on a direct passage to Falmouth, slower vessels will likely run out of fair tide before reaching the Manacles. In both cases the majority of the tidal set will have been between SW and NW until reaching the mainland (i.e. sailing against the tide).

Therefore, if heading for Mounts Bay, consider leaving Scilly about HWP-0400 (local LW+0130) from somewhere with deep water access. Over the next several hours the (predicted) tide sets initially N rotating through NE and E to SE at HWP+0200 when, at the nominal boat speed assumed, the Runnel Stone should have been reached. There is then an hour or so before the tide turns SW to cover most of the remaining distance into Mounts Bay. Admittedly, it will be too late to lock in to the wet dock at Penzance but there are alternatives. The second leg can then be timed to reach the Lizard at slack water as the tide turns E (HWP-0300).

Tidal height

The second consideration is the tidal height. Nearly all intra-island passages are strewn with rocks or other large drying patches. Therefore, vessel movements between anchorages take place in the top half of the tide, mostly in the period from local HW-0300 to HW+0100 (HWP-0200 to HWP+0200). This avoids the need to venture around the outside of the islands which is obviously more exposed. In the main summer months of June, July and August, arriving outside of these times could present a problem in finding a suitable berth, although there may be the option to anchor somewhere temporarily if the next occurrence of HW-0300 will still be in daylight. This will likely mean continuing around the N side of the islands to access the anchorages around Tresco.

Tidal range

The nature of the islands is such that neap tides considerably increase the amount of space available to anchor, so in the busier months and certainly for a first visit, a period of neap tides (meaning a coefficient below 70) is recommended.

Vessel

As stated, the assumption has been made that the vessel is well found and equipped. However, it should perhaps be noted here that craft which can dry out (away from a wall) have a massive advantage on Scilly because the additional anchoring options are many and varied and you can get out of the pervasive swell.

Approaching through Crow Sound using the TV mast on St Mary's as a clearing bearing

Crew

Be aware that medical facilities are limited and concentrated at St Mary's. Serious illness or injury normally requires evacuation to the mainland.

Dangers

The main navigational danger is traffic, in particular the Traffic Separation Scheme for commercial vessels heading N/S. The passage to Scilly, whether from Falmouth or Mounts Bay will encounter the TSS. Vessels crossing the TSS, including pleasure craft, are required to do so on a *heading* as near to right angles and at a constant speed as is practicable. This means motoring if necessary, and a course alteration on the route to and from Mounts Bay. The TSS is monitored by Falmouth Coastguard and it is unlikely that commercial traffic will be encountered outside of it, except fishing vessels, the ferry to Scilly (*Scillonian III*), and the cargo ship (*Gry Maritha*). What has been observed is the occasional vessel cutting the corner when joining or leaving the TSS at the S end. The Isles of Scilly Pilot Guide is the best source of information on local hazards, of which there are many, but it is worth mentioning here that the tides and swell go around, as well as through, the islands meeting near the Eastern Isles. The sea is always confused here.

Ports of refuge

There are none within the islands. Falmouth is the closest and Newlyn is suitable except in strong winds or large swell between E and S. As noted earlier,

Appletree Bay Tresco

significant weather from this quarter will make the return passage a risky proposition, so it is best to depart Scilly earlier to avoid it. The islands are in the Falmouth Coastguard area and there is an aerial on St Mary's. All weather lifeboats are based at Lizard, Newlyn, St Mary's, Sennen and St Ives.

System failure

This is covered in the main section. Mobile phone coverage on Scilly has improved considerably in recent years, but is by no means comparable to the mainland. It is a sensible precaution to take a second device (e.g. a mobile data dongle) which uses a different mast network to your phone/tablet. There is, however, plenty of scope for three point fixes! Repair facilities on Scilly are limited.

Reporting

Always leave your passage plan with a shore contact or coastguard. The RYA SafeTrx App should be used with caution here (apart from registering vessel details) as there will be no mobile phone coverage for extended periods on passage, which could result in misleading information being provided.

SUMMARY

Assuming you are not deterred by the above, what conclusion can be drawn at anchor in Falmouth with a decent weather window in prospect? Motor vessels will have no problem making the passage on a single tide in 6 hours or less so this analysis and summary refers to yachts.

Throughout, keep in mind that the additional distance involved in the passage via Mounts Bay is 7M (or 90 minutes at 4-5kn). For anyone who doesn't enjoy long passages, or has limited experience, the decision is a simple one – the gain from the direct route is not worth it.

Departure time is around HWF, dictated by the tidal gate at the Lizard. At neaps, HWF is 0100/1300 BST so it is immediately apparent that a single passage in daylight is unfeasible, even at 7kn, and a lunchtime departure means arriving before dawn. The trade off is therefore the additional 7M versus a 0100 start so two legs is the sensible option.

Midway towards springs, the departure time moves to 0400/1600. This phase of tide won't be ideal for first time visitors where a period of neap tides is preferable, but for others it presents the possibility of a single passage in mid-summer, albeit with an early start, or a night passage with the attendant increase in risk. In N winds, two legs may still be preferable, delaying the departure by a couple of hours and staying further offshore past Lizard Point which won't add much. A late afternoon arrival at Newlyn/Penzance would then be followed by a slightly earlier start the following day, but this may not be practicable in E winds, unless light.

The departure time advances to 0700/1900 around springs and a single passage in daylight is within scope for most yachts but still marginal for those with a cruising speed of 4kn who would be well advised to go via Mounts Bay unless prepared to undertake a night passage. Obviously, this is not a suitable time for a first visit.

Lastly, the period midway between springs and neaps gives a departure around 1000/2200. This is approaching a neap period window so is ideal for a first visit. A single daylight passage will only work for boat speeds of 7kn, but for a night passage this is probably the sweet spot, regardless of boat speed.

Isles of Scilly Passage Planning

The Cove anchorage, St Agnes with Porth Conger beyond the sand bar

It also appears to work really well for two legs, with leisurely starts and most of the mileage in the warmth of the afternoons, arriving in time for supper.

Now, folk will argue about what yachts should do for as long as people are sailing, so let us apply the mantra from the earlier passage planning section: 'Can you get out? Can you get in? Can you do the bit in the middle?' The first is covered off because departure is HW or just after, and the third can be assumed due to prior experience (having established above those with limited experience should not go direct). The second is the conundrum. On the direct route, passing Lizard Point at HWP+0300 gives arrival times at Scilly based on average speed over the ground as follows: 4kn HWP+0200, 5kn HWP-0015, 6kn HWP-0140, 7kn HWP-0245, 8kn HWP-0330. Compare this to the window when boats move between anchorages, allowing a bit of contingency (always wise). 4-5kn is later or uncomfortably close on a falling tide and risks a potential foul tide on the N side of the islands; 6kn is manageable but perhaps optimistic to have first choice of anchorage in high summer; 7 or 8kn (think motor-sailer) should be fine. However, given the small additional distance involved in going via Mounts Bay there is always a solid argument for this being the most prudent option. Those who do set out on a direct passage (in daylight) still have the option to divert if average boat speed drops below 6kn. At night there will always be at least one lighthouse in view and the deep water is free from hazards, except the TSS.

On balance therefore, two legs is always safer and is best for slower boat speeds, and also recommended for those with less experience. The direct route overnight works for most tidal ranges but only in more limited circumstances in daylight where faster boat speed is an advantage. For those with a 6kn cruising speed, which might well be a significant proportion, the conundrum remains: is the time saved worth the additional risk? Only the individual skipper can answer that.

For the return trip, the two hop passage via Mounts Bay is more optimal in almost every respect. One final note – dogs are not allowed anywhere in Newlyn Harbour which may be a factor for some.

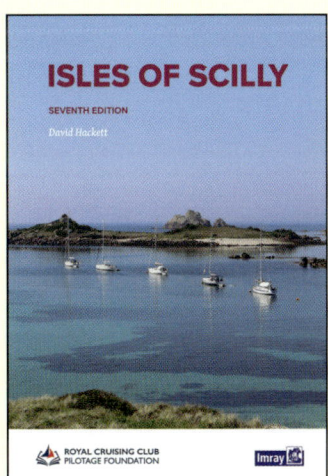

ISLES OF SCILLY
*David Hackett /
Royal Cruising Club
Pilotage Foundation*
Imray

The seventh edition of *Isles of Scilly* is an indispensable guide for anyone seeking to sail this stunning archipelago.

Meticulously researched and completely rewritten by RYA Offshore Yachtmaster skipper David Hackett, who has been navigating these islands for many years, this pilot offers detailed sailing directions and thorough anchorage information to ensure your safe passage around these challenging yet rewarding waters.

ISLES OF SCILLY

Isles of Scilly Anchorages

The following anchorages are only those accessible at LW with deep draught.

ST MARY'S

⚓ Hugh Town / ⚓ Porthloo

St Mary's Pool and Porthloo anchorage looking NE

Sheltered in winds from NE to S but exposed to Atlantic swell. Access from SE via St Mary's Sound or SW via Broad Sound. This is the main harbour for the islands.

St Mary's Sound

St Mary's Harbour with *Scillonian III* berthed

⚓ Porth Cressa

Porth Cressa, St Mary's anchorage. St Mary's Sound is left

Sheltered in winds from W via N to E, but subject to some swell in W and E winds. There are many cables on the seabed. Access from SE in clear water.

⚓ Watermill Cove

Crow Sound with St Mary's left and St Martin's right.

Sheltered from SW winds but affected by swell unless close in, especially around HW. Deep water but limited space. Access from ESE via Crow Sound.

ST AGNES

⚓ The Cove

The Cove anchorage, St Agnes with Porth Conger beyond the sand bar

Sheltered in winds from W to N except at MHWS±0100 when the bar is covered. Some swell in W winds. There are cables just W of the centre. Access from SE in clear water.

Isles of Scilly Passage Planning

TRESCO

⚓ New Grimsby

Moorings in New Grimsby Sound between Tresco and Bryher

Sheltered in winds from SW to W and NE to E but swell in SW winds. Beware of confused tidal streams at the S end. Access from NW via New Grimsby Sound.

Entrance to New Grimsby Sound, Tresco looking SE

⚓ Old Grimsby

Sheltered in winds from S to W but swell in W winds around HW. Access from NW via Old Grimsby Sound.

Yachts anchored off Old Grimsby, Tresco with Round Island in the distance and St Helen's Pool between

Entrance to Old Grimsby Sound, Tresco looking SE

NORTHERN ISLES

⚓ St Helen's Pool

Moderate shelter except from SE winds. Swell around HW in all winds, but several small islands create a lee from certain directions. Access (at LW) via the very narrow St Helen's Gap in daylight only.

St Helen's Gap looking with St Helen's Pool beyond and Old Grimsby in the distance

ST MARTINS

⚓ Tean Sound

Sheltered in winds from W or E. Deep water with strong tides and overfalls at N end. Access from N in clear water.

Tean Sound looking S towards St Mary's

⚓ N side

Several coves sheltered in winds from SW to S. Access from N between reefs in daylight only.

INDEX

A
Abbreviations 15
Albert Quay 122
Amsterdam Point 140
Anchor Stone 56
Anchoring 7
Anstey's Cove 38
Asia Pass 92
Aveton Gifford 77
Avon, River 75-77
Axmouth 21

B
Babbacombe 37
Balcombe Creek 69
BANTHAM 76
  Essential information 76
  Harbour Master's Office 72
  Local attractions 79
Barbican 93
Barn Pool 97
Batson Creek 66
Battisborough Island 78
Beer 21
Beer Head 12, 18
Beesands 61
Bere Ferrers 10
Berrills Yard 122
Berry Head 12, 40, 48, 51
Bigbury Bay 72-79
Black Head 157
Blackpool Sands 61
Bodinnick 118, 123
Bolt Head 13, 64
Bolt Tail 13, 64, 72
Bosahan Cove 152
Bovisand Pier 87
Bow Creek 59
BRIXHAM 46-47
  Essential information 48
  Harbour Master's Office 40
  Local attractions 48
Broadsands 45
Brunel Tower 24, 28
Burgh Island 72, 74

C
Cadgwith 158
Caffa Mill 118, 123
Calenick Creek 148
Calstock 110
Cargreen 108
Carne Beach 134
Carrick Roads 144-145
Cattewater 90, **94-95**
Cawsand Bay 80, 87, **88**
Cellar Bay 83
Challaborough Cove 74
Channals Creek 145
Chapel Point 126, 128
Charlestown 129
  Chart symbols 16
Church Cove 159
Church Cove (Gunwalloe) 162
Churston Cove 45
Clyst, River 29
Cockwood 27, 28
Combe 146
Coombe Cellars 37
Cothele Quay 109
Coverack 157-158
Cowlands Creek 146
Cremyll 98

D
Dandy Hole 104
Dart, River 50, **56-60**
DARTMOUTH 50-55
  Essential information 63
  Harbour Master's Office 50
  Local attractions 63
Devoran 145
Distances 3
Dittisham 56-57
Dodman Point **13**, 126, 131
Drake's Island 90, 92, 97
Duporth Beach 129
Durgan 151, 152

E
East Portlemouth 66
Eddystone Rocks 87
Elberry Cove 45
Erme, River 78
EXE, River 24-32
  Essential information 33
  Harbour Master's Office 24
  Local attractions 32
Exeter 30, 32
Exeter Canal 29
Exmouth 26

F
Fal, River 145
FALMOUTH 132-137
  Essential information 140
  Harbour Master's Office 132
  Local attractions 141
Falmouth Bay 132
Fishcombe Cove 45
Flushing 138
FOWEY **118-122**, 126
  Essential information 124
  Harbour Master's Office 118
  Local attractions 125
Frenchman's Creek 154
Frogmore Creek 68

G
Galmpton 57
Gerrans Bay 132
Gillan Creek 152
Golant 123
Golden Cap 18
Goodrington Sands 45
Gorran Haven 131
Great Mew Stone 80, 82
Grebe 151
Gribbin Head 118, 120, 126
Gunnislake 111
Gweek 154
Gyllingvase 134

H
Hallsands 61
Hamoaze 98-99
Headlands 12-14
HELFORD 150-153
  Essential information 154
  Harbour Master's Office 150
  Local attractions 154
Hemmick Beach 134
Hope Cove (Bigbury Bay) 72
Hope Cove (Tor Bay) 38
Hope's Nose 38, 40
Housel Bay 159-160

I
IALA Buoyage System 17
Ince Castle 104
International Port Traffic
  Signals (IPTS) 17
Isles of Scilly 174-181

J
Jennycliff Bay 92
Jubilee Pontoon 106

K
Kingsand 88
Kingsbridge 64, 69-70
Kingswear 52
Kynance Cove 160-161

L
Lambe Creek 147
Lamorna Cove 170
Lamouth Creek 146
Lantic Bay 120
Lerryn, River 123
Lizard Point **14**, 156, 157, 164
Loe Bar 162
LOOE 113-114
  Essential information 114
  Harbour Master's Office 112
  Local attractions 117
Looe Island 112
Lostwithiel 124
Low Lee 164, 165
Lower Exe 27-28
LYME REGIS 18-20
  Essential information 23
  Harbour Master's Office 18
  Local attractions 22

Index

Lympstone 28
Lynher, River 103-104

M

Maenporth 134
Malpas 147
Manacles 132
Merthen Creek 154
MEVAGISSEY 126-128
  Essential information 129
  Harbour Master's Office 126
  Local attractions 131
Millbrook 98
Millendreath 113
Mixtow Pill 123
Morwelham Quay 111
Mountbatten 90, 94
Mounts Bay 164
Mousehole 169-170
Mullion Cove 161
Murray's Rocks 74
Mylor 144

N

Nare Point 150
Neal Point 107
NEWLYN 166
  Essential information 171
  Harbour Master's Office 164
  Local attractions 171
Newton Abbot 34, 37
Newton Creek 84, 85
Newton Ferrers 85-86
North Sands 66
Noss Creek 85, 86
Noss Mayo 86
Noss on Dart 56

O

Oddicombe Beach 37
Old Mill Creek 56
Owen's Point 78

P

Padgarrack Cove 152
PAIGNTON 44
  Essential information 48
  Harbour Master's Office 40
  Local attractions 48
Par 126, 129
Parbean Cove 152
Parn Voose Cove 159
Passage Cove 152
  Passage Planning 3-7
Pelyn Creek 140
Penmarlam 123
Penpol Creek 145
Penpoll Creek 123
Penryn 138
Pentewan Sands 128
PENZANCE 167-168
  Essential information 171
  Harbour Master's Office 167
  Local attractions 171
Percuil River 140
Pill Creek 145
Plaidy Beach 113

PLYMOUTH 90-100
  Essential Information 100
  Harbour Master's Office 90
  Local attractions 100
Plymouth Sound 80, 87
Plymstock 94
Polbathic 105
Poldhu Cove 162
Polhawn Cove 89
Polkerris 129
POLPERRO 115-117
  Harbour Master's Office 115
  Local attractions 117
Polridmouth 120
Polruan 120
Polurrian Cove 162
Polwheveral Creek 154
Ponsence Cove 152
Pont Pill 121
Porth Creek 140
Porth Mellin 161
Porth Navas Creek 153
Porth Saxon 151
Porthallow 155
Porthcurno Cove 171
Porthkerris 155
PORTHLEVEN 162-163
  Essential information 163
  Harbour Master's Office 156
Porthluney Cove 134
Portholland 134
Porthoustock 155
Portloe 134
Portmellon Cove 128
Ports of refuge 5
Portscatho 134
Prawle Point 13, 64

R

Rame Head 13, 80, 87
Redlap Cove 61
Reporting 6
Restronguet Creek 144
Ropehaven 130
Ruan Lanihorne 146
Runnel Stone 165

S

Sailor's Creek 138
SALCOMBE 64-68
  Essential information 71
  Harbour Master's Office 64
  Local attractions 70
Saltash 98, **106**
Saltern Cove 45
Sand Acre Bay 103
Scabbacombe Head 51
Shadycombe Creek 66
Shaldon 34, 39
Skerries Bank **12**, 51
Smeaton Pass 92
South Sands 66
Southpool Creek 68
St Anthony Head 14, 132, 134
St Austell Bay 126, 129-130
St Germans 105
St Just 142
St Mary's Bay 48
St Mawes 139-140
St Michael's Mount 164, 168-169

Sunset in the Carrick Roads

St Winnow 124
Starcross 28
Starehole Bay 64
Start Bay 50, 61
Start Point **12**, 50, 61, 64
Stoke Gabriel Creek 58
Stoke Point 72
Stonehouse Pool 98
Straight Point **12**, 24
Sunny Cove 66
Sutton Harbour 93
Swanpool 134
Symbols 15
System failure 6

T

Talland Bay 117
TAMAR, River 102-111
  Essential information 111
  Local attractions 111
Tater-Du 164
Tavy, River 107
Teign, River 34, 35
TEIGNMOUTH 34-36
  Essential information 39
  Harbour Master's Office 34
  Local attractions 39
The Bag 68
The Bight 27
The Bridge 92
The Ness 34
The Salty 34, 35
The Sands 45
Thurlestone 72
Tidal streams 8-11
Tiddy, River 105
Tides 4
Tolcarne Creek 145
Tolverne 146

Topsham 30
Tor Bay 40-49
Torpoint **99**, 102
TORQUAY 42-43
  Essential information 48
  Harbour Master's Office 40
  Local attractions 48
Totnes 50, 59-60
Trebah 152
Trefusis Point 136
Tremayne Quay 154
Tresillian 147
TRURO 147-148
  Essential information 149
  Harbour Master's Office 142
  Local attractions 149
Tuckenhay 59
Turf Lock 29-30
Turnaware Beach 145
Turnchapel 94

V

Veryan Bay 132

W

Warren Cove 61
Wearde Quay 103
Weather 4
Weir Quay 108
Wembury Bay 82
Wiseman's Pool 123

Y

YEALM, River 72, **80-86**
  Essential information 86
  Harbour Master's Office 80

West Country Pilot • 183

'Troy' class dinghies at Fowey

Southpool Creek, Salcombe

Plymouth tidal curve

Mean spring and neap curves
Springs occur 2 days after New and Full Moon

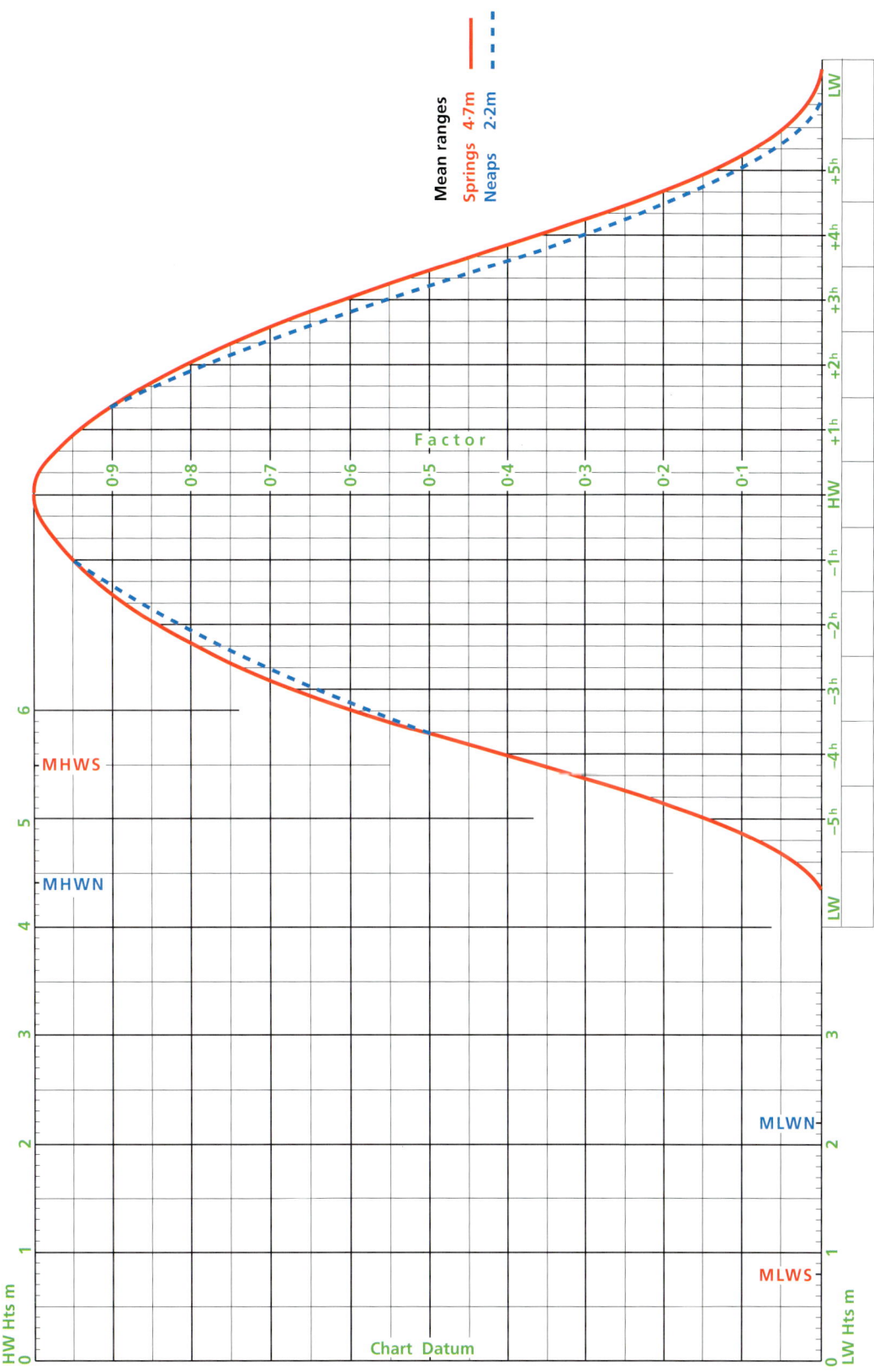